VODKA & SANDSTORMS

VODKA & SANDSTORMS

LUKE RICHMOND

First published in 2020 by Luke Richmond
and OLOC Adventures.

Port Arthur, Tasmania, 7182 Australia.
www.olocadventures.com

10,9,8,7,6,5,4,3,2,1

Copyright © Luke Richmond 2020

All rights reserved. No part of this book may be reproduced or transmitted in any form or by any means, electronic or mechanical, including photocopying, recording or by any other information storage retrieval system, without prior permission in writing from the publisher.

National Library of Australia Cataloguing-in-Publication entry:
Vodka & Sandstorms: What is life but one big adventure / Richmond, Luke.

ISBN: 978-0-6485947-0-3 (paperback)

Category: Memoir / Adventure Travel

Cover and internal design: Nada Backovic
Cover image: Luke Richmond and iStock

The paper in this book is FSC certified. FSC promotes environmentally responsible, socially beneficial and economically viable management of the world's forests.

For Elise.

PRAISE FOR **VODKA & SANDSTORMS**

'Ranulph Fiennes meets Andy McNab. For anyone interested in exploration and adventure, this book is the real deal. A fascinating and gripping account of endeavour, determination and courage, which packs the punch of a thriller, scarcely leaving you time to catch your breath between pages.'

JAMIE MASLIN - author of *The Long Hitch Home*

'How has one bloke managed to cram so much into just one life? I've done some serious expeditions in my life and reading Luke's book has made me feel like I've just scratched the surface of what I am….what we are all capable of. Brutally honest and told at breakneck pace, Vodka and Sandstorms is the perfect kick up the bum I need to get out there and get the most out of life.'

JUSTIN JONES - World record setting explorer, documentary producer and storyteller.

'The "dignity of risk" is a human right and the human races greatest accomplishments have often been on the back of enormous risk to human life. Luke embraces risk as a necessary means to an end in this inspiring account of his incredible adventures. A true inspiration and a reminder to those who discourage the expression of risk in today's workplaces, schools and playgrounds that you will never get much back out of life without taking risk".

KEN WARE - Founder of NeuroPhysics Therapy

'An instant adrenalin experience in a book, could not put it down. From one crazy adventure to the next. This book will leave you inspired, excited and planning your own adventure.'

JAY - 12 year Australian SAS and Commando veteran.

'Strap on your parachute, grab your oars, lace up your boots and get ready for the read of your life. Once again Richmond reminds us just how many incredible things there are to do in this world if we only take that first step.'

GRANT 'AXE' RAWLINSON - Human Powered Explorer

'I get energised and inspired for the day's adventure whenever I sell my books within 100 metres of the incredible Luke Richmond at Salamanca Market. Read *Vodka and Sandstorms* and feel the force!'

JAMES BOYCE - Author of *Van Diemen's Land*

ABOUT THE AUTHOR

Luke Richmond is an Aussie adventurer who has conquered the odds during many internationally acclaimed expeditions. Growing up on various cattle stations across the Northern Territory, Luke joined the army at 17 years old, which gave him the discipline and world knowledge he needed, and lit a fire for adventure that he pursues to this day. Luke has climbed the highest mountain on six continents, completed a world record ocean row across the Atlantic, and was the first Australian male to trek 1800 kilometres across the Gobi Desert in Mongolia, dragging a cart that contained all his food and water. Luke's lifelong passion is to make adventure accessible to everyone, and to inspire others to feel the reward of conquering a physical and mental challenge. His life motto is OLOC which stands for 'One Life One Chance,' a belief that has driven him into harder and longer challenges every single year.

CONTENTS

- PROLOGUE — 1
- Chapter 1 - The Beginning — 3
- Chapter 2 - Building. Antenna. Span. Earth. - Tonsai — 7
- Chapter 3 - The 'B' in BASE - Pattaya — 13
- Chapter 4 - Frenchmans Cap — 19
- Chapter 5 - The 'A' in BASE — 28
- Chapter 6 - Crossing the Gobi Desert — 33
- Chapter 7 - Everest Base Camp — 104
- Chapter 8 - Mount Satopanth — 133
- Chapter 9 - The Ganges — 162
- Chapter 10 - Rowing the Tasman — 169
- Chapter 11 - Thumb and a Book Tour — 189
- Chapter 12 - The Murray River — 227
- What's next? — 274

PROLOGUE

I thought at first that it was seasickness, or maybe I was missing my wife Elise, who I wouldn't see for eight weeks. But as the days passed and we rowed further and further away from Australia, I realised what it was: a feeling of impending doom. This was accompanied by the gut-wrenching thought that I would never see Elise again. Rowing across the Tasman Sea to New Zealand wasn't my first rodeo, I had a career full of dangerous expeditions behind me, including 55 days rowing the Atlantic and regular BASE jumping, a sport that will bring you closer to death than any other. Yet through everything, I'd never experienced what I was feeling now.

The dread marinated inside me until Day Four, when I knew I had to say something to Grant. I told him I had a bad feeling about the expedition and although I didn't want to alter his mindset, it needed to be discussed. Grant is an emotionally intelligent guy with a long history of expeditions under his belt and he treats gut feelings seriously. We discussed it for over an hour and ran through everything that was going well on the expedition and decided to push on. Two hours later we were battling through gale-force winds on the eastern edge of Bass Strait, a notorious stretch of water between mainland Australia and Tasmania.

I was on deck for my rowing shift and the sea conditions were big, so I jumped on the oars and hooked in. I attached the metal safety line to the carabiner hanging from my waist to tether me to the boat in case the unthinkable happened and I was thrown overboard into the frigid waters. Halfway through my shift a rogue wave rose up on our left and I turned the boat to line up with it. The wave was huge and doubled in size before we made its crest. The lip of the wave started to break above me.

A guttural growl escaped my lips as the boat's stern lifted and we were carried skyward. We were going to be pitch-poled, flipping end over end, but at the last second the bow dug in and with violent speed we were capsized down the face of the monster. I was upside down and underwater with the roar of the ocean all around me. I tried to push free but something was wrong, my foot was trapped in the rowing plate. I felt ropes around me and my first panicked thought was, 'I'm going to be tangled up'. I yanked my leg hard and felt the plate give way. Desperate for air I spun around and pushed upwards to the surface underneath our upside-down rowboat.

I was connected to the boat by the safety line, which was the only thing that stopped me being pulled away by the current. Grant was in the cabin with the door tightly sealed. He would have gone from dozing to being thrown around and upside down. As I was assessing the chaos, my lifejacket self-inflated and almost tore my head off. I'd forgotten to tie the crotch straps and now it was riding high and choking me.

'You okay, bro?' I yelled to Grant.

'Yeah,' he replied.

We were in a bad situation and we had to get the boat upright before the next set of waves came down on us. The boat was supposed to self-right but it was struggling to do so.

I had an idea: to unclip my safety line, slide down along the boat and re-clip at the back. Once there, I hoped I could use my strength on the rudder to turn the boat. It was a risky move: if I was separated it was a death sentence. I tentatively undid the screw gate on the carabiner and paused. Was I making the biggest mistake of my life in the middle of the Tasman Sea?

I unclipped my line and started swimming.

Chapter 1

The Beginning

I can honestly say I'm living my dream adventure life, but this wasn't always the case. I woke up in jail once with no idea how I got there. It was 2009 in London, I was a drug addict and the police were hosing me down because I was covered in my own filth. This wasn't the man I was meant to be.

I was raised by two loving parents, Clive and Mandy Richmond, in the wild freedom of the Australian outback. I grew up fishing, hunting and living a country kid's dream. I joined the army at seventeen years of age, with Mum and Dad's permission. I served for four years and was deployed on peacekeeping missions to East Timor, a proud young man in his twenties. Upon discharge I wanted to travel and explore the world. I flew to Europe with all of my possessions in a backpack, to discover unknown lands and have adventures. I'm not sure where it all went wrong.

The pity in the eyes of those police officers filled me with an overpowering shame, and it was at that moment I knew something had to change. I was released from jail the next day but I was in a bad way and kept taking drugs. I had to get out of London. I called an old army buddy of mine, Liam, and told him

I needed his help. Liam was an avid kickboxer and he told me to fly to a place in Phuket he had visited for training, called Tiger Muay Thai. I hung up and booked my ticket there and then, high as a kite. I finished the remainder of my drugs in the taxi on the way to Heathrow and flew out to Thailand as I started going into withdrawal.

I landed in Phuket and went cold turkey while completing six hours per day of Muay Thai training. Every punch I threw, every kick, every elbow, every drop of sweat that hit the canvas, I was cleansing myself of the drink, the drugs and the shame. While I was an addict, everything inside me had been suppressed, but by the end of that first month my emotions were reawakening. Dreams, goals, aspirations: everything was coming alive again.

I started to regain control, and in the process, my desire for adventure took hold. I had grown up reading Wilbur Smith and Jack London novels. I read about the great Antarctic explorers Shackleton, Amundsen and Mawson. I wondered if I was made of the same stuff as those stoic men. I needed to find out. But first I needed money.

I flew back to Australia and found a job in the mining sector during the boom. For six months I worked twelve-hours shifts in an underground coalmine. I built up a treasure chest of money and when I had saved enough, I went online to find my first adventure. I found a list, the 'Seven Summits', the biggest mountain on every continent. I set myself the lofty goal of climbing them all in one year. I bought every piece of equipment the website recommended and I found myself a place on a climbing team heading to South America. I was the guy with all the gear and no idea, but I was going to find out what I was really made of.

At the end of that year I had climbed Mount Aconcagua in Argentina, Denali in Alaska, Kilimanjaro in Tanzania, Vinson Massif in Antarctica, Carstensz Pyramid in West Papua, and failed to summit Mount Elbrus in Russia. I was held captive in the jungle, witnessed climbers frozen on the side of the trail and had an AK47 pointed at my head. I dragged sleds, rescued climbers out of crevasses, was caught in an avalanche and built snow walls during gale-force winds. I climbed on snow, ice, rock and officially became a mountaineer. I found my purpose and went back to work to save money for more adventures.

Out of the blue I received a phone call from a British rowing team. The team were planning a Row2Rio expedition. They were two guys and two girls who had ridden their bicycles from London to Portugal. From there they were planning to row a boat across the Atlantic Ocean to Brazil and ride their bikes into Rio de Janeiro as part of the Olympic Games celebrations. After they arrived in Portugal, one of the guys was struck down with appendicitis and had to pull out of the team. They were going to cancel their row and were drowning their sorrows in a local pub where they met a mate of mine, Mathew. Upon hearing their story, he said, 'Hold on, I might know a guy.'

I received a Skype call from the team that night. 'Do you want to row across the Atlantic?' they asked. 'Yes,' I said immediately. Then I asked my girlfriend at the time Elise, if I could go. Fortunately, she said yes.

I quit my job the next day, flew to Portugal and within ten days of taking the phone call I was making my first strokes out into the Atlantic. We had to maintain two hours of rowing, two hours of rest, 24 hours per day, and I had never rowed before in my life. We had 250 kilograms of dehydrated food in the belly of the boat and a water maker for our drinking water. We were attempting an unsupported crossing in the hope of setting a new Guinness World Record.

Fast forward 55 days and 6400 kilometres of beautiful misery, we landed on a beach on the coast of Brazil. I jumped out to meet my waiting family and friends and fell over. I couldn't walk. I'd lost 15 kilograms in weight and had adapted solely to being able to row. It took three weeks for my balance to come back to a point where I wouldn't crash into walls while heading to the toilet at night. I had never suffered like that before. The sleep deprivation, the twelve hours of rowing each day, the salt sores and boils on my backside, the infected rashes, the uncomfortable existence and the insecurity. We had achieved a world record and I had become an ocean rower.

I met my beautiful wife Elise on Tinder when we were both working in the health and fitness industry in Sydney. I was trying to be a 'real' adult and I had opened my second gym while she was working as a personal trainer in the city. We connected online, met up for a coffee and have been inseparable since.

We sold all our assets in Australia and went travelling together. Eighteen months after we met, we were married in a hot air balloon above the desert near Las Vegas. After exchanging our vows and sealing the deal with a kiss, we climbed onto the edge of the basket together and jumped – plummeting towards the earth 5000 feet below, before pulling our parachutes and landing safely in the grounds of a casino. It seemed the perfect way to start our life of adventure together.

I was a humble kid from the Australian outback who took off to see the world and seek his destiny. I had a stumble or two along the way, but that's how experience is measured. Two things in my life are certain. I have an unwavering love for my wife, family and friends. And when adventure calls, I will answer.

Chapter 2
Building. Antenna. Span. Earth. – Tonsai

It was 5.30am when I crept out of the bungalow, doing my best not to wake Elise. She had watched me jump so often she would rather sleep in than tag along. I knew, however, that she would most likely lay awake worried until I returned.

The power had been turned off before dawn, as it was every day. The cluster of shacks owned by an elderly Thai lady would be without electricity for the next twelve hours. The budget travellers didn't seem to care; this place was all about the beach, the climbing and the jump.

The first thing I noticed was the stillness in the air, not a breath of wind; this was the key to pulling off the mission. I looked up through the gap in the jungle canopy and saw clear skies. The weather was on my side.

The cicadas sang as I walked along the path towards the beach. Some macaque monkeys ran along the branches high above me and I could hear the rumble of a generator supplying power to the expensive hotel nearby. I thought about their humming air-conditioners as the first beads of sweat rolled down my bare chest. The humidity was thick, monsoon season wasn't far away, and its arrival would bring with it an end to the period of perfect weather for jumping. I read the environment as I walked, the stillness of the palm trees confirming there was no wind. I couldn't hear any breaking waves, another good sign of the wind staying away. With this new hobby of mine the wind could literally kill me.

I stepped onto the sand and turned left towards a small bar sheltered underneath the cliff. This famous hangout would be bustling by the afternoon but for now it was all mine. I laid out the contents of my bag on the wooden platform overlooking the water. There was moisture on the tables that told of rain overnight. The rock would still be wet and more dangerous to climb. I went through my mental checklist and ticked off everything I needed. Parachute: check. I packed it yesterday and it was ready to go. Pin tension: check. These two little pieces of metal had to open or it was game over. Helmet and pads: check. GoPro: check. Poncho to wrap my parachute in, as I'd soon be sweating profusely: check. Shoes for climbing: check. My last check was to look up at my objective.

Tonsai wall towered over me, 110 metres of limestone and hanging stalactites. I had been watching YouTube videos featuring Tonsai for years and finally I was going to jump it. I scanned upwards from its base, moving my eyes over every little bush and piece of grass protruding from the rock face, checking for signs of wind at different altitudes. The bottom was clear, the middle was calm and the exit point at the top was also perfect. It was time to climb.

I walked along the beach and made a mental note of the tide. The water was still a little high but by the time I was ready to jump it would be lower and give me a bigger landing area. The sand crunched underfoot as I entered a recess in the rock shielded by jungle and approached the back of the cliff. An overhang opened up where the climb began. It was still dark under the thick canopy of trees so I moved with caution. If I stopped for too long the mosquitoes would swarm. I moved at a steady pace, placing my hands and feet on the permanent bamboo ladder. I ascended the five metres to the top of the first wall; this was the easy part. From the top the muddy trail turned into the jungle, with no more ladders and no protection. I was on my own.

My eyes adjusted as the night lost its battle with the rising sun, the strengthening rays filtering down through the dense trees. I love the jungle. I could feel life all around me, from the bugs and insects in the leaf litter to the monkeys in the ancient trees, it was energising. I cautiously made my way along to the next section of cliff: ten metres of moist rock full of small pockets and cracks, ideal for climbing if it was dry. The route wasn't hard but it was vertical, and a fall could have serious consequences. When asking a fellow jumper about the safety of the place, I had been told, 'The only death recorded on this cliff was on the climb, the jump is safe.'

I wasn't sure if it was nerves or the fishcake I'd eaten the day before from a roadside stall, but I needed to take off my pack and run into the bush to relieve myself. Returning with a spring in my step, I pulled on my rig and made the first move heading up. The rock was wet but sharp, allowing a firm grip on the soles of my cheap running shoes. Halfway up some thick vines had grown out of the limestone, making for a good spot to pause and catch my breath. The climb would be terrifying normally, but compared to what I was about to do there was no contest.

I moved again and made the top. Sweat was pouring off me and mosquitoes were enjoying a hearty breakfast. I didn't stop for long, I could see the next section of cliff through the trees a few metres ahead. This vertical section was higher and had a tree growing in front of it. I thought about using the trunk as a support, but after tapping it with my knuckles, the hollow sound convinced me otherwise. The rain overnight hadn't saturated this wall and I felt more confident on the holds as I climbed. The technical climbing movements flowed well as I ascended, and my mind cleared as I started to think about the task at hand.

This state of mind is referred to as a flow state by extreme sports men and women, a point of absolute clarity while going about a dangerous endeavour. Anytime I climbed, especially without ropes, and even more so when I was heading to a jump, I entered a flow state. At the top of the second wall I couldn't remember the short climb. The two hardest sections were behind me and I moved off along the muddy trail.

The path entered a clearing containing a large open-mouthed cave that looked as if it had been home to someone or something in the past. I looked up through the gap in the canopy and saw clouds beginning to form. I needed the weather to hold off for just a little while longer. On the edge of the clearing, standing vigil was a huge tree. It was arrow straight and had grown tall in the meagre sunlight penetrating this special place. The trunk must have been at least four arm spans in circumference and as I happened by I whispered a greeting, 'Hey, big fella', and softly patted its bark. The odds would have been against this tree having grown so big in such a dark, damp place, surrounded by hundreds of other trees competing for the same resources. But it had, and now it was the dominant totem to which the others yielded. A great lesson from nature about resilience.

The third section of vertical climbing was only six metres and mercifully it was also dry. It started with a scramble, before I had to stem between two walls. Stemming is putting one foot on one wall and one foot on the other to create enough force to move upwards. The technique came naturally to me and allowed me to use very little grip in my hands to complete the ascent. At the top, the cliff eased off into five tiered sections of easy climbing on a slight angle. I increased my pace and settled into a rhythm.

Sweat was pouring from my body as I reached the point where the wall ended. Directly in front of me was a sheer drop-off. This was the point of traverse where I needed to move to my left to carry on up an adjacent wall. I paused, took a deep breath, and surveyed my surroundings. This natural formation between two cliffs was a great place to check the wind – just a light breeze, enough to cool my sweat but not enough to cause me to abort the jump. I moved left and climbed.

For the following ten minutes I was in the zone, moving confidently up the easy climbing until there was nowhere higher to go. The sunlight blinded me as I exited the jungle and stood on the razor-sharp ridges of the tower. I was on the back of the mountain and had a short traverse remaining to take me to the cliff edge on the ocean side. The rock had been eroded over time, leaving pinnacles and sharp edges everywhere that tore my cheap runners to shreds with their sandpaper-like texture. I looked across from my hand placement. There, stretching below me, was the white sand and blue water of Railay Beach. Too early for the sunbathing tourists, I was the only witness to its incredible beauty.

I 'down-climbed' to the cliff edge directly above the beach and traversed until I found the spot I was searching for. I needed to have an overhang of cliff with a clear drop directly to the sand below. This was the spot. I moved back a few paces from the edge and unpacked my parachute, pads and helmet. Once unloaded my bag was folded and shoved away into my pants, I would leave nothing behind. Surviving in this sport was about following a checklist and ensuring every detail had been double-checked. I went through my gear-up procedure, mentally ticking off essentials one at a time. First to go on was my parachute, last was my helmet and camera. I retraced my steps to the edge, while fear and adrenaline built inside me for the second time this morning. It was go-time. My hands shook as I made the last move to the very edge of the rock cliff overhanging the beach.

My toes protruded over the edge with nothing but air below them. I looked down at the beach to where I had started my climb and checked the palm trees for any signs of wind. The landing area was large and inviting, and the trees were still. A gust of wind could alter how my chute opened and could send me on a collision course with the cliff. It wouldn't be the first time. I spat over the edge and watched it fall. The movement pattern of the saliva during its descent could tell me more about what was happening with the wind. If it moved left or right I knew there was a crosswind, if it enlarged as it fell I could have an updraft. On this morning it fell straight and perfect.

My hands continued to shake as I went through my final mental checklist, once again checking every little detail as a last line of defence. By the time I finished, my hands were no longer shaking. My fear had turned to excitement and I wanted to throw myself out into the void. I looked towards the tiny islands off the coast and I counted.

Three, two, one…Go! I jumped.

No words can do justice to the feeling of freefall but I can say that time slows down. The mere 2.5 seconds of falling, totally free from the stress, pressures and realities of normal life, felt like minutes. You see and feel everything with amazing clarity: the cliff face rushing by behind me, the stalactites to my left, the air roaring in my ears, my speed increasing as gravity accelerates me to the ground. The only thing that forces me to leave this euphoric moment is the sandy beach rushing up to meet me.

I threw out my pilot chute, which catches the air, inflates and pulls the pins on my parachute. My big white canopy exploded open with the boom of a shotgun.

I was flying.

My canopy opened on heading facing away from the cliff, and I flew out over the water. I made a right-hand turn and flew parallel to the beach for fifteen to twenty seconds, before completing a 180-degree turn back towards the bar underneath the cliff.

I landed in the sand in front of the wooden tables from where I had begun and let out a yell more primal then celebratory. My heart rate jacked as adrenaline pumped through my veins. I took off my gear, sat down on the seat and looked out across the bay, taking a deep breath.

This was the jump I had seen a guy make over a year ago, while sitting on this very spot, and it had inspired me to take up the sport. And here I was, one year later, having jumped it myself. I was at the beginning of my BASE jumping career. I had jumped out of planes first to learn skydiving and jumped the famous Perrine Bridge in Idaho for my first BASE jump. I went on to jump cliffs in Moab, and a balloon on my wedding day in Vegas with Elise, who skydived alongside me. The sport had terrified and excited me in equal measure.

As my sweat cooled, I remembered a text I had received from a mate a few days earlier, it read: 'I'm coming to Thailand, have you jumped a building yet?'

Chapter 3

The 'B' in BASE – Pattaya

The plane banked low across the water as it made its final approach towards Pattaya's airport. I could see the fishing boats and the waves curling into whitewash on the surface of the ocean. I scanned the horizon, searching for the next objective, just as I had scanned dozens of mountain ranges before. This time, however, I was looking for a man-made structure. Adventure can be anything and take you anywhere, it doesn't have to be to the highest peaks in the Himalaya or the driest deserts. It can be in your backyard, a nearby town or, in this case, one of the most famous cities in Thailand.

My heart skipped a beat as the plane turned another 90 degrees and I saw some buildings. They were not big enough for what we had planned. My mentor, army buddy and all-round best mate, Jimmy, was meeting me in town. He had held my hand, metaphorically speaking, through my first BASE jumps and was going to do it again. This jump wasn't going to be like Tonsai; there would be no climbing up wet vertical rock, it would be stairs and elevators leading us to the exit point. I continued scanning the horizon for buildings, like a husband scanning arriving passengers at the airport for his wife. The plane made its final turn away from a storm cloud on its way towards the runway and I saw them. Through light blue fog the towers rose upwards, giants forcing their way to the heavens, marvels of human engineering.

Nervous energy had me twisting in my seat as I visualised the mission ahead. The plane touched down on the tarmac and taxied to the terminal. I was surrounded by Thai locals and tourists coming to enjoy the beaches and nightlife of this crazy city. They had no idea what I was about to do, and it made me feel like James Bond on some secret endeavour behind enemy lines. This was the part of BASE jumping I loved the most: the mission.

If we chose to accept it, our mission was to infiltrate and jump off one of the biggest buildings in Pattaya. Jimmy had experience in this field and he was showing me the way. Over the previous month I had jumped Tonsai cliff a dozen more times and trained with my landings for accuracy. I would draw a target on the beach and try to hit the bullseye every time. One thing Jimmy had warned me: 'The landing areas are tight, so practice.'

I cleared the airport and jumped in a taxi, not bothering to haggle on the fare. The city was about an hour away and I wanted to get going. The driver picked up on my haste and floored it. I had grown used to the chaotic nature of the roads and drivers in Thailand, so I settled back and watched the scenery whip by. We passed a coffin shop displaying its latest models. Not exactly the best thing to be seeing before attempting to throw myself off a skyscraper but I thought it was great how Thai society was confronting mortality.

With the coffin display they were saying, 'Yes, everyone dies, and here are the boxes you end up in.' In Australia we never really confront death; we hire funeral homes, never handle a body and refer to death as 'passed away.' This keeps death on our periphery and we rarely acknowledge our mortality until it's too late. Death doesn't have to be a negative aspect of our lives. It can be one of the biggest motivators in getting the most out of every single day. The realisation that we are a bag of meat, bones and electricity, should persuade us to eat healthy, drink less and take better care of ourselves.

Knowing that death is coming for us all, sometimes much earlier than we would like, will allow you to think deeper about what you really want out of your life. If you only had a few years left, would you really care about your next promotion and a bigger house? Or would you spend quality time with family, be a better person, and tick off things from your bucket list. Death is our own personal drill sergeant and he is screaming at you, 'Don't waste time!'

I had been jumping 110 metre cliffs in training, but as we entered Pattaya I watched the buildings grow to twice that height. Jimmy had sent me the name of his hotel and I headed straight there. Rain started to fall as the car pulled up, and there he was, my old mate Jimmy, appearing at the window with a grin on his face.

We embraced like brothers.

'No jumping with this rain, hey?' I asked.

'Yeah, not today, but we will go on a recon anyway.'

We spent the afternoon moving between buildings, some derelict and others just recently constructed. Jimmy gave me the theory lesson behind jumping buildings safely. He had completed jumps off dozens of buildings in this area and shared his hard-earned knowledge.

Come nightfall, we devoured a seafood dinner back at his room, and while I was chewing through delicious king prawns, Jimmy casually asked, 'You want to know what we are jumping in the morning?'

'Hell, yes!' I blurted, showering him with chewed seafood.

He paused with a half smile and a glint in his eye.

'You are sitting in it.'

We were staying on the fifteenth floor of a 57-floor, 190-metre, beast of a tower positioned right alongside a beach.

'This one is good to go,' said Jimmy. 'But we will need to hit it really early.'

'I'm in a hundred per cent, let's do this,' I said, with nervous excitement.

I had a restless sleep, repeating the jump over in my mind a thousand times, analysing countless 'what if' scenarios, until the alarm beat its drum at 4.45am. I had a quick shower, a shot of coffee, and a nervous bathroom stop before exiting the room with Jimmy. We walked four metres to the fire escape door, which Jimmy wedged open with a sock.

'What's that for?' I asked, pointing at his sock.

'It's just in case we can't jump. We will need to get back to our room, these doors lock from inside.'

We started the walk up the stairs carrying our gear. The stairwell had no ventilation and we were sweating immediately. We trod lightly, not talking and pausing every ten floors to catch our breath. At level 57 we stepped outside and were greeted by the pale glow of pre-dawn light. We climbed a set of maintenance stairs to access the very top of the building. I climbed over a rail towards the beach side and there it was: the edge. Nothing protected the drop-off; we had a clear six-metre run-up to the exit point. We put down our gear and crawled on our bellies to the edge to look over the side.

There was a large shallow pool directly below us surrounded by palm trees and sunbeds. Balconies were stacked like dominoes on the two other large buildings flanking this one and created an area of calm. We both completed a spit check and watched our saliva fall with zero deviation. There was no wind and we were good to go. The beach was a lot closer than I had thought it would be when staring up at the building's roof from ground level, so I had no concerns about making the landing area. The plan was to fly parallel to the ocean as far away from the hotel as we could. There was a small road 200 metres along the beach, which would be our rendezvous point.

We slid back from the edge and prepped our gear. We talked through potential problems, including what would happen if we were arrested. Once we both had parachutes on, helmets on and cameras rolling we checked each other one last time.

'I'll go first,' I said, sounding confident but quietly shitting myself.

'Sounds good, you know what to do.'

I walked back to get a run-up at the edge; separation away from the building was important. This structure didn't overhang like Tonsai, so I needed every centimetre of separation I could get in case my canopy opened backwards, towards the building.

I stood still for a moment looking at the edge. I went through my checklist, ticking off everything I had to do. Once I was ready, I took a deep breath.

'Okay, bro. Three, two, one…Go!'

I ran, my last foot placement hit the edge perfectly and suddenly I was airborne. Balconies whipped by and the pool rushed up to meet me. The details of the fall are still vivid in my mind, the white balconies and pot plants moved in slow motion as I plummeted towards the ground. I pitched my pilot chute, it caught the air and the canopy exploded above me, opening on heading. I flew away from the building and turned left along the beach, I was still very high and cursed myself for not enjoying a longer free fall before pitching. I heard Jimmy's canopy crack open behind me and whoever wasn't awake before definitely was now.

The radios of security guards were chattering away below. I knew there was no way they could miss us, but they wouldn't know where we were just yet. I flew down the beach and landed on the sand near our evacuation road. Jimmy touched down close by and we skipped the celebrations and started grabbing up our parachutes. I stuffed everything away and calmly walked down the small road away from the beach. Jimmy met me in the middle and we headed towards a taxi rank in the distance. As we reached the main road a security guard came walking around the corner of the intersection and stopped in front of us.

'You jump?' he said in puffed broken English, pointing at us then back down the road.

'No mate, we came from airplane,' said Jimmy, mimicking the sound of a jet and holding out his arms like wings.

The guard was just a normal guy, not a big boss and looked at us baffled. He wasn't sure what to do and during his confusion we started walking again.

'See ya later,' we said together, and gave him a wave.

We made it to the waiting taxi and woke up the driver. He was startled yet happy to have a fare so early in the day. We piled into the back seat.

'Take us for breakfast,' we said.

'Holiday Inn, very good,' he replied.

'Sounds great.'

He accelerated away, and Jimmy and I turned to each other with big smiles.

Over bacon and eggs, we celebrated. It was an awesome jump and we had got away clean with no injuries. We had arranged a small room in another hotel a few blocks away to stow our gear, then we could get a taxi back to the building like a couple of guys coming home from a big night. We would then pack up and move locations. I loved this side of jumping, it wasn't just the rush of the jump but the whole mission made for a great adventure. Especially when I was with Jimmy. It was like we were still in the army tracking down bad guys.

Before we made our way back, and while settling into another cup of coffee, I said to Jimmy, 'Thank's for helping me with my first building jump, I really appreciate it.'

'No worries at all, you did great. But I have a question for you.'

'Yeah, what is it?' I asked, intrigued.

'What is left for you to jump now?' he asked with a cheeky smile. Without allowing me to answer he continued on, 'I know what it is because I haven't jumped it either, and it's time we did.'

I knew what he was saying. BASE stood for buildings, antenna, span and earth, and I had jumped everything but an A.

'Well, where in the world should we go for that?' I asked.

'I know a place,' he said with a smile.

Chapter 4

Frenchmans Cap

I landed at Hobart airport with Elise, and the first thing that hit me as we walked down the stairs onto the tarmac was the crisp clean air. It had a very similar smell and feel to the South Island of New Zealand. A feeling of remoteness, cold and adventure.

Ten minutes from the airport, we were standing in the middle of the capital city, Hobart. It was first established in 1804, as a collection of tents and huts at the mouth of the Derwent river. It is Australia's second oldest city and was settled predominantly by convicts, Royal Navy Marines and a small contingent of free settlers. It was already inhabited by Aboriginal's who had called it home for tens of thousands of years.

The settlement swelled in the shadow of Mount Wellington, it's 1270 metre prominence and exposed rock columns, impossible to miss from the tranquil harbour at the city centre. It had the rare combination of a big flowing river, a harbour with an unbroken view out to sea, and mountains all within eyesight. In 1804 the new colony was known as Van Diemen's Land and the settlers pushed the frontier into the wilderness.

By 1856 the state was renamed Tasmania and evolved from an inhospitable corner of the world, to a thriving hub of industry.

With a population of 225,000, Hobart is more like a big country town than a city. Cut off from mainland Australia, Tasmania is an island state and it really did feel like a different world. There was a stress-free country atmosphere that I had grown up with as a boy and I felt right at home.

Jimmy flew in the following day from a remote area of the Northern Territory where he worked in the mines. He had a perfect roster, two weeks of mining followed by two weeks of jumping somewhere in the world. The high-paying job was funding his life and love of BASE. We had two objectives for our mission to Tassie, as it's known to the locals. Trek out and jump Frenchmans Cap, an incredible 300-metre cliff buried deep in the western forest. Then tick off the last object in the BASE acronym.

We picked up a hire car and drove 214 kilometres northwest to the start of the trail head leading to Frenchmans Cap. Ben, a fellow BASE jumper I had met in Tonsai, had arranged to meet us at the start but upon arrival he was nowhere to be seen. We had agreed if he was a no show at the carpark we would push onto the trail without him.

Getting to the mountain was going to be a physical challenge. I had to carry all my personal kit and camping gear on my back and all my BASE gear on my front, a load of 30 kilograms altogether. During my army years or when I was in peak climbing condition, this wouldn't have been an issue, but with limited build-up training it was going to be a shock to the system. Jimmy was in a physical condition referred to as 'getting off the couch.' He hadn't done much training and his job involved driving enormous mining trucks for ten hours per day. Elise would carry all of her own camping gear, food and the teams gas for cooking.

We stepped off onto the trail undaunted.

We called the first rest break after an hour. The weight was burning my shoulders but it felt great to be out in the bush again.

'What do you think so far?' I asked Elise.

'It's so nice to be away from the city,' she replied.

Jimmy chimed in, 'Can't wait to jump. But I should have brought a hat for my bald head.'

As we rested amid the constant buzz of march flies, Ben bounded towards us.

'Hey guys, sorry I missed you. I was hitchhiking and had no phone service,' he yelled.

'Welcome brother, it's great to see you,' I said as we shook hands.

I looked at the small backpack he was carrying.

'Where is all your gear?'

'I travel light, I'm all good.'

The four of us started out again. The trail was estimated to take five hours to walk to Lake Vera, the halfway point where we would camp for the night. My ego said we could do it in four.

The landscape changed from an ancient forest of trees seven arm spans in circumference to marshland and dense scrub. The trail was in great condition, wooden walkways had been constructed over the boggy ground to aid trekkers and preserve the fragile land. The funding for the project came from Dick Smith, one of Australia's most successful businessman and philanthropists. He injected $1.5 million into maintaining the trails with another $1.5 million coming from the Tasmanian government.

My underestimation of the route and my overestimation of our abilities had us walking into Lake Vera six hours after departing the car park. It wasn't the picturesque alpine lake I had been hoping for. The scrub was so thick there was nowhere to camp except the wooden tent platforms built by the national park. There was also a small hut for trekkers to cook and sleep in. I boiled water from the freshwater tank attached to the hut and made us all some meals: leftover dehydrated ones from past expeditions that were packed with calories and enjoyed by all.

The hut housed a few trekkers who were bedding down for the night and there was plenty of room for us to squeeze in. After our dinner, and not long after the sun had disappeared, I crawled into my sleeping bag with stiff legs and passed out. I slept for eight hours and woke up sore yet recharged, and ready to attack the day. In the guidebook, the second half of the trek was estimated to take four hours. After the previous day's effort, we decided to just see what happened. Water bottles were filled and we set off at 6.30am.

The trail paralleled the tranquil lake and the surrounding trees were beginning to shed their burden. At one point, a breeze rattled the branches and their tiny leaves, no bigger than five-cent pieces, started to fall. The yellow flakes were highlighted by the rising sun to create a golden snowfall. The birds were abundant and joined in the chorus as we started an uphill slog shortly after leaving the hut. We were taking multiple breaks as we climbed higher to the top of a ridgeline. The large trees disappeared to be replaced by short scrub bush. In the distance, named after its resemblance to headdress worn by French cooks, towered Frenchmans Cap.

The sheer prominence stopped us in our tracks. The grey vertical rock face rose high above the surrounding valleys, dwarfing everything else. During the early years of Van Diemen's Land, Tasmania's original name, escaped convicts from Macquarie Harbour Penal Station were known to use the peak as a navigation tool. They would try to cross the remote western wilderness towards the settled districts to the east. The peak was first climbed by a European, James Sprent, in 1853, with his trigonometrical party. The entire area became a national park in 1941 and Frenchmans has been the unwavering sentinel throughout it all.

'Well, this has made the walk worth it,' Jimmy panted as he made the top.

'Sure has, buddy,' I replied.

'I can't wait to get up there,' Ben said, dropping his pack on the ground.

We sat and analysed the face among the incessant march flies until Elise said, 'Okay boys, let's get there.'

The trail dropped down into what can only be described as prehistoric country. It was a maze of thick roots and tough unyielding scrub. To try to traverse this land without following trails would be hell on two legs. We had been carrying our loads for six hours, two hours over the estimate, as we walked into one of the most beautiful lakes I had ever seen. Lake Tahune was nestled directly underneath the giant cliffs of Frenchmans. It was four football fields in size and the water took on a tea colour due to the tannins from the surrounding trees. The postcard scene wasn't lost on me, but I was exhausted. We found a tiny sand beach on the lake's edge to drop our gear, and I stripped down to bike shorts and plunged into the icy water.

We realised quickly that camping spots were in very short supply. The hut that was supposed to be there had been demolished at the start of summer and was being rebuilt. Finding a place to sling a hammock in the bush surrounding the lake was almost impossible due to the dense scrub. Three pairs of climbers had beaten us there and snapped up the only flat ground, leaving us the small beach. We laid out our kit on the sand and devoured some lunch with strong coffee.

Jimmy was a little worse off than the rest of us after the hike and when I suggested we should go up to scout the landing areas, he declined.

'I'm done. You go. I need a rest.'

'I'm in, let's do it,' piped up Ben.

'I'll go for a walk to the summit for photos while you boys do your thing,' said Elise.

Jimmy lay down on the shore for a well-earned rest, while Ben and I hiked off to assess what this jump would be like.

The landing area is a critical part of every jump. There were countless cliffs to jump off in the world, but the rare combination of high, overhanging cliff with a safe landing area was the key. Every jumper has a level of risk they are willing to accept, accompanied by their own skill set. Jimmy and Ben were by far the more experienced jumpers, I had to make the assessment for myself. We hiked to the bottom of the cliff and tried to envision the freefall, flight time and likely landing areas.

'Bloody rocks everywhere, bro,' said Ben.

'Yeah, ankle snapping territory,' I replied.

The most logical area was a small grass slope directly under the cliff, but it was littered with boulders and not an ideal spot for landing. If one of us was injured, we were two days' hike from the nearest road. Helicopter rescue was available of course, but what we were attempting to do was still frowned upon, if not outright illegal in Australia, and our rescue would arrive with a $10,000 price tag. I heard about a jumper who had a bad opening and landed halfway down a cliff near Sydney. He couldn't get off and needed to call the helicopter. He cut off his parachute and threw it down to a waiting friend who then disappeared. When the rescue service arrived, he was just a hiker who had slipped on the edge. I'm sure they didn't believe his story but without proof he got the free lift out.

Ben and I hiked around the face and started climbing towards the summit.

'Let's go find the exit point and see what we can see,' I suggested.

The climb to the top was an easy 45-minute scramble following a well-trodden path. Once on top the view was incredible and we peeled away from the trail to the cliff's edge and started to hunt around for the best spot to jump – once again looking for the combination of a flat exit point, run-up if possible to aid separation, and a vertical/overhung cliff. We found what we were looking for – a flat rock directly overlooking the grassy slope 270 metres below. We could see the lake off to our left separated by a rocky ridgeline. The small sandy beach was visible as well.

Ben had an idea.

'Have you got the laser range finder?' he asked.

'Sure do,' I said, pulling it out of my pocket and handing it to him. The little gadget could measure exact distances and angles to any cliff, tree or outcrop we were seeing.

'Perfect, I have a plan,' he said, as he started measuring.

Ben took distance and angle readings of the ridgeline. After a few minutes he pointed to the sharp rocky ridge and said, 'We can clear that'. He told me his plan and it made sense, we didn't have to risk the boulder field. We could turn left after opening and fly over or around the ridge. Then fly down into the lake area, circle around the lake and land on the small beach where we were camping. I liked the idea, it would be an incredible flight and if it didn't go to plan we had a second option to land in the water. The key to the jump was to clear the rocky ridge first and get above the lake.

We trekked back to our camp and shared the idea with Elise and Jimmy. I cooked up some meals and gave one to Ben, who had only brought a bag of nuts with him on the trek. An hour after he devoured the rice dish, he threw it all up. He couldn't blame my cooking skills, he was most likely suffering some exhaustion and dehydration from the day's effort, and he crashed out shortly afterwards.

Ben had his tiny tent, Jimmy was in a hammock and Elise and I slept on the beach. Alarms went off at 5am and I made a batch of coffee for everyone. We prepped our gear and started up towards the top. While we were ascending, I could feel a breeze moving across the face of Frenchmans.

We all felt it.

'I don't like that wind,' said Jimmy.

'Me either,' I replied.

We arrived at the diving board rock we found the day before and started doing our checks. I crawled out on my belly and spat over the side, watching my spit for any movement or change in its shape. It was perfect. I had a surge of excitement before Ben pointed at the ridge and said, 'Shit, look at the ridge, boys.'

The small shrubs clinging to the rocky ridge were getting buffeted by a crosswind, the same wind we felt on the climb up. It looked strong, and after our canopies opened we would turn left towards the lake into a headwind. BASE canopies don't have much forward drive and a headwind would stop us in our flight. If we didn't clear the ridge, we would be in serious trouble. Our one safe-ish landing area on the small beach was ruled out. Our options were the original boulder field or to wait for the weather to improve. I had learned quickly in the BASE world to voice my decision immediately and with confidence. I jumped once as a beginner when conditions were not perfect, but the other more experienced guys were jumping and I was swept up in their enthusiasm. I had a 180-degree off-heading and almost hit the cliff. I learned a valuable lesson that day. So as I stood looking out across the green forest from the top of Frenchmans I said, 'I'm out, boys. This one isn't for me.'

Jimmy and Ben both agreed we should wait and we trekked back to the beach together. Over breakfast we discussed the jump and asked the other campers what the weather was doing. It wasn't looking good. The builders working on the new hut told us a large storm system was forecast for the afternoon. It seemed our window for this jump was closing.

'I'll go up onto the ridge and check it again,' I said to the boys, picking up our wind flag.

'Take the walkie-talkie so we can chat,' said Jimmy.

I tore up the mountain and peeled off onto the ridge. I could hear and feel the wind before I unrolled the flag. I held it up and we all watched it bend under the increasing force of the gusts. I spoke into the handset, 'I think we are done, lads.' Jimmy's voice came back, 'I think you're right. That's BASE jumping.'

With only limited days in Tasmania we decided to leave the mountain and focus on two other jumps we were determined to hit. The slog out was harder than the approach, after limited sleep and multiple treks up and down Frenchmans I was exhausted. Elise was in a similar state and Jimmy was struggling. Ben decided to skip Lake Vera and push out to the highway in one go. His light load was the envy of us all as we bid him farewell.

It was a scorching hot day. We took regular breaks and stumbled into the Lake Vera hut in the late afternoon. I dropped my pack, peeled off my clothes and waded out through the reeds into the ice-cold, tea-coloured water. I looked around at the dense forest from the centre of the lake. Its beauty was a veneer to its harshness and as much as I was suffering from the hike and disappointed in not jumping, I was absolutely loving it. The outdoors is where I belong.

Around midnight the forecasted storm front came through with a vengeance. It battered the tin roof of the hut and I was glad we weren't still camped on that small stretch of beach. At 6am the rain had stopped, and we crawled out of our sleeping bags to pack up and get going. The trail entered flat lands shortly after leaving the hut and travel was much easier. We passed by dozens of people enjoying the country for the long weekend: fathers with daughters, friends, couples and climbers on a mission. It was great to see so many people immersed in nature and away from towns and technology.

We were exhausted after covering over 50 kilometres to the mountain and back. Every bend in the trail had one of us voicing, 'That has to be the last bend before the car park,' but it never was. Jimmy sat on the ground, soaked in sweat, and yelled out in frustration, 'I'm done, guys. Go on without me!'

He was totally spent.

'We're almost there, let's finish it,' I said.

After a rest and more encouragement, he picked himself up and we stumbled on. We turned a bend and this time it was the last one. We all saw the car park and burst out laughing. Jimmy had had his breakdown 200 metres from the end.

Chapter 5

The 'A' in BASE

The last object I needed to jump was an antenna. Jimmy, who had hundreds more jumps than me was yet to jump one as well. We received an invitation from Ben two days after the aborted Frenchmans Cap jump which read, 'Come and see me, lads. I have found an antenna for you, it's ready to go.' Intrigued by his message, we loaded up the car and hit the road.

Ben was a manager at a pub in the small town of Cressy in central north Tasmania. Cressy is known as Tasmania's trout capital, after all the great fishing in the area, and has a population of 670. I wondered how tall the antenna was; jumpable ones range from around 35 metres right up to 400 metres. Ben had organised some accommodation in town for us. We enjoyed a steak dinner with him and over a cold beer he gave us the plan.

'It's an hour's drive away, not massive but it's easy to access and safe to jump,' he told us.

'What time are we leaving?' asked Jimmy.

'We have to jump at dawn, so let's leave here at 4am,' replied Ben.

'Game on, boys,' I said with excitement as I finished my beer.

We were on the road at 4.14am on a freezing morning. I had checked my gear the night before and was jacked on coffee as we drove for over an hour. The antenna stuck out from the surrounding green fields like a fly in milk. At 51 metres high, it would be the lowest jump I had ever made if we pulled it off. It was towering close to a small town and we would need to be extremely quiet as we gained access to avoid alerting the local authorities.

Elise reversed the car into a side road, where she would wait for us to jump. The three of us grabbed our gear, jumped the fence into a paddock and started walking towards the steel structure in the semi darkness. Dawn wasn't far away.

A barbed-wire fence surrounded the base to keep out people like us. It wasn't a big hindrance, and we easily climbed over using a corner post and dropped down inside. Whether it was nerves or the coffee, Jimmy needed to go to the toilet. 'I'm busting, I'm gonna shit myself,' he said to me and Ben, laughing as we prepared our rigs.

'Just go,' I said. He peeled away to the corner of the fence and sorted himself out.

It was a freezing five degrees as we started to climb the steel ladder. The structure was square-shaped, two metres by two metres, with the internal ladder going all the way to the top. Ben was first, followed by Jimmy, and I brought up the rear. My hands went numb against the cold metal in the first 10 metres. The frigid air mixed with the adrenaline had me puffing hard and I needed to rest every 15 metres on the steel platforms. Once my hands warmed up and I caught my breath, I'd start up again.

At the top of the structure were some broadcast dishes and we had no idea if they were giving off radiation of not. We played it safe and stayed well clear of them, selecting a platform five metres below to launch from. Due to the low height we were going to do PCA jumps, pilot chute assist. This meant holding onto the pilot chute of the man in front, so when he jumped we would literally pull the parachute out for him and let it go. This allowed the parachute to open immediately with no freefall. The last jumper would tie his pilot chute to the antenna and use break cord to achieve the exact same result. The cord would pull out his chute and break at a certain tension, allowing him to fly away. It's a tried and tested method for jumping low objects.

Jimmy agreed to give Ben and me a PCA and then jump last using the break cord. He tied his cord to the structure and then tried to climb to the outside, from where he would help us jump. As he moved around a steel beam, I saw the pins on his parachute container open.

'Jimmy stop. Your rig's gonna fall out, your pins just popped,' I told him.

'Ahh fuck, really?' he replied, knowing exactly what that meant.

Jimmy stood still while I held the back of his rig together.

'Ben, let's get you off mate, then I'll fix my rig,' he said to Ben, who was ready to jump.

'Sounds good,' replied Ben as he climbed to the outside of the tower and turned around with his back towards Jimmy.

Jimmy held onto Ben's pilot chute and double-checked all was ready to go. 'I'm set, jump when ready,' said Jimmy.

'Thanks,' said Ben, taking a deep breath. 'Three, two, one… Go.'

He jumped, falling a short distance before his parachute cracked open beautifully. He flew down to land safely next to a big tree in the centre of the paddock. The sun was over the horizon by this stage and soon the town would be waking up and we would be in a vulnerable position.

Jimmy climbed back inside the tower and when he shuffled himself into a position above me, his whole parachute came sliding out of his rig and landed in my lap.

'Fuuuuuuck,' was all Jimmy could say.

'Shit, we're in a bad spot now,' I said.

A truck drove past us on the nearby road and I thought we were about to be busted for sure. We were two guys up an antenna, making a load of noise with a huge parachute bundled in my lap that was trying desperately to escape.

'We have to go down. Let's down climb as best we can,' I said.

We started making our way down, me holding Jimmy's parachute to my chest and Jimmy above me trying not to get tangled in his canopy lines. We must have looked ridiculous.

'This won't work, let's ditch it over,' said Jimmy after a few minutes of struggling. He undid his rig and together we hurled the whole thing out away from the tower and watched it fall to the ground. It was then that I noticed Ben climbing up below us with speed.

It didn't take him long to reach us.

'We better get down lads, we will be busted for sure,' I said.

'You're ready to go, I'll PCA you now and Jimmy can climb down,' said Ben.

It was our last chance.

'Let's do it,' I said.

Ben and I raced back up to the top. I climbed outside the tower and turned away to face out into the paddock. Ben readied himself behind me and then I heard the words, 'I'm set, jump when ready.'

'Cheers bro,' I said. I took a deep breath and counted out loud, 'Three, two, one…Go.'

I leapt from the structure and felt my canopy open above me, the ground was already close. I was caught off guard and missed my steering toggles on the first grab. I found them on the second, flared my parachute but had botched it. I hit the ground hard and rolled out my landing next to the big tree. I stood up and gave a thumbs-up to the tower, Ben was climbing down.

Jimmy grabbed his rig from the ground and the three of us walked quickly back to the car, feeling more like the Three Stooges than extreme sportsmen. As Elise drove us away down the highway, she broke the silence.

'How did that go, boys?'

We all burst out laughing and when we finally caught our breath, we said in unison, 'That's BASE jumping.'

◆◆◆

I entered the world of BASE jumping with clear objectives in my mind. I wanted to jump the four objects, also a balloon, a dam and jump my top four locations: Lauterbrunnen valley in Switzerland, Lake Garda in Italy, Moab in the USA and Tonsai Beach in Phuket. I accomplished all of this in two short years. I have received my BASE number, a token number acknowledging my place in the sport, and I will be forever part of this unique community. After the first two years I found myself in a position with no clear objectives moving forward. I also had months away on other expeditions and hadn't jumped enough to stay safe.

BASE isn't a sport to be taken lightly or with complacency, it will kill you. Knowing this, I have, of late, pulled back from the edge and drifted into 'retirement'. A career in the sport was never my goal and as Jimmy likes to tell me often, 'There are no old BASE jumpers.'

The ability to walk back from the edge when conditions are not perfect is a fundamental asset. I have stood on the top of cliffs and decided the jump wasn't safe, only to watch four other jumpers throw backflips and jump off. Everyone will have their own level of risk and assessment. If you don't have the confidence to decide for yourself, and step back while your idols step forward, then this sport is not for you. Every time I evaluate a jump I tell myself, 'This could be the last thing I ever do, is it safe?' If it's not, I step back, take off my gear and go home.

BASE has taught me a lot about myself and about my emotions. It's the only sport where I will have a near-death experience and then rush back up to do it again. I have learned how to control my fear and how to execute a mission when the only outcome for failure is death. These skills I now carry into other expeditions and my life is richer because of it. When I give keynote talks around the country, I talk about BASE. I play a video for the crowd featuring one of my jumps, then open with an honest statement and a touch of humour.

'BASE jumping is the most incredible, breathtaking, electrifying and intoxicating thing you could ever do, but I do not recommend it to anyone.'

Chapter 6
Crossing the Gobi Desert

As a boy I had spent a number of years growing up in the Simpson Desert in a tiny community called Birdsville, located in the south-western corner of Queensland. I knew the country well and when not trapped in school, I spent my days fishing in the brown water of the Diamantina River. I also hunted rabbits with Dad in remote areas along red sand dunes. I would sit on the roof of the truck with a shotgun, while Dad slowly drove next to the dunes. When a rabbit popped its head up or made a run for it, I would unleash hell.

One of Dad's jobs was to rescue tourists who got bogged or stranded out in the desert. He would pick me up from school and we would drive out to find them, fix their vehicle or tow them back to civilisation. One time we drove hours to find some stranded travellers who over the radio reported their truck was bogged in the sand. They were low on water and needed our help. When we arrived, Dad took one look and shook his head in annoyance. He let some air out of their tyres to increase the surface area of the rubber and drove the truck out. A simple bit of knowledge about off-road driving could be the difference between life and death in the outback.

I had experienced the Australian desert, and I wanted to explore somewhere I had never been before, so when Elise asked, 'What about the Gobi Desert?' my interest peaked straight away. The Gobi is the fifth largest desert in the world and spans 1.3 million square kilometres. It covers regions of North and Western China and Southern Mongolia. Temperatures fluctuate from minus 45 degrees in winter to plus 45 degrees in summer. The fierce winds were known to whip up sandstorms that could block out the sun. This was a place I had to explore and test my endurance in. We planned a crossing from west to east, dragging carts containing our supplies through the centre of the Gobi. It would be a route stretching 2000 kilometres through a place still shrouded in mystery.

During my research into Mongolia I was learning a lot about its history. One of the more widely known facts is it was home to Genghis Khan. Pronounced 'Chinggis Khaan', the ancient ruler was born in 1162AD and united the nomadic tribes forming the Mongol empire. His armies invaded bordering countries and at the height of his power the empire covered China, Russia, all of Central Asia and most of Europe. His fierce armies spread across Eurasia and left in their wake large-scale massacres of the civilian populations. The great Khan died in 1227AD, yet his empire lived on under one banner until 1294AD. It was the largest empire of all time and I was excited to go and see the land that gave birth to such a unique history.

We needed to build some carts to haul all of our supplies and water, so I consulted Google on cart designs and sent out emails to anyone who had crossed a desert or built human-drawn carts. I received a reply from Tim Jarvis, an Australian adventurer who crossed the Great Victoria Desert. His cart design was solid but his trip was much shorter than ours would be and we needed something bigger. I also received a reply from Ash Dykes, a young British guy who crossed Mongolia on foot dragging a cart. His design looked more feasible and I began working on our own design, picking his brain for details. I gave my dad a call about the build and he suggested we try to make them out of alloy instead of steel. 'Remember the bull bars on the truck at home?' he said. 'They're alloy.' I remembered the protective frame mounted on the front of the truck and also recalled the countless impacts we'd had with kangaroos at full speed over the years; the frame never buckled. He said this would reduce the weight substantially yet still be incredibly strong. I took his advice on board and employed a local welder to start construction.

My initial thoughts regarding wheels and tyres were to have big wide tyres to spread the weight, a lesson I learnt from Dad watching him rescue tourists. After doing more research on the type of desert the Gobi was, it was sounding like a place of very little sand. I emailed the contacts I had made online and they confirmed my research. There was a section of huge sand dunes 180 kilometres long and 15 kilometres wide in the southern part of the Gobi. Beyond this section it was hard, baked earth, rocks, grass and desert scrub. I decided on a design with four wheels on one axle. This allowed two smaller wheels on each side but would also distribute weight better than one wheel.

I tracked down a company in London that manufactured extremely tough wheels fitted with solid rubber tyres – the perfect combo for dragging heavy carts across rough terrain. It was around this time that a good mate of mine, Mathew, joined our Gobi expedition. I owed Matty my ocean row across the Atlantic in 2016. He met the British Row2Rio crew in Portugal while he was preparing for his own Atlantic row. He and his team went on to break the five-person world record across the Atlantic in the same season.

Matty seemed to relish the expedition life. Born in England, he served in the military before becoming a stockbroker. He was successful in the game of numbers and made a swag of cash. He invested his money into building a care home for abused children and grew his business to a dozen homes providing incredible safe havens for some of England's most vulnerable kids. He had a talent for blending into any circle of people within minutes and having them in fits of laughter shortly after. During his Atlantic row his team raised over £100,000 for the NSPCC, a children's support charity. I call him semi-retired at 38 years old, and all he wants to do with his spare time and money is to explore the world.

The carts were completed and Matty joined us for some build-up training. Our fitness program included two sessions per day of strength and conditioning, followed by cart dragging at progressively heavier weights. Two kilometres with 150 kilograms, three kilometres with 160 kilograms, six kilometres with 175 kilograms and upwards to an overloaded weight of 200 kilograms for seven kilometres. I was monitoring the wear and tear on the carts and equipment the entire time. The frames were absolutely solid, the inside wheels and tyres showed more wear and tear than the outside set, yet nothing that would lead to failure. The harness, however, was fraying from the anchor points. The stainless-steel loop linking the cart to the harness was a friction point and I began thinking of ways to repair them if they did fail during the crossing. A repair kit containing webbing and a thick sewing thread was going to be a necessity.

The deserts annual weather data led me to the conclusion that to try a crossing in winter would be impossible, the minus 45 degree temperatures and fierce storms would stop us in our tracks. Equally tough would be the 45-plus degree temperatures in summer, when sandstorms were reported to be at their worst. We planned to start at the end of winter, on the western edge of the desert at the base of the Altai Mountains. If all went to plan, we would be finishing before the brutal heat of summer kicked in. How long it would take was open for speculation; conservatively, we guessed around 70 days to cover 2000 kilometres.

The amount of fresh food we would need for that length of time would weigh a tonne, so we sourced dehydrated meals. Similar to the meals I consumed during the Atlantic crossing, they were lightweight and calorie dense. We would also have protein supplements from Australian Sports Nutrition. ASN custom-made all of our supplements depending on our expedition needs, and they would play a vital role in getting enough calories into us each day. With the departure date secured we had to break down the carts, load them onto pallets and get them shipped to

Mongolia. Matty flew back to the UK to sort out his equipment and, in his words, 'Eat pies and drink beers' to gain some fat in preparation. We would next see him in Ulaanbaatar.

While sorting out shipping logistics I contacted a Scottish guy named Peter Syme. He owned and operated a company called 1000 Mile Journeys and had crossed the Gobi twice with camels. He was a wealth of knowledge and filled in the information black holes I was encountering. I told him our planned route, and although he said it would be extremely challenging with carts, it could be done. He also informed us that to find water we had to find the nomad families. Each family who lived out in the remote regions would have their own well; one family, one well was the rule. He told me there was one stretch of roughly 400 kilometres where not even the nomads could survive; there was no water at all. This posed a big obstacle on our route. The only way we could overcome this section was to carry up to 100 kilograms of water in barrels, which would be near impossible, or have some form of support with camels or vehicles. We were hoping to go totally unsupported, so I digested the information but left the final decision for a later date.

The day finally arrived, and Elise and I boarded a plane for Mongolia. We had a five-hour stopover in Hong Kong and then we flew across China towards Mongolia. Staring out the plane's window, I noticed small communities in northern China, but once we crossed into Mongolia I couldn't see anything but desert below us. We flew over the south-east portion of the Gobi on our way towards the capital Ulaanbaatar. The desolate orange landscape reminded me of the Simpson Desert. Was it sand or gravel I was seeing? I studied every contour and river, trying to pre-empt what the desert could throw at us. Processing what-if scenarios in my head was a trait I had picked up in the military and a tool I used to manage the risk on expeditions. Below us in gullies and on top of the mountains, snow was holding strong from the extreme winter. Elise and I were sharing a window, taking it all in as Ulaanbaatar came into view.

The ancient city had a skyline born from the Soviet Union; the drab black and grey architecture was unmistakable. Not even the modern skyscraper in the city centre, mimicking the arc of the Burj Khalifa, could pull it from the era of Russian dominance. The pilot circled the city and on the fringes I noticed people were living in suburbs formed of gers, with a small fence or rock wall around them. The ger or yurt is a portable, self-supported round tent covered traditionally with skins but now with white canvas, and is typically the home of nomad people. I would learn in the coming days that the ger communities were the poorer neighbourhoods and the concrete jungle of apartment blocks belonged to the more affluent.

The pilot touched down with a softer than usual landing and we disembarked into the lone building at the airport. We breezed through the non-existent customs and into the waiting hall, where we were confronted with a wall of Mongolians holding up signs. Among the round-faced, heavily coated locals, we spied our names written on a sign held by an expressionless man in a black leather jacket. This man was Tumuro. Standing next to him was his plump, non-smiling, taller son Orgil, also in a black leather jacket.

We approached with beaming smiles and shook hands with the men who would ultimately be responsible for getting us into and out of the desert. These guys were the local arm of a western company I'd found online. They had supported many trips into their countries remote regions and were fully prepared to help us with our mission.

Tumuro was overweight to the point of being round, yet looked like he could handle himself well. It wouldn't have surprised me if he was a former KGB agent. He didn't speak a word of English but seemed to understand what was being said. He had served in the military as a helicopter pilot before retiring to a life guiding tourists into the outdoors. Orgil knew the basics of the English language after recently completing a course, and would act as interpreter. He appeared to be part of the generation born into a more comfortable life. He was overweight, stood six foot two inches tall and had the appearance of a young man who had never endured any physical or mental hardship. He was undecided what he wanted in life, instead choosing to play video games throughout the long winters.

They were men of very few words I discovered as we departed the terminal and headed towards a green van in horrendous condition. This derelict vehicle was owned and driven by Tumuro's friend, Dafka, who apart from looking like a skinny Mongolian version of Luigi Mario, gave us the first smile we had received since arriving. We wedged into the seats while Orgil slammed the door by pulling on some tattered upholstery. It was peak-hour traffic heading into the city and we passed a number of coal-fired power plants billowing black smoke into the eleven-degree afternoon air. The land surrounding the city was bleak, snow still covered the hills and dull grey dominated the scene. They stopped at a viewing point and we climbed out to a pile of rocks on the side of the busy highway. The view overlooked the power plant and the condensed buildings of the capital. Under our feet were dozens of shattered vodka bottles and although we weren't overly excited about the setting, we were happy to be starting the expedition.

The following morning Tumuro and Orgil picked us up from the no-frills hotel we were staying in. A combination of jetlag, traffic and cold had me sleeping soundly within seconds of my head touching the pillow. Wearing their black leather jackets and pants, with Orgil also sporting a French cap, they took us to the black market to buy equipment.

'Keep hand on money, many stealing here,' warned Orgil as we pulled up. We entered a fenced outdoor area spanning many acres, selling every item you could imagine. If we were on our own it would have taken days to sift through the chaos and find what we were looking for, but with help from the lads we went straight to each item. First were 20 litre water barrels, fourteen in total. They were pre-loved Coca Cola, juice and detergent barrels but at $3 a-piece they were a bargain. We would each carry four and have two spares. This would allow us to carry up to 80 litres each in areas with no water. We found tarps for covering the carts, a small shovel, lightweight folding stools and gas.

After the market we had lunch at Tumuro's house and checked the carts, which Tumuro had received and stored. In my mind I had envisioned a lovely ger house with a backyard I could construct the carts in, but the reality was the sixth floor of a ghetto concrete apartment block. Tumuro's wife was absolutely lovely. She served us tea, fed us sliced meats and made us feel part of the family. Their apartment was tiny, and I couldn't see the carts anywhere. Orgil took me out onto their narrow balcony where I was shocked to see them in the corner, wedged upright together and covered in filth.

I wanted to build them entirely to make sure all the parts had arrived but that was impossible. We couldn't carry them down the stairs just to check and bring them all the way back up again. I actually had no idea how they got them up there, going by the physical condition of both the men. They said they were trying to save us some money on storage fees and had kept them safe for us. I appreciated their effort and couldn't get angry. The next shock came when Tumuro pulled out a map of the Gobi Desert. His map was ancient and of a huge scale showing very little detail.

He pointed to our starting position and told us, through Orgil translating, that we could drive there in one big day, no problem. This didn't sound right to me. I had calculated at least a three-day drive to our chosen start point. I looked at the map and noticed the village of Bulgan he had his finger on wasn't the right one. I moved my finger 1000 kilometres west to the edge of the desert and found another Bulgan. 'This is where we start,' I said.

The whole family erupted in conversation. I didn't know what was being said but I could judge by their reaction they had no idea what we actually wanted to achieve. I was disappointed in our western contact for not passing the information along. A few minutes later I had detailed exactly what our mission was and what we expected from them.

'This very big,' said Orgil warily, as it all finally clicked into place.

'Yes, it is mate,' I replied with a big smile.

Tumuro had never travelled that far into the desert or been through the area in the middle we wanted to try and cross. I told them water was our biggest concern and Tumuro echoed the words of Peter Syme: 'One family, one well.'

'How were we supposed to locate these families?' I asked Tumuro.

He thought for a moment. With Orgil translating, in his broken English, he said they would need to drive ahead and find them before we arrived. The families moved all the time, sometimes the water wasn't good and it was possible some families wouldn't have enough water to share. This didn't sound good. It dawned on us that we were going to need more support than we originally thought. We needed the lads to find the families and guide us to them, otherwise we were running the serious risk of being stuck somewhere with no water. If that happened, we might need rescuing.

We asked Tumuro if he was willing to drive ahead of us through our proposed route from the start to at least halfway. He paused for a moment and thought, then replied with a nod and what, if I didn't know better, looked almost like a smile.

I think he was getting excited.

Tumuro wanted a second vehicle as back-up in case he became bogged or broken down. It made sense. He suggested Dafka. Apart from my concerns about Dafka's vehicle being reliable, my first impressions of him were good. He seemed to be a happy guy and was much fitter than Tumuro or Orgil, which could be a big benefit. I agreed. We all shook hands, with everyone finally on the same page. We ate biscuits, drank tea and I asked Tumuro's wife to take a photo of us to mark the occasion.

When she handed back the phone, Elise checked the photo and cracked up laughing. She showed me the picture and I had the same reaction. The snap of the four of us on the couch showed Elise and I beaming huge smiles while Orgil and Tumuro were stone faced. It was hilarious, made even more so when we looked up on the carpeted walls of their home to see their family photos. The men, Tumuro's wife and Orgil's sister, all not smiling year after year.

'Why are you not smiling?' I asked Orgil.
'This is Mongolian way,' he replied.

◆◆◆

The following day was spent collecting our dehydrated food and extra equipment from customs. It was a frustrating day but eventually we had everything in our possession. Afterwards Orgil took us for 'khuushuur,' a local pastry similar to a fried pizza pocket filled with carrot, cabbage and cheese. While outside waiting for the food I noticed a cow chewing on a plastic bag. Its hips were sticking through its malnourished tight skin and I felt sad for it in this unforgiving environment. The temperature had plummeted overnight, and the day was cold. On the horizon, the power stations looked more insidious than usual, spewing their toxic fumes into the frigid air. They were helping destroy one thing while keeping another alive and I yearned for the quiet of the outdoors. I wanted to be left alone with my thoughts as I walked along through the remoteness. I knew the desert would calm my mind, we just had to get to the start line.

When Matty left after our training camp he was in peak shape, and by the time he arrived in Mongolia he had packed on ten kilograms of fat in preparation for the crossing. Apparently the 'pies and beers' phase was his favourite part of the whole build-up process. We crammed into the guesthouse and set to work packing up the food and equipment ready for departure the following day. The Scottish outdoor company Highlander had supplied us with a heap of kit, including six 120-litre duffel bags to pack our dehydrated food into. We got to work and by the end of the night we had jammed the food away, divided up team supplies and sorted the protein supplements into weekly ziplock bags. If anyone had walked in halfway through dividing up the white protein powder we would have looked very suspicious.

The first lesson I had to learn on departure day was that it didn't matter how prepared or excited I was to get moving,

Mongolia had its own time. After agreeing to pick us up at 8am, Tumuro, Orgil and Dafka rolled up at 8.42am, in two vans. We loaded up all the food bags and equipment and climbed aboard. We looked like the Beverly Hillbillies off on an adventure. The lads then needed to fuel up the vehicles and buy themselves mobile sim cards, jobs they could have taken care of the day before. By the time we were ready to leave, we had the added bonus of peak-hour traffic as we drove out of the city. When the buildings and pollution finally disappeared behind me, the stress from the last few days disappeared too.

'Are you happy to leave the capital behind?' I asked Elise. She passed me her journal she had just finished scribbling in:

'I've never been in a place that can seem deserted despite crowds of people and raging traffic jams. The medium strips of dirt and skeletal trees created an eeriness only broken by the beautiful bundled faces of the babies. With cheeks as plump as freshly ripened peaches, they reminded me of lifelike Cabbage Patch dolls from when I was a kid. It's as though the city was abandoned many years ago and then stumbled upon again in a desperate time. The paint stripped buildings reflect the harsh seasons of this place.'

The road was straight and puckered with holes, and our average speed throughout the first day was 70 kilometres per hour. At times Tumuro would become overexcited about some mountains or sand dunes in the distance, gesturing wildly and rattling on in Mongolian to Orgil for a good fifteen minutes. We would be waiting for Orgil to turn around and fill us in on the nature, history and culture of his country as it revealed itself. He would turn and say, 'There is sand,' before turning back to stare out of the windscreen. Elise, Matty and I would look at each other with rolling eyes. It was apparent communication was going to be an issue and we would not be receiving much information.

We made frequent stops at specific piles of rocks called Ovoo, on the side of the roads. Some were small stacks and others were enormous mounds draped in prayer flags and resembling temples. Tumuro would jump out, walk around them three times in a clockwise direction and grab a handful of grass seeds from a bag to throw in the air, he would then toss two or three cups of milk into the breeze. This custom traced back to ancient Mongolian folk religious practices. In modern times they are a place to worship heaven, gods and hold ceremonies led by elders or shamans. I was all for acquiring as much good luck and protection as we could for this expedition, so we all started joining in.

Late in the afternoon we arrived at a small town called Hurarong, nestled among featureless hills. We pulled up inside a fenced area containing six large gers, one of which would become our hotel for the night. Staying inside the traditional Mongolian home was on my to-do list, so I was excited to get this chance on our first night. I stepped through its tiny doorway into the round tent and felt right at home. The thick walls were supported by a wooden frame and in the centre was a cast-iron stove for heating and cooking. The floors were covered with carpet and the timber beams were elaborately decorated with bright colourful patterns. Around the exterior were beds, a set of shelves, a small washbasin and a mirror. There was everything I needed; I could picture myself living in one on a block of land somewhere back home in Australia. For Matty the stay wasn't quite so comfortable: he didn't fit the beds due to his six foot four inch, 120 kilogram size and wasn't overly impressed.

After Hurarong, rough dirt tracks and potholed tarmac roads were the norm, as we ticked over 1000 kilometres since Ulaanbaatar, and it dawned on me how far we were going to have to walk to get back. The foothills of the Altai Mountains began to show themselves on the southern horizon and we paralleled the incredible snow-covered peaks for an entire afternoon. The valley we were driving through opened up into a flat section, stretching to the west and north. The ground was covered in a veneer of fine grass, proving the rumour that the Mongolian grasslands in summer were bathed in green. After seeing the land for the first time I couldn't imagine it transforming from barren to beautiful in a couple of months. As we drove through this valley, however, we started to see the first signs of life buried beneath the soil.

Wildlife appeared in the form of a two-humped Bactrian camel. We had never seen one in the flesh, so we stopped to get a closer look. Excited during our first encounter, we took dozens of pictures of the hairy beast, with the Altai Mountains offering the postcard backdrop. Ten minutes further down the road we saw a group of five camels and before long they were scattered everywhere across the planes. As we pulled into the small town of Altay at the end of another long day, we felt we were finally in the real Mongolia. We were away from the city and getting closer to our start point.

We arrived at the edge of Bulgan the following day and pulled off at a flat area of dirt beside the road. We unloaded everything jammed inside the vans: carts, wheels, food bags, barrels, tents and accessories all out ready to be checked and repacked into the carts. Slowly and methodically, we assembled the components. It wasn't a complicated procedure, but we didn't have an endless supply of bolts or tools and I wanted it done right the first time. The two main body sections bolted together, then the front pulling arms were attached. Wheels went on next, were tested for alignment and then we loaded them up. Two 120-litre food bags per cart and 88 kilograms per person of dehydrated meals, enough to last 70 days. Four 20-litre water barrels per person went in next, enough to last ten days if we didn't come across any wells or water sources. The little remaining space was loaded with tents, personal kit, sleeping rolls, a spare wheel each and camera gear, including a drone. For cooking we had a box of gas canisters and for power we were using solar panels and battery packs from Goal Zero.

It was a mountain of equipment because we wanted to try and do the crossing unassisted if possible. Matty had been in touch with Guinness about a world record for an unassisted crossing but he was yet to hear back. If there was a chance to get one, we wanted to give it a shot. The last job was to attach the sponsors' logos to the side of the carts and get some pictures and video with the drone. We were set to go. I had been studying the maps and had a plan in place for our first few days. But one thing I had come to realise is that when it comes to adventures, plans have to be adaptable, if not changeable.

Our plan was to go cross-country, and I had our first bearing set in the compass and I moved to take the lead. Elise fell in behind me and Matty brought up the rear. The day had got away from us with all the preparations and we took our first steps into the desert at 3pm. The carts weighed 180 kilograms each and when I took those first few steps and felt the harness pull tight, the cart buried itself into the sand.

'Oh shit,' whispered a little voice in my head.

The ground underfoot was firm but when the cart crossed over it the four wheels cut deep. I immediately regretted relying on other people for information and not trialling bigger wheels. But it was too late to do anything about it. We worked together pushing one cart at a time through sandy riverbeds, where it was impossible to pull through solo. We took regular water breaks and when I looked back I could still see Bulgan clearly in the distance. We were moving desperately slow.

We decided to camp for the night after three hours covering only eight kilometres. In planning I knew we had to average 30 to 40 kilometres a day if we had any hope of getting the job done before the extreme summer temperatures. We set up camp and the boys drove the vans back to see us. I'm sure they were thinking we were out of our depth, but they didn't let on. They got a fire going and set their camp up close by. We hadn't eaten for most of the day and were exhausted. We boiled water to make meals and the three of us looked at each other in silent shock.

> *Elise's journal: 'The next step, water break, is all I can think of. The end is just this myth that lies somewhere on the horizon far to the East. It was a relief to step off, to have a break from it all; no traffic or artificial noise, no money exchanging hands, no bills to pay. The only currency we know now is water.'*

I woke up at 3.30am, starving and thirsty, and shovelled the dehydrated dessert I'd prepared before bed into my mouth. As I stuffed my face, Elise woke up. 'Come and eat your dessert,' I whispered to her.

One thing we needed was calories, especially Elise, who was pulling the same weight as me but was 30 kilograms lighter. We polished off the meals, guzzled down some water and fell back to sleep.

At 8am we broke camp and set off into soft sand and a slight incline. A four-wheel-drive track came into view and it was heading in our general direction. All thoughts of avoiding roads were suppressed by the effort it was taking to move the cart. I pulled onto the track and felt the relief instantly. Apart from the ground being firmer, the path was also clear of bushes, rocks and holes that stopped us in our place. We moved along at a slightly better speed but needed regular rest and water breaks.

As per our plan, we wanted the boys to drive ahead and find the next water source. Once they located it, they could call us on the satellite phone to relay the GPS coordinates and we would make our way to them. Two things happened on the first day that made this crucial part of the plan impossible. The spare GPS broke in the morning and the satellite phone supplied to the boys had a broken aerial and didn't work. As I said, all plans were adaptable; our backup plan was to send them ahead to find the nomads and the water. They would then leave one vehicle there and drive back to us in the other van to relay the information. We hoped there wouldn't be too much back and forth and after repeating the new plan multiple times, the boys departed.

The track we followed began to make its way towards a gravel road in good condition. We were still heading in the right direction, but I was adamant about not using the new road. After stopping for a coffee and a dehydrated meal for lunch, we carried on into the afternoon where the sand underfoot was breaking my soul. I knew Elise was struggling as well. She had dropped back behind Matty and at times was falling face forward into the dirt. It was hard for me to know what to say.

Elise's journal: '*Sand, about three inches deep that seemed to grab my wheels and pull them into the earth. At one point it took me nearly 45 minutes to move not much more than one kilometre. I tripped up constantly, heading face first into the dirt, looking up to see the boys moving further and further away. This was harder than I could've ever imagined. When I reached the boys I looked at them, panting, willing them to say how hard they were finding it. It was a relief when they did.*'

The physical toll was stacking up. The going was so much harder than any of us had thought. At one point in the afternoon as I stopped to relax my shoulders and catch my breath, I noticed for the first time the environment around me. The snow-capped peaks were on our northern side watching over us in the distance; to the south were camels grazing; and in front of us stretched the desert bathed in an afternoon glow. It was a beautiful moment and I smiled despite the hardship. Still smiling, I bent into my harness, focused on the ground two metres in front of me and used my trekking poles to start the slow trudge forward again.

Tumuro and Orgil drove back to us and we were surprised to see them so soon. They told us ten kilometres away there was a river where we could top up our water barrels. This was great news to hear, we were each carrying two full barrels, which were a huge weight to haul. The boys disappeared again and knowing water was so close we each dumped 20 litres to bring the weight of the carts down. Not long after they departed a camel herder cantered over on his horse and dismounted. He looked to be in his fifties and was dressed in traditional clothing. He had bowed legs from a lifetime of riding and his wrinkled face had endured many harsh winters. I shook his hand and the roughness of his grasp and the firmness of his shake caught me off guard. Here was a man who seemed to be thriving in this harsh environment. We were just tourists struggling along on a suffer fest holiday to get a taste of his life and share in his knowledge.

We communicated as best we could through smiles, drawings in the dirt and charades before the man mounted his horse again. He paused before riding away and looked again at our carts. Raising his hand he gestured towards the gravel road close by and seemed not to grasp the reason why we were in the sand struggling when the road was there. I watched him ride away and I failed to grasp the reason either. Our goal was to cross the Gobi. Looking at each other, in our battered and beaten condition, I said to the agreeable audience of Elise and Matty, 'Let's jump on the road.'

The hard gravel was like skating on ice and we made great progress for the remainder of the afternoon. We pulled off the road near a pile of rocks and set up camp before dark. We could see a small village in the distance that we assumed would be located on the river the boys mentioned earlier. The rock pile shielded us from the wind and we settled in for a well-earned dinner and sleep. We had covered 22 kilometres – a massive improvement on the day before – and as I crawled into my sleeping bag I thought, 'We can do this.'

The wind picked up during the night and evolved into a solid gale as we packed up and hit the gravel at 7am. With our new outlook and the sheer impossibility of dragging the carts cross-country I asked Tumuro to use the dirt roads and nomad trails to get us to the next water source heading east. Checking over the maps together he pointed out a large river we should cross the following day.

'Perfect, show us the way there.'

He seemed happy with the new approach, and nodded enthusiastically before driving off and leaving us in the dust.

Elise's journal: 'I have to keep reminding myself that although I'm strong, the boys are bigger and stronger, and are going to move more efficiently. For every one of Matty's steps I take three, so I'm always comfortably 500 metres to one kilometre behind them. At this point my cart weighs 160 kilograms. At 5'4' and 65 kilograms, I have the leverage of a cheap spoon through hard ice cream. If I hit a stone or a mound of desert grass I get pinballed to the side or completely stopped dead.'

Our trail turned south-east and we trudged on through a frustrating headwind. We had multiple visits from locals riding horses. They would dismount, remove their gloves and shake hands with us, a beautiful show of respect to strange foreigners crossing their land. We had a massive third day covering 28 kilometres before we set up camp in constant wind. Matty lost his glove during one intense gust. It was snatched away and carried off out of sight. He was also hit with a plastic bottle, hurtled at breakneck speed across the ground. It smashed the big man straight in the leg and I laughed to myself watching him hop around.

On Day Four we were up early again. I felt as if I'd played back-to-back games of rugby. Elise and I shared one tent, while Matty went solo next door. Our morning routine was wake up, get some water on the boil, make breakfast and drink coffee, then crawl out of our sleeping bags, pack up everything inside the tent, pull on clothes and get outside. The temperature had dropped well below freezing overnight and turned the tops of our water barrels into ice blocks. I was wearing the same clothing I wore in Antarctica during my expedition to climb Vinson Massif, testament to the Gobi Desert's brutal weather. Morning rituals would be completed one at a time as we strolled off into the desert with our single fold-out shovel. Tents would be broken down and packed away and carts loaded for another day of dragging.

Balancing the weight of the cart was important. If the weight was too far forward the handles would bounce up and come crashing down, pulling on the harness. If it was too far back, the handles would lift up and slam into my elbows and armpits. The first part of the day always involved a few stops to fine-tune the load. My body was screaming during the first hour after setting out, but as it gradually warmed up, I settled into a steady pace behind Elise and was able to drift away.

My mind was either a powerful friend or lethal enemy depending on the day I was having. When the dragging became monotonous, without interruption from rocks, bush or conversation, it could really wreak havoc. I could be enjoying a super-positive morning and then find myself riding an Alice in Wonderland spiral of negative emotion, burrowing myself deeper and deeper into the rabbit hole. I could break the cycle by stopping for a moment, having a look around and appreciating where I was and what we were doing. For the following few hours I would be on top of the world only for the pattern to repeat itself again. It could be maddening at times. I was sure Elise and Matty were having their own battles adapting to the new world we found ourselves in. For me, these mental gymnastics were shaping up to be one of my toughest obstacles.

By the afternoon the wind had died down, the sun was shining and we had made it to a wide flowing river at the 28-kilometre point. It was time to call it a day and enjoy the last couple of hours of sunlight. We crossed a small bridge and found the boys parked underneath, having a wash and warming themselves by a fire. We dropped our carts, grabbed the empty water barrels and went down to the river. Although the water was flowing, we had to filter it to make sure we didn't get sick. We were using 10 litre gravity-fed Katadyn filter bags to clean the water of bacteria. We filled two barrels each for the next few days and then got down to the business of washing our bodies. The water was freezing but refreshing and before the sun set I was clean, hydrated and had a hot meal in my belly.

> *Elise's journal:* '*As the sun went down a herd of horses waded through the water and rolled in the sand. As I splashed the freezing water on my face and dunked my mummified feet, willing them to carry me for two more months, I couldn't help but smile. This moment, these simple memories, are why I am out here.*'

Over the following two days we covered 55 kilometres, sticking to our new daily average. We were getting visits from locals every few hours as we walked on the road, so to help better communicate with them, we asked Orgil to write us a letter about what we were doing. We could then give it to people to read instead of playing a complicated game of charades. The letter was always well received and everybody who stopped would always try to give us something. Pieces of candy, bottles of water, or my new favourite, a goat's milk biscuit called Aaruul. It smelled like Parmesan cheese and was hard enough to crack stone, but it was delicious. Elise and Matty didn't like them at all, so there was plenty for me.

By the end of the first week we had adapted well physically and emotionally to the near constant dragging. We now headed along a dirt trail, which turned towards a mountain range in the distance. The mountains were the barrier to the interior of the Gobi, a place where even the nomads sparsely travelled. We would need to cross the range to stay on course. How we would do that we had no idea, but Tumuro seemed to think there would be a trail through the peaks somewhere. He was doing a great job finding locals and gaining information of what lay ahead, so I didn't doubt he would find a way.

As we ventured further away from anything resembling civilisation, we increasingly came across herds of animals owned by nomad families: horses, camels, goats and the occasional dog. In the early afternoon we met a shepherd boy tending a herd of goats. He came over to us and walked along smiling as he watched his herd. Young goats were headbutting each other, kids were sucking milk from their mothers, and they were feeding on the fresh grass popping up with the approaching summer. The boy had a keen sense for his animals and upon hearing a faint whimper, he ran to pick up and carry back a newborn that had been separated. He placed the baby goat on Elise's cart and we continued on together. We arrived at two gers where a small cluster of adults were busy working. We asked the boy if they were his family and he nodded enthusiastically.

We unharnessed ourselves and smiled as a group of children and their dogs ran over to greet us. They all beamed smiles back, then led us over to where it looked like their parents were busy doing something. Once we got closer, I could see five goats were tied down to the ground on their sides and wide eyed with fear as the adults worked away at them with a type of brush. They were brushing the hair from them and collecting it. I had read that goat and camel hair was used as insulation in traditional homes and here was the first step of the process. The elders smiled and stood up to shake our hands before returning to their work. The eldest man said something to a younger woman who smiled and gestured for us to come inside their Ger. She made the international hand signal for drinking and I guessed we were being invited in for tea.

I stepped inside through a satin curtained doorway followed by Matty and Elise. As my eyes adjusted to the light, I could see the cast-iron fireplace in the centre of the small circular room. The walls were decorated in bright colourful patterns with carpets on the floor and a pile of thin mattresses and pillows stacked in one corner. There was a shelf for cooking utensils and a religious shrine on the wall in front of the door. The children clambered in and settled themselves on a mattress and began watching a tiny television powered by a truck battery. They were smiling and giggling at big Matty and the foreigners sitting cross-legged on their floor. We were given tea, followed by biscuits and bread. There was an assortment of creamy sauces and some form of hardened animal fat, but we played it safe and stuck to the tea and biscuits.

Their generosity was heart-warming and once we were full and couldn't eat or drink another thing, we exited and took some group photos with the rest of the family. We bade them farewell, returned to our carts and covered as much distance as we could during the last few hours of daylight. As we laboured through the foothills leading into the mountains, I thought about our encounter: the generosity, the simplicity of life and the overwhelming happiness the family were projecting. It was these encounters I would remember forever, how they could transform a tough day into one of the best days of the expedition.

We set up camp at an elevation of 1813 metres, where the steady gain in altitude and the coolness in the air at sunset meant another cold night. We had discussed our finishing point a number of times before the expedition and, with the edge of the desert not represented by a road, fence line or a sign reading 'You made it', we relied on others who had gone before us. Peter Syme, who had walked the Gobi with camels, designated a town called Sainshand as his finish point, and it also became ours. After studying the maps I figured we had another 1600 to 1700 kilometres to go. When I came to this realisation, I couldn't even begin to think how long it would take us judging by our current progress. The land was constantly changing and throwing obstacles in our way, the mountains were ahead of us and we didn't know if there was water on our route. I put my thoughts to the side and focused on one day at a time. Kilometre by kilometre we would get closer, and one day in the future it would all be over.

◆◆◆

Our second week in the desert began at 2.30am, when an old car containing a few drunken Mongolians pulled off the trail and stopped within three metres of our tents. Their headlights lit us up like a New Year celebration and they started blasting their horn. We had heard reports about the drinking problem in Mongolian society and had seen it firsthand in the capital. Even out here in the middle of nowhere, any dirt road with a lot of traffic would be littered with vodka bottles. Tumuro had two full crates of vodka in his van for nightly drinks and sacrifices to the gods. I lay in my sleeping bag as the horn penetrated my soul. Matty cracked first, he unzipped his tent, stuck his head out and yelled, 'Fuck off.' The driver received the message loud and clear as he stopped honking, reversed away and drove off into the night.

A few hours of restless sleep later and we were packed up and starting our day, which began with eight kilometres of steady uphill hiking. It felt like we had been walking uphill almost every day. Just as I wondered whether the desert would ever be flat, we hit corrugations in the trail. Corrugations are a formation of parallel ridges in the ground very similar to a corrugated-iron roof. They typically form on dirt roads and if not flattened out, they get bigger and go on for longer. As a boy growing up in the Northern Territory of Australia, I saw dirt roads like these all the time. With Dad driving a truck built for the conditions, he would increase the speed and float across the ridges, producing a loud hum from the tyres. The vehicle would have less steering control but there would be no damage. If he drove slowly, the corrugations would make the truck vibrate violently and cause problems.

The corrugations wreaked havoc with the carts; we couldn't move fast enough across them to smooth out the ride and the tyres fit neatly between the ridges, creating a breaking effect every time they dropped in. This motion sent the carts bucking left and right and the handles would bury into my hips or slam my rib cage. Elise, with less body weight, was in a worse position but even big Matty wasn't getting through unscathed. We battled on, each taking turns to stop and scream if we received a rougher than usual jab to the ribs. The trail finally flattened out as we entered a small village of five gers and four mudbrick buildings.

This village was a group of families who lived together for one reason: water. In the centre of the village was a natural spring, bubbling to the surface. We stopped for a rest and took the time to fill up a barrel each. Tumuro and Orgil had returned from questioning all the locals and told us the water could be drunk straight from the ground. We walked over to the partially fenced spring and the water was very clean and very cold. But it was also loaded with goat shit. We decided to filter it just to be safe, as a dose of diarrhoea out here would make the rough days even more so.

I noticed the families had built large enclosures half buried into the ground and I asked Orgil what they were for. He explained that in winter when it was extremely cold, the animals needed to be undercover. With temperatures reaching minus 45 degrees Celsius, that made sense. Having their animals penned also made it easier for the nomads to collect the cow and goat dung, dry it, and use it as fuel. Through the long winters that's all they would have for heating and cooking.

We left the village fully loaded with water and spent the afternoon dragging through sporadic sections of corrugations, uphill grinds and downhill slogs, and even some sprinkling rain late in the afternoon. We had endured a battering, and even though we covered 25 kilometres, only 20 kilometres was a straight line towards our destination. Lying in the tent that night, I thought we would need to do some big days soon or we would never get our journey completed in time.

Elise's journal: 'My mind had its first beating today, and I was exhausted from it all. A dehydrated lasagne, a big drink of water and bed. Tomorrow will be better.'

◆◆◆

Never in my wildest dreams or expedition planning sessions would I have expected hail. Yet, at dawn on Day Nine, tiny ice spheres fell from the sky in abundance, which were spun and whipped across the plains by the relentless Gobi winds. We were held in our tents for an extra hour by the storm. When it cleared a beautiful blue sky appeared, the sun came out in full force and we couldn't find any excuse to steal more sleep.

'What shall we do today, team?' I yelled out the question that had become part of our morning routine.

'I think we should go for a walk!' answered Matty and Elise, enthusiastically.

'Okay let's go!' I shouted, and we started packing up.

Some 20 kilometres after the hailstorm, we arrived at a large river with a nomad family perched on its bank. I had seen the river on the map days before and had prepared myself for our first river crossing with the carts. We had planned to unload the carts, ferry the gear across and then carry the empty carts across one at a time. But our plans were squashed when we laid eyes on the river. It wasn't the waist-deep meltwater I had expected; it was frozen solid. Winter hadn't released its grip on the Gobi. We parked the carts next to the family's ger to take a closer look at the ice.

The husband and wife were busy trimming their goats with a pair of scissors as we approached. They stopped to come over, say hi and shake our hands. Two little girls about two or three years old with beaming big smiles came out of the ger but kept a safe distance at first. They were filthy dirty and super cute, creeping closer and closer until they were touching the foreign carts. Tumuro had driven back along the river where he had been scouting a crossing for the vehicles and pulled up next to us. He started talking to the husband and after a few minutes spoke to Orgil, who turned to us. 'The carts can cross no problem, cars must go around,' he said.

I was sceptical at first. I walked down the bank and tentatively out into the middle of the river. Once I realised it was solid, I began to figure out a path to take the carts across. Most of the ice looked good but some sections were thinner. By thrusting my trekking poles into the ice and fanning out like a soldier clearing a minefield, I had a good scope of the places to avoid. If the carts' wheels broke through, we would have a mission on our hands getting them out again.

I crossed first, with Matty walking close behind to lend a hand. When my cart's wheels lodged in a small ice gulley, one shove from the big man and I was free again. The wheels cut into the ice and left small trenches, but there were no breakthroughs and I made it safely to the other side. Matty crossed second, easily hauling his across the gully that held me. Elise went last and made it across with no problems at all. We waved at the family from the opposite bank, the two little girls and their parents waved back smiling. We dragged the carts up the bank and journeyed seven kilometres towards the 3000-metre high mountains that were now bearing down on us, before calling it a day. We had racked up 27 kilometres, one hailstorm and one ice river crossed.

I always think about factors of sleep when I'm on expeditions and how when I'm at home in a comfy bed, with a climate-controlled room and a perfect pillow, I sometimes can't sleep. Out in the Gobi, after a full day of dragging, I could be lying on sharp rocks with a book under my head as a pillow and sleep for ten hours. I often tell people at my presentations, 'If you want to know what a good sleep feels like, come on an adventure.' As I poked my head out of the tent at dawn, after enough time flat on my back to recover and do it all again, the peaks blocked our path ahead. We knew this day was coming, it was the day we would find out if there was a mountain pass to cross or if we would need to go on a five-day detour to the south to get around.

Our first 13 kilometres of the day was slightly uphill and warmed us after another chilly night. Tumuro came back to deliver the news that we would need to take the detour, the pass was still covered in snow. I was annoyed at first but had guessed this was the most likely outcome. We changed our bearing south to follow Tumuro's tyre tracks and paralleled the mountains until just after lunch, when we came across a nomad family living at the base of the peaks.

The local man spoke to Tumuro and Orgil, answering all their questions. Once we had caught up to them, Orgil informed us there was apparently another trail through the mountains that was only used by the locals and was free of snow.

'Should we try?' he asked us.

'Hell yeah, let's go for it,' we all replied.

Anything that could save us five days was worth a try. We stopped to eat, rest and prepare ourselves. The track was going to be steep and it wouldn't be easy getting our carts through.

Matty took the lead, Elise went next and I brought up the rear. The trail was a steady incline in the beginning but quickly wound its way through steep cliffs, getting gradually steeper. We were battling across rocks and around fallen boulders and the carts were taking a battering. Matty's cart lost a tyre, forcing us to halt for some quick repairs and we were all stopping regularly to catch our breath. The steepest section came into view and we could see the boys had parked their vehicles at the top to indicate the summit. As steep as this may sound, if I didn't have a 160-kilogram cart attached to me it would be regarded as a pleasant uphill stroll. But with the added weight it was a genuine test of will.

Matty chugged up first, crested the top and collapsed in a heap to furious applause from the boys. They knew we were stubborn foreigners not wanting any help and once I saw Matty complete it solo, I was determined to do the same. Elise went up next, but her body weight just couldn't get the leverage and she needed a push from Matty. Then it was my turn.

'I'll be right,' I told Matty, and inched my way up, digging in my trekking poles to the point of snapping them and using every ounce of strength to stop sliding backwards. Ten metres from the top, gravity snatched the life out of me and I began to slide down. There are not many things that scare me, but when I'm attached to a huge weight on wheels and it wants to roll backward down the hill, my eyes will begin bulging. Matty sensed the tipping point and brought his weight to bear, saving me from backflipping to the bottom and most likely being injured. It was a necessary intervention and even though I was annoyed at my weakness, I was over the moon to reach the top of the pass.

The view was incredible; it plateaued out into a lush green valley with a small lake, shadowed by another peak reaching higher than the pass and covered in snow. We rehydrated and cooled off as rain started to sprinkle down followed by snow. We carried on into a freezing headwind, meeting one nomad who galloped up at full speed on his horse, away from a large scattered herd of sheep. We were bundled up in Arctic clothing, while he wore a humble traditional coat. He was in his late twenties and looked in peak physical condition. When he dismounted to shake our hands, his grip was like a vice and he beamed a huge smile as we handed him our note detailing our adventure. We shook hands again before he vaulted onto his barebacked steed and galloped away to tend his animals. We had covered 26 kilometres of uphill torment and had one thing on our minds: sleep.

The night was freezing, camped high on the mountain pass. The wind was howling, sporadic rain came in and when we woke at our regular time the following morning, we were being battered by a snowstorm. We decided to wait it out in our sleeping bags, while the wind intensified and pulled the tent pegs from the ground. The temperature dropped to minus five. By 11.30am the snowfall had eased to a sprinkle and the rain was holding off. The wind was still fierce, but we wanted to get going and do as many kilometres as we could.

I knew we had to get down off the pass to warmer temperatures and more stable weather, so we packed in lightning speed and started trudging up a steady incline as fast as possible to warm ourselves. Elise has never been good with the cold, and when we had previously discussed Antarctica as a possible adventure location, she said she wouldn't be able to handle it. But here she was bundled up and stomping into a freezing headwind with numb hands and frozen feet. The conditions were some of the nastiest I've had to stomp through, but when it came to those kinds of hardships, I absolutely loved them.

Elise's journal: 'I now know the real meaning of trudging; I felt like I was going backwards. A few hours in, my head was giving out on me. I just couldn't find something to take my thoughts off the stomp. The relentless winds were like a frozen brick wall. I had my buff covering my face and so much snot was coming out of my nose that it blocked me from breathing through my mouth. Just as I ripped it off in a fluster, I heard from behind me, "Now THIS is living, isn't it, babe?" I replied, "You're sick, Richmond." If I wasn't strapped into my harness, I would have punched him.'

The snow clung to my beard, and my fingers and toes were numb. These were the days I relished: everything against us and no option but to dig in and keep moving forward. I looked to my right and saw an eagle gliding next to me. Brown feathers covered its powerful wings and the majestic master of the sky was close enough to touch. The force of the wind kept him adjacent to me as time stood still. At one point he turned his predatory head and my eyes locked on to his. In that fleeting moment we were engulfed by the howling wind.

We made camp early, still on the mountain pass but with the knowledge we would be heading down in the morning.

> *Elise's journal:* 'Overnight my wet clothes and wet blanket attitude dried out. I've picked myself up a little desert flu and Luke has been trying to get me to bush blow (hold one nostril and shoot snot out of the other onto the ground) for years now. I have always said I didn't have the nasal power for a clean blow and it's not necessary when tissues are accessible. I have now found my nasal power. Bush blowing is way more convenient out here than wasting precious baby wipes.'

Four kilometres from our camp, where we woke again in below-freezing temperatures, we began our descent out of the mountains. For the next three hours we wound our way down rocky trails and gorges. Some sections became so steep that it wasn't safe for us to try to descend by ourselves. As a team, the three of us took one cart down first, then we walked back up to get the next cart and then repeated the process a third time. It was time-consuming and taxing on our energy levels, but if we took a tumble with the weight of the cart bearing down from behind, it could crush us.

We dropped 600 metres in elevation and the temperature rose to 25 degrees Celsius. We went from freezing our arses off to sweating buckets and having to shed all our layers again. Our descent levelled off and the trail formed into a sandy riverbed. The ground underfoot slowed our progress and we arrived at two gers, attended by their owners. I could see thick green grass and some small trees sprouting up from the sandy floor close by and I knew there must be water. Tumuro, Orgil and Dafka were parked and talking to the nomads as we pulled up exhausted.

Tumuro relayed important information he had learned from the locals: the water here could be the last clean water for a long time. We were about to enter part of the desert where water was very scarce and even the nomads couldn't guarantee there was any ahead. Tumuro was nervous and wanted to fill all of the extra water barrels and keep them in the van as a reserve.

'Can we fill all?' asked Orgil.

As adamant as we were about carrying all of our own water and doing as much as we could ourselves, his idea made perfect sense. To risk running out of water and sending the boys off for a very long drive to find it just didn't add up.

'Do it, lads. Let's play it safe,' I said.

◆◆◆

As you may imagine, physical contact for Elise and I was one of the first things to be sacrificed once the expedition began. We were filthy dirty, physically and mentally drained, and the last thing on our minds was cuddling. Conversations adapted to the conditions and in the normal world where we would discuss training regimes and where to drink our next flat white, we now discussed how to stick to our daily ration of four baby wipes and the best technique for morning rituals.

Elise's journal: 'Intimacy is dead in the desert. It's compounded by a few things. 1. By the end of the day we are so shattered that making dinner is an effort, let alone anything else. 2. I'm pretty sure Luke thinks the dirtier he is the more legit of an adventure it is. 3. Luke is reading Mike Horn's book Conquering the Impossible. *Luke rates him as the greatest adventurer of modern times.*

"Babe, do you want to know what Mike Horn does with his snot?"

"Please, do tell."

"He rubs it all over his face. He says it's the best for protection against the elements."

I said to him, "We are not there yet, babe, use the SPF 50." Intimacy is dead in the desert.

◆◆◆

On Day 13, I noticed an object moving in the distance. I could tell immediately it was coming fast towards us. My mind began running what-if scenarios and I thought, 'Is this a bunch of desert bandits coming to rob and kill us?' As I contemplated what I would do if it was, I realised it was a group of large animals heading our way. I wondered if bandits rode horses for a second, before realising it was five Bactrian camels at full gallop. We stopped and watched the animals run – they were going to pass close by – and then I noticed the boy.

Wedged in between the two humps of the biggest camel was a small herd boy with a whip. He was driving the camels hard and didn't slow his pace even when he noticed us staring at him. We didn't know where he had come from or where he was going, and I'm sure he thought the exact same thing about us. It was a beautiful moment that's etched in my memory forever, something very few people on this planet will get to witness. Boy and animal surviving together and supporting each other in one of the harshest environments on earth.

We set up camp at 6.30pm, with the sun still roasting us. The lads had parked up close by and Dafka was busy collecting animal dung for their fire. Tumuro came over to stand with Matty and me as we stared out at the incredible desert.

'Gobi start now,' said Tumuro without a hint of emotion, before walking back to his van.

I turned to Matty in shock.

'I knew that bugger spoke English,' I said.

We laughed before looking back at the scene in front of us as I thought, 'The Gobi starts now.'

My body had been adapting to our new life and the extreme elements. We were consuming close to 5000 calories of dehydrated food and protein shakes per day, but I was still dropping weight at a rapid pace. All my body fat was already gone, and my legs seemed to be getting skinnier by the hour. Matty was also dropping weight fast but wasn't too worried due to his pre-storage before the trip. Elise looked the best out of the three of us, the amount of food we were consuming was decent for her body weight and she hadn't noticeably changed. Due to weight restrictions, we couldn't carry excess food and snacks, and as the days ticked by my cravings for fat, sugar, bread and butter, were becoming insatiable. Matty was the same: at most breaks the first topic of discussion was about what foods we would eat upon returning home. This is a conversation inevitably held by anyone who has taken a long expedition, but for me it had started earlier than normal. I thought I was beginning to starve.

The following day, two hours into a perfect morning, Tumuro was parked on the side of the trail and straightaway we could tell it wasn't good news. We needed to head east but the nomad trail turned north towards a number of small hills in the distance. Our choice was simple: head east overland, through the rocks, sand and desert scrub, or follow the trail. Orgil said the detour could be many hours but it was too rough to risk the vehicles overland. We knew how hard it was to cross overland with the weight we had behind us so we didn't have much choice except to follow them.

The day was dry and hot and the wind had picked up. After lunch the trail began to veer north-east and by the afternoon we were heading south-east. It was frustrating at times, but I knew we had no other option but to follow the trail. The wind increased by the middle of the afternoon and the sandstorms came out of nowhere, stopping us in our tracks. We would drop the carts, huddle behind them for a few minutes until the storm passed and then resume. We had to wear our ski goggles and face masks to protect ourselves from the sandpaper effect of the wind.

Our trail intersected a gravel road that connected Mongolia to China. Tumuro, Dafka and Orgil were waiting for us at the crossing to tell us they planned to drive 90 kilometres north to a village where they could restock their food and get fuel for the vehicles. It took me a moment to realise we hadn't fuelled up since leaving Bulgan, and it made sense to get the job done using the good road heading in the right direction. We would carry on down the trail and they were to find us when they returned later that night.

As the lads were about to pull away, Orgil leaned out the window and asked a question that stopped me cold: 'Need any snack?'

Before realising I had spoken, I had ordered two loaves of bread, a tub of butter and a can of coke.

'Beers!' yelled Matty.

'Haribo lollies,' said Elise, with a cheeky grin. Supported or unsupported, it didn't matter in the slightest. I was losing weight like a prisoner of war and we had 50 plus days to go. It was for survival – at least that's what I told myself.

We carried on until late afternoon and decided to set up camp at a point where the trail began to ascend towards another hill. For a desert supposedly flat and not very sandy, the Gobi seemed to be either going up or down, and covered with sand. We had covered 29 kilometres, our biggest total so far but after going through my routine and plotting our course on the map, we had only covered 17 kilometres towards Sainshand.

I was feeling low after dinner, realising how much the detour had cost us, but then I heard a sound that picked me up instantly. The honk of the horn sounded the arrival of the snacks. When Orgil laid out the spread in front of us, the light from my head torch made it seem like Christmas had come early. I tore into the fresh loaf of bread, cutting slabs of butter like cheese to put on top. It was absolutely delicious and the rush of energy into my body jacked my heart rate. I heard Matty crack his can of beer and he yelled out from his tent, 'This is the life.' The sugar from Elise's lollies kicked in and we were chattering away like schoolkids and fell asleep when the crash took over moments later. With a belly full of bread, I slept content, forgetting about the lost kilometres and the hill in the distance.

◆◆◆

Elise's journal: 'There is no such thing as an easy day out here. Easy days are a fantasy that exists only in the early hours of the morning when we are just waking up. When we can't yet feel the aches or pains. When the weather is cool, and we can't see past the mountains to what awaits us. Within the first hour or two of the day, the fantasy is usually over. There are hard days, brutal days and there are soul-destroying days. But no easy days.'

Day Fifteen will be eternally remembered as Hell Day. It started like any other but after the first hour the ground underfoot turned into deep sand. Added to an uphill trajectory, it was the worst possible scenario for us. The carts' four wheels buried into the ground, cutting deep tracks through the desert. Progress was slow and energy-sapping.

I was breaking trail, with Elise following and Matty in the rear, but after 50 steps I would need to stop and catch my breath before repeating the process. After a few hours of this, with random expulsions of profanity, I was almost finished. Elise and I changed positions and she broke trail for a while. She battled forward, and I knew how hard it must have been for her.

Elise's journal: 'The wheels seemed like they were being pulled underground. I kept turning back, certain Luke was being hilarious and holding back my cart, but it was just the deep sand engulfing my wheels. I stopped and screamed at the top of my lungs the worst vocabulary I could offer. Then the tears came, not enough for the boys to figure out, just enough so my body and my mind were both on the same page.'

The heat had been building throughout the day, and by midday it was adding fuel to our struggle. Absolutely exhausted, we stopped in the shade of a rocky outcrop for lunch. The frustration of the sand was easy to read in all of us.

I spoke first. 'I chose the wrong wheels, if it's like this the whole way we are finished.'

Matty said, 'We might have to cut the weight down.' This received slow nods from Elise and me. Reducing the weight so we could move easier through the sandy sections was an option. But it was a last resort and we decided to carry on and see if conditions improved.

Elise's journal: 'My body was on a 45-degree angle trying to leverage the cart uphill through the bog. Sweat was seeping from every part of me and I found myself missing the freezing weather from a few days before. This heat, this terrain, was not only slowing us down but was making the journey dangerous. Our bodies had already dropped weight from the sheer volume of the work we were doing each day. Luke is wasting away in front of my eyes and we are only a quarter of the way in. To continue ruining our bodies like this as the temperature only gets hotter would be crazy.'

The trail didn't improve after lunch, if anything our exhaustion made the ordeal even worse. We all went through random outbursts of swearing at the sand. Our composure was well and truly gone. We were moving so slowly that Tumuro drove back to check we were okay. Orgil's squishy face wasn't what I needed to see at that point in time and when I said, 'It's very hard', he simply replied, 'Yes, Gobi starts now.' I could have killed him right then and there. He picked up on my frustration and they left us alone to continue battling.

We arrived at a flat section of ground late in the day and I was the first to throw my harness off, slam the cart down and collapse to the ground. Elise came in second looking totally destroyed and collapsed next to me. Matty arrived last.

'I'm fucking done!' he yelled, slamming his cart to the ground near mine. 'I'm finished, I'm calling a plane, fuck this!'

I pulled out the video camera to capture Matty going off; he was saying what we were all thinking. I had been in his position on other expeditions and realised how priceless the footage could be. He calmed down after a while and I made him a protein shake: red frog raspberry, his favourite flavour.

We didn't start our evening routine, instead we decided to sit together to discuss the events of the day and how we were feeling. It had been a tough two weeks and an extremely tough twelve hours.

'If there are too many days like this, we won't make it across,' I said. They agreed.

'Let's drop one food bag,' said Matty.

'Yeah, I think so too,' said Elise. Our options were to keep battling on, avoid sand as much as we could and take our chances. Or we could scale back some weight into the vans and hopefully make dragging easier. We bounced ideas and goals back and forth and, in the end, we came to a realisation. The style of crossing we were attempting hadn't been done through this area without support. I had also made a mistake with the wheel size, which was hindering us, although we also concluded the weight was so heavy that bigger wheels might not have helped.

We also wanted to enjoy what we were doing. For twelve hours I had been fixated on the ground two feet in front of me, not looking around and thinking only about the pain. We wanted to carry all our own food and supplies but not if it meant a torturous two months we would end up regretting. The other point was about gaining the title of an unsupported expedition. Initially, I wanted an unsupported crossing, but in reality, once we chose to have the vehicles close by, and had ploughed into bread, butter and beer the night before, it was technically all over.

Support could be considered many things: emotional, physical or simply knowing that rescue was a phone call away. Satellite phones, and our ability to log on to the internet from anywhere on earth has essentially given support to all expeditions that utilise the technology. In my opinion, the only fully unsupported expeditions that have earned their title were the first expeditions to Antarctica by Shackleton, Amundsen and Scott. These pioneers were exploring the unknown interior of a frozen continent, risking their lives to be the first and were away for years without contact or support from civilisation. Yet they were supporting each other through the hardship, so what really is 'unsupported'? Is it something saved purely for the solo adventurer with no communications, no assistance and no chance of rescue? If that's the reality, then I'll probably never be unsupported. The risk would be too high, and dying, even while doing something you love, is still dying, and what a waste that would be.

We decided to unload one 40-kilogram food bag each and load it into Dafka's van. If all went well, we would get it resupplied in 25 to 30 days. This brought the weight of our carts down from 170–180 kilograms to a more manageable 130–140 kilograms, depending on how much water we carried. It still wasn't going to be a walk in the park, and I knew many more tough days were waiting for us, but we made the call and now we would live by it. I slipped into my sleeping bag feeling like an 80-year-old man who had just tackled a buffalo. As I drifted off to sleep, I wondered what the Gobi had in store for us next.

◆◆◆

The following three days were the morale boost the team needed. After scaling back the weight, we could move quicker across the sand and even when it became tough in places and we needed to help each other, it was nothing compared to hell day. Our best day before hell day was 28 kilometres, now we had clocked up 64 kilometres in two days and were on track for another 30-kilometre day on Day Eighteen. It wasn't a huge improvement, but over time those few extra kilometres would add up.

In the afternoon the winds increased to such a force that we could not take a single step into it head-on. We tried our best to tack across it like ships on the sea but it was pointless. We had to stop. Setting up tents in a gale-force sandstorm is no easy task, it took three of us 20 minutes to set up one. Matty needed to lie spread-eagled on the tent while Elise and I placed in poles and hammered in pegs.

> *Elise's journal: 'In storms like this we cover up as much as we can. Jackets, goggles, buffs up to our eyes. I've never liked small spaces and find it hard to breath when my buff is over my face. Breathing through my mouth deepens my desert flu and my nose starts to run, making the process even more uncomfortable. You either stay trapped in a buff full of snot or get a face full of dust and storm. Today got particularly bad; I went to try and rotate my buff for some relief and what I thought was snot was actually blood. The nosebleed soaked my buff, but I had no choice but to let it flow until we got some cover in our tents from the storm.'*

We were safe inside our tents as the wind raged outside. Tumuro and Orgil had set up their camp near to us. When the weather was miserable, they all slept in the vans and had converted Dafka's into a cooking space. The wind eased off close to sunset and Tumuro brought over a bottle of vodka to share. We crawled out of our tents and stood in a circle with Dafka and

Tumuro, who treated us to the Mongolian custom. Orgil wasn't allowed to drink, so he managed the cup and held the bottle.

One at a time we were given a cup full of the white lightning. The general rule was to flick a single drop to the desert spirits then drink it back in one gulp. The cup was passed on to the next person and refilled to the brim. The process continued until the once full bottle was empty. We each had two cups and because we were dehydrated from dragging, it went straight to my head. The boys returned to their vans to crack another bottle as I crawled back into my sleeping bag and lay down to watch the tent spin for a few minutes. We were battling against Mother Nature one minute and then half drunk on vodka with our smiling guides the next.

◆◆◆

Maintaining our hygiene was important to fend off bacteria, but staying clean in the desert was a challenge. We had to save all the water for drinking and couldn't spare any to wash ourselves. The baby wipes we carried became a new form of currency, more valuable than money, and could be shared or traded for food if times were desperate. We each had a ration of four baby wipes per day for a 70-day expedition. I needed two for the morning ritual, one to wipe my face and important bits at the end of the day, leaving one spare for back up. Toilet paper could have been more economical, but the wipes had disinfectant qualities, a cleaner feel and fewer accidents with the more robust material.

> *Elise's journal: 'The dust penetrates everywhere. Earholes, nose holes and places you wouldn't think to use a baby wipe. When I crawl inside the tent expecting relief, it's not there. Dust follows you in, ready to fill every crevice, get in your dinner and settle on your skin reminding you where you are. I haven't washed my hair since the start of the trip and have*

only taken a brush to it once. It's just not worth the hassle but it's starting to itch.'

The wind blew for 48 hours straight, the temperature dropped near zero during the nights and, like clockwork, the dust storms reared up in the afternoon along with the heat. Through all of it we maintained our average distance per day and were disciplined in getting up and moving on every morning no matter what.

On Day 20 we noticed a small village in the distance, the first major village we had seen since leaving Bulgan. We entered the seemingly deserted town of a dozen small single-level buildings and I noticed powerlines connecting them. I realised quickly that where there was power there could be cold drinks.

One thing adventure has given me over the years is perspective; for example, when I'm in a freezing environment like Antarctica, a warm cup of water is the best thing you have ever enjoyed. Similarly, in the desert after drinking nothing but ground temperature water for almost three weeks, a cold sugary beverage would be the greatest thing ever. It's human nature to adapt to our environment and when I'm back home for a few months, I sometimes catch myself getting annoyed at my less than perfect flat white coffee. When I notice this behaviour, I know I have lost perspective and it's time to get back into the wild.

We found the vans parked next to a mud shack, where Orgil waved for us to join them inside. We dropped the carts and ducked our heads at the doorway to enter the small shop. A lady stood in the corner working away with dough next to a large steel bowl of boiling oil. We had arrived at a Khuushuur shop, selling the delicious fried pastries we had sampled in Ulaanbaatar. My mouth began to water as I sat down at the wooden table. I felt and looked as if I was starving. When the lady started bringing pastries over, I devoured them two at a time. Matty was of a similar mindset and together we inhaled a dozen in as many minutes. I washed them down with four cups of sweet coffee.

Elise was more restrained and although she was a vegetarian at the time, that didn't stop her devouring the meaty filling.

After our public display of binge eating, Tumuro and Dafka went to refill our water barrels from the village well, while Orgil walked us to the local shop. Walking without a cart attached was a foreign feeling; I felt like I was floating and stumbling at the same time. We entered the shop and laid eyes on a treasure chest of snacks. Matty and I shared a cheeky grin that said, 'Here we go.' I walked out with three loaves of bread, butter, honey, jam, four packets of chocolate wafers, and a bag of the '3in1' instant sweet coffee I had enjoyed at lunch. I also had a cold Coca Cola in my hand, which I finished in three gulps. Elise loaded up on lollies, some shampoo satchels and a small plastic bucket she said was going to be her washtub. Matty's arms were full of snacks similar to mine plus a sixpack of local beer. We all had smiles on our faces from ear to ear.

We were buzzing as we took some photos with the locals and then made our way out of town. Overloaded with extra water, we decided to set up camp earlier than usual to give ourselves a couple of hours to drink a beer, eat some snacks and wash ourselves properly. We made camp near a prominent pyramid-shaped 2275 metre mountain named Eej Khairkhan. Orgil told us it was a sacred place of worship for the local people, called 'Mother Mountain.' It was a relaxed afternoon watching the sunset and washing off the layers of grime built up over the last 20 days. Even the guides took the afternoon to have a bath and dry in the sun.

Elise's journal: 'The old soul tunes were playing from the van's speakers and it was time for some serious dirt admin. As Luke (bless him) helped me wash my hair while Matty got stuck into some clothes washing. The sun was shining and we were kicking around the Gobi Desert in our underwear, enjoying our first proper wash in three weeks. As I write this, I'm watching the sun fall behind the sacred mountain; my hair is clean, my belly is full of bread, my mind is silent, and my heart is peaceful. I guess Luke was right, this is living.'

◆◆◆

On Day 21 we crossed the 500-kilometre mark and took a minute to congratulate ourselves on the effort so far. We still had a long way to go and I didn't want to think about how many more days it would take us to finish. We also had our first encounter with bulldust, a fine dust like talcum powder that fills up holes in the trail and once disturbed hangs in the air and clings to everything. I had grown up with bulldust and knew it well; the outback regions of Australia are renowned for it. On a scale of difficulties in the desert, the deep soft powder didn't really register next to the wind, rocks, holes and sand. It was just another element to clean off ourselves at the end of the day.

Dalanzadgad is a town in the central southern area of the Gobi, located fairly close to our halfway point. It was 530 kilometres away and positioned on a main highway linking Ulaanbaatar through to China. Dalanzadgad was also a tourist hub for people who wanted a quick glimpse of the desert before returning to civilisation. Large ger camps for tourists were constructed in the desert close to the town, where they enjoyed day trips to the sand dunes. The luxury of a ger camp is what I shifted my focus to and we decided to push hard to one of these camps and then take two full days of rest. Setting realistic goals and having something to aim towards was important to keep up morale. The finish line was still too far away to think about, but a halfway camp with cold beer and showers was exactly what we needed for motivation.

The land was flat as we started our fourth week, the temperatures hot and the scenery desolate and unchanging. We covered 104 kilometres in three days, our biggest totals so far and we were all moving at the same steady pace with our eyes fixed on the horizon. During the long hours of nothingness my mind travelled inward, dissecting my mistakes, regrets, triumphs and tragedies: hours of thinking and following chains of thought down rabbit holes of enlightenment. It's only on expeditions that I begin to think in this way, back home I'm surrounded by constant sensory stimulation and a moment of daydreaming, in a manner like the Gobi induces, would be considered temporary insanity.

New ideas were conjured up daily to be put into play on my return to the 'civilised' world. We were in a place that would be considered the absolute middle of nowhere but in reality, this was someone's somewhere. This place was the whole world to the nomad family we were camped close to at the end of Day 24. A man, his wife, three beautiful smiling kids, two dogs, 200 sheep and a bunch of camels – this was their home. The sun set over the family's ger, bathing it in a glorious yellow light. I was slowly evolving as a man and learning new things about myself in the absolute middle of somewhere.

◆◆◆

Our days were broken up into manageable chunks of distance and time. After breakfast and packing up the carts, our first morning block of dragging was 90 minutes, followed by a 20-minute rest. This was repeated twice more before a 45-minute break for lunch. The heat built as the trip progressed and our lunchbreaks evolved into a quick inhalation of food, before crawling under our carts for a nap out of the sun. In the afternoon, depending on how we were feeling, it was usually one more 90-minute block and then a single hour to bring us to our camp for the night. By staying disciplined and sticking to our strategy, we hit a 35-kilometre total on Day 25 after ten hours of hauling. My body would be screaming for rest by the time we made camp, and every time I took off my boots I asked myself, 'How the hell do I do that again tomorrow?'

Elise's journal: 'The body is an amazing thing. We are in a 24-hour degradation/regeneration cycle. At the end of a 10-hour day, we undo our harnesses at around 6pm. In the short time it takes us to sit down, debrief and make up a protein shake, our mind has already told our muscles, "It's cool, you can shut down now, you're done." Minutes later as we attempt to stand, our backs freeze, hamstrings tighten, hips stiffen, and our entire bodies grind to a halt. We spend the next hour hobbling around, being careful not to stray too far from our small tent's radius until our bodies finally scream, "For god's sake get prone already. And don't you dare do this again to me tomorrow." Most nights in agreement with my body, I go to sleep thinking I can't possibly do that again.'

During the monotony of desert life, and I guess in any circumstance where you spend a large amount of time in close proximity to other people, small things start to grind on you. One thing Matty did was starting to drive me insane. In normal life it would barely register but out here it was becoming something I would obsess about for hours. We both had some hearing damage from our military service, but he also had a habit of saying 'Pardon?' after almost everything I said to him. This lovely act of manners was really pissing me off. Some days after a few injections of 'Pardon?' I would simply stop talking to avoid the response, leaving long spells where we wouldn't communicate and with me coming off as a grumpy prick.

During this period where I was getting wound up, he was feeling the same about Elise and me. He was on an expedition with a couple and was in a tent by himself. I didn't realise that sometimes when Elise and I were laughing and chatting at night, he was feeling left out. It was an oversight on my behalf and over the weeks of dragging, it became a point of obsession for him. While Matty and I had our issues, Elise was feeling the same way about how Matty walked off faster in the mornings, leaving her behind. In normal life she would assess this as him having a much bigger stride than her and wanting to warm his body up with his normal pace. Out in the desert, however, it felt like he was doing it on purpose and subtly telling Elise to 'hurry the fuck up.' It wasn't long before all of the built-up tension started to get to us and we needed to do something about it.

'We need to talk,' I said to Matty as he was pulling on his boots one morning.

It's funny how those four words are like the international words of warning that something's about to go down. He knew what was coming.

'Yeah, what's up?' he said, with a prickly tone.

From there I unloaded all my silly grievances; not with malice or personal attack, just to get it all out. He then returned the torrent back at me and got everything off his chest as well. It was then Elise's turn. Once we were all done there was a moment of silence before it was time for hugs and a laugh at each other.

After unloading all the tension in the morning, I had one of the best days of dragging. I had no negative thoughts consuming my time, I was happy and at each rest stop we all chatted like we had in the first few days. We were back on track emotionally and the importance of communication during the monotonous act of crossing a desert wasn't lost on me.

On turning north, we slowly inserted ourselves into the foothills and mountains. The barren section of the Gobi to the south fell away and we started to notice the changing of the seasons. The surrounding peaks had captured rainwater, allowing grass to sprout around their bases and in the valleys connecting them, heralding the arrival of summer. This brought in the herds of goats, camels and horses to feed on the leafy greens they hadn't eaten through the long winter. The constantly changing environment was incredible; one moment we were in barren flat sand, being belted by sandstorms, two days later we were watching animals feed on grass in pleasant temperatures.

Elise's journal: 'It was like we discovered a completely different Mongolia. "Can you guys smell that?" Matty vocalised my thoughts. We were smelling grass. For the last four weeks our noses had been filled with our own body odour, dust and camel shit. The grass smelt like this year's prize-winning flowers from Chelsea. It smelt like life.'

A man and a little old lady on an ancient motorbike stopped by to say hello. She smiled and handed over a big handful of homemade biscuits. They smelt like sour yoghurt and were rock hard. She gestured to her knees and then to her mouth, which I interpreted to mean the biscuits would be good for our joints. I bit into mine and didn't mind the sour flavour. Elise and Matty couldn't stomach them so once again I was to inherit the lot. They rode away while giving us big waves. The generosity of these people who had so very little was amazing.

We were lucky during the Gobi expedition because Matty had secured sponsorship from Inmarsat Global, a satellite communication giant. They had given us satellite uplink equipment with unlimited data and I began to understand very quickly how this type of technology could be an emotional double-edged weapon. Sending out our blogs and pictures was incredible for everyone at home following our journey. Also having a 24-hour reliable satellite phone gave us a sense of security, while receiving emails and messages from friends and family was a huge morale booster. However, too much of it could make you wish for home and chip away at your resilience.

We balanced out the risk by sharing the blogging duties and I limited my online time to once every three days. On the night of our twenty-seventh day in the desert, I received an email from Dad. He had been working away on a book about his incredible life in outback Australia and sent me a poem he had written as part of his memoir, *Southern Cross Gypsies*. Dad had struggled with depression in his fifties and I had a small dose of it during my twenties after leaving the military. The subject line read 'Black Dog', and as I read his words they struck a cord.

Don't let the Black Dog stalk you in the quiet of the night.
When your defences have been shattered and
    you've given up the fight.
He will wait until you weaken, like a vulture at your gate.
He has no good intentions and he will surely seal your fate.

Like a hound from hell he searches to feed on souls of men,
Men who have been beaten down, with broken hearts within.
So before your last hopes fade and he takes you to his lair,
Let him wait a little longer as I have some words to share.

We blokes think we're just too tough; we never cry unless alone.
A woman shares her fears and tears and makes
    her feelings known.
Let me hold you now, old mate, like a man might hold his brother.
There's only me and you here now, and I won't tell another.

You can even cry for all I care and let it all come out.
If we can't help a friend in need, what the hell's this life about?
It won't mean you're weak or soft; it might even make you strong,
And you might find a way back up from this life
    that's all gone wrong.

I long to see you smile again, and that old larrikin in your eye,
Come on, mate. Talk to me; let's give this thing a try.
Don't let the Black Dog take you; by God he's had his share,
Chase him back whence he came and chain the bastard there.

And if he ever growls and prowls again,
    to have his heartless hunger fed,
Don't turn that gun upon yourself;
    shoot that mongrel dog instead.

– Clive Richmond

Depression in our society seems to be growing every year. It could be a product of our work–life balance and the growing amount of habitual stress the normal person lives with every day. It could be a feeling of disenfranchisement in a world where unlimited knowledge is at our fingertips. Or a lacking sense of purpose even though a child born into today's western society can choose to become anybody they want to be. I have found that a life full of positive feedback from actual lived experiences has maintained my mental health. Every dollar I have earned has gone into adventures and although my life doesn't fit into the normal brackets of society, I wouldn't change it for anything. When talking to anyone dealing with depression I would say, 'Don't bottle up those emotions. Talk to someone and let's go on an adventure.'

◆◆◆

The following three days of monotonous dragging were broken with moments to remember. Two young boys on horseback rode up to shake our hands and say hello. They were very interested in what we were up to and posed for photos, beaming huge smiles. The elder brother had a two-way radio around his neck that crackled to life with an older Mongolian voice. The boys snapped to attention and made ready to leave. The elder bounded up onto his barebacked horse with ease but his little brother struggled. He was going in circles, trying to climb up onto his horse. His brother laughed at him for a few seconds before riding over to help him up. They both galloped away while waving back at us and never losing their smiles.

Then there was a visit from the Mongolian version of the Backstreet Boys. A four-wheel-drive vehicle pulled up in a cloud of dust and out jumped four well-dressed young guys looking out of place in the desert. One spoke broken English and he told us his friend was one of the most popular singers in Mongolia and they were on tour. We all took photos and they told us they were excited about what we were attempting. Before leaving they gave us a copy of their CD and a big bottle of vodka as a parting gift. They drove away to their next gig and we stomped on till dusk.

We handed the bottle as a gift to Tumuro, who was baffled how we came to have it in our possession despite our best efforts to explain. It was better quality vodka than the stuff he was drinking, and he immediately brought out the cup of death and opened the bottle. The cup went around to all of us three times before the bottle was empty and our heads were swimming. Elise didn't enjoy the cultural drinking experience but never wanted to be rude, so she swigged it back. Thankfully Tumuro went back to his camp, but it was short lived. He came back with vegetable soup and a second smaller bottle of vodka. Two more shots each and we were well and truly ready for bed.

By the end of Day 30 we had been covering big distances daily and our bodies were showing signs of wear and tear. My right foot was giving me issues, my left knee wasn't playing ball and my overall condition resembled Tom Hanks from *Castaway*. The increasing heat was making us sweat and soak our clothes through, adding an extra dimension to our layers of filth. As much as we were struggling at times, and the uncomfortableness of life definitely had its challenges, the simple process of walking and existing was something I truly enjoyed.

> *Elise's journal: 'There is certainly nothing glamorous about living in the desert. We sleep on the ground, we pee in bottles, we rest in the dirt, we wash at 10-day intervals, we shit in holes, our skin is peeling, and our fingers are cracking. I'm constantly blowing blood out of my nose, the boys are cultivating an ecosystem in their beards, we smell revolting and my leg hair has reached its full potential. What the journey lacks in glamour though, it makes up for in simplicity; and there is true beauty in simplicity.'*

We had clocked up 885 kilometres since departing Bulgan, which if my map skills were accurate was our halfway point. We also passed through the biggest village we had yet to encounter: Baynlig. We repeated our routine from the last village and devoured deep-fried Khuushuur at a hole-in-the-wall shop. This time two ladies inside worked overtime with dough on the bench and a slab of unknown meat sitting on the floor at their feet. I tried not to think about the hygiene standards and waited patiently for the delicious treats. I downed seven, Matty six and Elise five. They were super greasy and contained chunks of animal fat that I knew was going to deliver much-needed calories, if we didn't have any issues from the unknown floor meat. Next was the local store to load up on our favourite snacks and then we were heading for the desert once again.

On the way out of town we passed a school that seemed quiet, until lots of smiling little faces started popping up at the windows and yelling out to us. Before we blinked, we were surrounded by 50 kids who had decided we were much more interesting than what was happening inside their class. They were all smiling, laughing and posing for photos. We handed out some of the lollies we had just bought and like the Pied Piper, the kids followed us through the village. They all waved while yelling out some of the English they had been learning in school. 'What is your name?' 'Hello, how are you?' It was heart warming.

Elise's journal: 'Throughout this entire journey there is one thing that has truly stood out for me, the children. Whether they are running behind us in an excited cluster, riding horses through the countryside or being thrust into our arms by their parents for a photo, they are all full of endless energy, curiosity and pure innocence. At the same time, I am being sent photos from Australia of my friends' newborn babies, whose parents can't hide the love they already have for these beautiful little humans. These children, just as I did, have the simple gift of growing up knowing what it feels like to be cared for, to be held and to be loved.'

The meaty goodness inside the deep-fried treats passed through us in the first few hours after leaving town. One at a time we would scramble for the shovel and venture away from the carts to cast out the demons. Maybe putting the meat on the floor in the heat wasn't the best place to keep it.

We met up with the boys and the vans just before it was time to camp. They had parked on a fork in the dirt trail and we had another decision to make. It felt like déjà vu. Ahead, if we chose to go straight, the trail turned to sand and would be very tough. Our other option was the longer route along yet another trail to the north. As a team we decided that since we had taken two big detours already, we would follow the shortcut as it would gain us back two days. We pushed on for our last hour and then called it a day, with 35 kilometres in the logbook.

The following day gave us our first taste of what the rest of the expedition would be like. The heat rose faster than normal and peaked at 34 degrees Celsius just after our lunchbreak. We cowered under our carts at each long break and our water intake doubled from four litres per day in the cold mountains, to eight litres per day in the hot barren flat lands.

Elise's journal: 'A hot breeze made it bearable and when it hit our sweat it almost felt cool, almost. "Well you know what they say about shortcuts. If it was easy, it would just be the way." More words of wisdom from Luke as I try to convince myself we've made the right choice.

There were large numbers of camels grazing by the trail in the afternoon. The increase in heat seemed to have had an impact on them as well, and they were all starting to shed their winter coats. The two-humped beasts looked extra dishevelled with half of their hair gone. We noticed a large herd of them bunched together in the distance, and as we got closer, we saw it was a well. Buried in among the cluster of camels was a nomad hauling up water to give to his animals. His smiling wife stood by, tending to the calves of the herd. Upon seeing us he stopped what he was doing and came over to shake our hands.

We must have looked fairly dishevelled because shortly after saying hello he turned to his wife and said something. She nodded in approval and he ran off to his motorbike and tore away to his ger in the distance. His wife gestured for us to wait and we took turns hauling up water for the camels. They were bustling to get to the trough and their stench was ripe. They were drinking greedily and after each big gulp they would lift their heads, slap their big lips and shake their heads wildly. They were beautiful creatures and one day I would love to do an expedition with them.

The man arrived back with a big plastic jug of white fluid and a small bowl. He filled the bowl and took the first drink himself. He then refilled it and handed it to me. I was thirsty and worn out from the hot day and took a small sip then gulped it down with glee. It was camel's milk mixed with sour yoghurt, it wasn't cold but it wasn't hot either, and it was delicious. Elise was next but she couldn't get down more than a few sips, so I drank hers. Matty wasn't keen on the camel brew either, but I forced him to drink his bowl in payback for his enthusiasm during the vodka drinking sessions. We thanked the couple and hung out with them taking pictures and shooting some video. We said our goodbyes before it got too late and carried on for only a short while before setting up camp. I fell asleep with a grumbling stomach. Elise said it best: *'Between the vodka, the meat from the floor, and the camel yoghurt, my stomach doesn't know what's going on.'*

Before departing the following morning, I dispatched the lives of two small desert creatures. A camel spider and a small yellow scorpion that decided to make our tent their home. It could have been the bad karma of killing that set us up for one of our toughest days. We struck corrugations straightaway and as soon as the sun put its head over the horizon, I knew we were in for a scorcher. We were 130 kilometres from the town of Bulgan, where the tourist camps we were longing to get to were located. By 3pm the heat was unbearable, and we were withering under its power.

Elise's journal: '*It's Day 33 and our conversations went something like this. "It's hot." "Fuck me, it's hot." "It's so damn hot." Pretty riveting, but it was 36 degrees today and less than a week ago we were wearing three layers. Heat stroke is a real risk for us now and we really need to make sure we look out for each other. Before now I've been having breakfast then mixing up two dehydrated meals to eat little bits at a time on the five breaks we were taking during the day. But in this heat, munching on "Louisiana red beans" or "Kathmandu curry" is about as appealing as dragging my cart straight over the sand dunes in the east. (Really hope that's a mirage.) Now I will eat breakfast and a main meal before 9.30am, then only drink water until 3pm. My daydreams have been replaced with Willy Wonka's cold beverage factory. I guzzle a cool beach ball-sized coconut then slide down a tropical Frosty Fruit into a river of frozen coke. I'm harshly snapped back to reality with an unrefreshing sip of my 30-degree water.*'

Heat exhaustion and heat stroke are no joke. When I was serving in the military I had witnessed, and felt, my fair share of both. After Christmas holidays each year, our unit was taken to the North Queensland town of Tully. It was the wettest place in the country as well as being incredibly hot and humid. We were made to march into the jungle with full packs on to kick off the start of the year. Here was a bunch of guys, fresh off holidays where drinking beers was prioritised over training, thrown straight into a forced march in the tropical heat. One year we started with a full platoon of 30 men, and lost ten to heat exhaustion on the march in. It set in so quickly, it seemed almost as if the guys were faking it. One by one they would drop, and a medic would take them away to the shade of the closest tree to administer fluids.

Another time I was out in the bush on a navigation exercise with a soldier named Clarey. It was blistering hot and we were running between the checkpoints trying to be the first pair back to base. After four hours of pushing hard, Clarey stopped and stared out into the bush, then took off his webbing and hurled his rifle into the trees. I went over to him and noticed he wasn't sweating anymore, and the salt was dried on his skin. He was delirious and didn't know where we were or what we were doing. I sat him down in the shade, poured some water on him and told him to rest. I raced off to collect the last checkpoint, then walked Clarey out of the bush to get treatment.

I was reflecting on these experiences as we struggled through the afternoon heat. I was keeping an eye on the others and they were keeping an eye on me. The days were only going to get hotter, so as we set up camp we decided as a team to start an hour earlier the next morning. We planned to walk more kilometres in the cooler hours and lay up under the carts for a longer break in the middle of the day. Unlike the military where medical treatment was ready at hand, our closest hospital was a thousand kilometres away, so we had to play it safe.

◆◆◆

We were up early and cracking on in the pre-dawn light. As the heat rose, I descended into myself and drifted away into thoughts and daydreams. A single dream could make 90 minutes feel like seconds. But a negative spiral of thoughts could make seconds feel like hours. Through the monotonous heat my mind was a battlefield as I fought the negative forces and tried to stay positive. I knew the mental struggle well and had come to expect it. Matty had dealt with similar stuff during his Atlantic crossing but I was worried how Elise was dealing with it. I grew more concerned when she went silent for hours at a time.

Elise's journal: 'Today I pondered my way through an oasis, through sand dunes and across rolling hills. I pondered over the last five years of my life and what the next five may hold. I pondered through sharp pains in my left knee and aches in my back. I pondered up a new business plan to start when I got home. I pondered the details of my next adventure and what it will take to get me there. I pondered away a full 34 kilometres of the Gobi, with no breaks in thoughts at all. It's rare to have the time to let thoughts evolve like they do out here. I don't think I've ever really come close to the true art of pondering until I found myself walking the desert at four kilometres per hour in the blazing heat.'

We had covered another 34 kilometres and were chuffed with our efforts. We set up camp, ate as much as our bellies could hold, drank copious amounts of water and lay down in the tent with aching bones. We decided to leave all the flaps and zips of the tent open to get some cool air overnight. I woke up choking on dust and the tent being torn from its pegs. The wind was howling and the dust blasted through the open door. I jumped out of my sleeping bag, zipped up everything and lay back down coughing. We hadn't experienced wind of this magnitude and the tent was getting flattened on top of us. I was expecting to hear it tear apart but it held strong. After 30 minutes I was too tired to worry anymore and drifted back to sleep.

Getting out of the tent in a violent sandstorm wasn't something I looked forward to, so when I needed to take a leak during the night, I had my pee bottle at hand. For a guy, using a bottle was no big challenge because of obvious anatomical reasons, but for girls it was a different story. A small device called a 'SheWee' aided Elise to become, as she would describe it, 'more of a man' in the act of peeing into a bottle. Without getting too descriptive, it was a moulded plastic cup with a spout. I had used the pee bottle, almost filled it and hoped I didn't have to go again before dawn, then went back to sleep with the storm raging outside.

Elise's journal: 'Luke and I have an "inside tent" communal pee bottle. As I reached for it, I was devastated to find that Luke had beaten me to it and filled it to the brim. I cracked open the zip on the tent just enough to tip the contents of the bottle outside. As I brought it back in, I felt wet. I'd tipped the contents into the bottle's attached lid and now it was all over me and my sleeping bag. At the start of this trip I would have been so disgusted by having my husband's pee on me, but new dirty Elise took one baby wipe, made a half-arsed attempt to clean it up, peed in the bottle and went straight back to bed.

◆◆◆

We had walked over 1000 kilometres when Bulgan, one of many towns named Bulgan in Mongolia, finally materialised. This was a place I had focused my hopes and dreams on for the past two weeks. It appeared on the horizon and a short time later we were in the middle of the village. We unstrapped the carts and quickly realised there were no tourist camps nestled in among the dilapidated buildings. After asking around, Tumuro told us the first tourist camp of the season had just been built 14 kilometres to the north-east of town. The news did not dampen my spirits, I knew we would be there in a few hours and in the meantime I had my eyes fixed on the village store. I was starving. We loaded up on our usual favourites: bread, butter, ice cream and beer. We also piled in eggs, salami, sauces and various other goodies for our rest day. Half the village had gathered around our carts to fiddle with them and I sat down to watch the townsfolk and eat my ice cream.

I noticed a few drunken guys in the crowd stumbling around and bumping into people. Nobody seemed to care and simply let the men stumble on to the next person. Mongolia is void of concern for the predominantly male drunken behaviour and unconcerned about the vodka bottle graveyards scattered around the village. The consumption of alcohol, particularly vodka thanks to Russian imports during the communist period, has evolved into a daily habit. For the modern population these habits have transcended health and reason and become ingrained in the culture. But I'm sure some reflective locals might catch themselves asking, 'How did we get here?'

I have noticed a similar trend in Australia. 'A hard-earned thirst needs a big cold beer' was a catchy marketing line carved into my subconscious as a boy. Having a few beers after work is absolutely normal behaviour and downing a dozen drinks at a barbecue is the 'Aussie way.' In Australia we have grabbed the consumption of alcohol with both hands to become masters at it; it has surpassed heritage and become a daily habit for a large portion of the population, and is now part of our culture.

Like the Mongolians, we no longer push the boundaries of the frontier. Perhaps if we were still outback settlers working the land from sunrise to sunset, a few beers per day would be of no real concern. The health consequences of our current lifestyles, however, are painfully clear. Don't let me mislead you into thinking I'm a saint, far from it. I had my own battles with drug and alcohol addiction in my early years and take full ownership. Sometimes, however, I reflect upon those demon days and wonder how much of a role our Australian culture had to play in it.

We loaded up our treats and charged out of town to the oasis waiting for us 14 kilometres away. Just before lunchtime we arrived at a large group of gers and a cluster of small brick buildings built at a high point overlooking a valley, in the distance I noticed some large red sandstone cliffs. These were the Flaming Cliffs of the Gobi Desert, a famous site visited by palaeontologists since the 1920s. Dinosaur eggs and other rare fossils were unearthed here and since those days it has been a fixture on the tourist trail. We were the first tourists of the season and the lady who greeted us at the gate wore a big smile and directed us to our gers. Elise and I were in one and Matty's was next door. Our host showed us around, pointing out the kitchen where we could use gas to prepare meals, the laundry for washing our filthy clothes and the showers. The Flaming Cliffs disappeared from my mind as three thoughts filled the void: shower, food and bed. Our ger contained a full-length mirror and I hadn't looked at my reflection for over a month. It was a shocking sight: I was wasting away. I stripped off my clothes to get a closer look.

Elise's journal: 'It's been a surprising treat not having mirrors to stare into for five weeks. For so many years I would use what I saw as a reason to beat myself up, so to forgo the burden of a reflection on this trip has been refreshing. The camels don't care about the state of your hair or a few pimples. Luke and I undressed and stood in front of the mirror pulling on the flaps of skin where our muscles used to be. Luke said, "We should hurry this thing up babe, or there won't be anything left of us."'

In normal life a shower is just another task to complete during a busy day. Out in the Gobi after 39 days of dust, sweat and filth, this shower took on its own life force. The water was hot and when I stood underneath it I exhaled with a moan. It was relaxing, invigorating and morale boosting all at once. The dirty water flowed into the drain as I scrubbed weeks of dust from my pores. I stopped the flow to lather up with soap and repeated the process four times before I was satisfied. When I exited the building I was clean, glowing red, and resembled a drowned rat. It was time to eat.

We lit the gas stove and made ourselves sandwiches filled with fried salami and eggs, all soaked in tomato sauce. The grease dripped through my fingers as I bit into it. The flavour took me back to the bacon and egg breakfasts I enjoyed on Sunday mornings with my parents. Matty and I devoured three of our Gobi burgers, while Elise polished off two. We washed them down with a cold beer and I felt the effects of the alcohol within minutes. A local lady who worked in the kitchen was watching us and smiled as we sat back to rub our full bellies. She offered to wash our plates and pan for us and we retired to our gers for one of many naps.

I woke on our first full rest day of the expedition. It was Day 40 and not a single kilometre would be walked. With no cart to drag, I set myself the task of eating as much as I could, drinking plenty of water, showering again and doing the small repair jobs on the carts. We sat together after another large feed of Gobi burgers and talked about the last stage of the expedition. Our daily averages were staying above 35 kilometres per day and while analysing the maps and plotting our course, I estimated we could be walking into Sainshand within three weeks. My birthday was seventeen days away and Matty suggested we should aim for it. I crunched the numbers and it was doable. We planned our departure from the camp and set June 11th as our new finishing target.

There was roughly 570 kilometres to go, and as I pulled on my harness ready for departure the number was firmly fixed in my mind. We thanked the staff at the camp for their hospitality and turned once again towards the east. My body was feeling strong and although we walked into a blasting headwind for the first few hours, it didn't bother me in the slightest. We followed a powerline that on the map went straight into the large city of Dalanzadgad, three days' walk away. The dirt road next to the line was perfect for our carts and we covered 36.5 kilometres before calling it a day.

Elise's journal: 'Yesterday "uncomfortable" was swapped out for our old comforts and it didn't take long to feel like the people we were before this journey began nearly six weeks ago. Today, as we strapped into our boots and harnesses, I felt the first drops of sweat drip slowly from my neck to my naval and the wind hit me head on, making my nose leak and back ache. I felt uncomfortable again. Unlike the first few weeks though, this feeling only lasted momentarily. My brain remembered what I was doing in an instant and what I previously knew as uncomfortable had lost its title and had now become, "just the way things are". My swag is no longer a piece of foam, it's my bed. Our tent isn't a flimsy piece of canvas, it's our bedroom, dining room, kitchen and home. My damp pink piece of towel isn't just a wipe down, it's my shower. I thought about all the things I didn't do in the past because it would have made me feel uncomfortable, things that with time could've become my comfort.'

◆◆◆

The nomads were in full migratory swing and we witnessed a family moving west towards the greener valleys in the mountains. The family seemed to be better off than others we had come across and they were moving large herds of goats, horses and camels. A truck fully loaded with collapsed gers and furniture drove over and stopped, and an elderly man hopped down. He didn't say much as he hobbled over but he was intrigued by our carts. He picked one up and pulled it around for a while before shaking his head and sitting down. He showed us a pair of ancient binoculars he was using, accepted some of our wafers and then said goodbye. Not a word was exchanged between us, just big smiles and an understanding.

Elise hadn't slept well the night before and I could tell by her silence that she was in pain. Her feet were giving her some grief, but she wouldn't complain and just carried on with the job. We had big totals to hit each day and she didn't want to be the weak link in the team. I was in awe of her strength. We had 36 kilometres in the bank before she finally admitted defeat.

> Elise's journal: 'At 2am I was still awake. I tried the impossible task of silently unzipping the tent so I could escape the wheel my mind was trapped in. As I clumsily poked my head out, it was as if I was seeing the universe for the first time. Stars blanketed the world above me and I stood butt naked in the open, utterly amazed by it all. I stayed outside star gazing for nearly 30 minutes, sucking it all in before deciding I was finally ready for sleep. I spoke about ten words all day, my body rapidly declined as the sun moved over us. Of the ten words most of them were, "I'm fine," as Luke tried to figure out what was wrong with me. Sometimes I just don't want to talk and after six weeks there are not many conversations we haven't had. After no sleep and something seriously painful going on with my feet, if I have to have another chat about calculations, how many kilometres we have to go or when we will be finished, I will lose my fucking mind. So I stay quiet.'

My mental vision of Dalanzadgad was green grass and a crystal-clear lake with a traditional Mongolian village built around it. In reality, it was as far from a tranquil oasis as we could get. By lunchtime on Day 43 we made the outskirts of the city and were greeted by many vehicles full of staring locals and vodka bottle graveyards. The population of Dalanzadgad was 20,000, and was the crossroads for highways leading north to the capital and south to China. It was the biggest town in the southern region of Mongolia. The dirt track turned into tarmac as we skirted the city's small airport and headed into town. Our wheels spinning freely on the highway were a blessing but the traffic we had to navigate wasn't. We were a hazard to motorists and as a precaution we tried to avoid the main roads. The backstreets weaved through suburbs of derelict houses, wrecked cars, coal-fired power stations and factories. Dogs barked from every backyard and the locals were not the smiling nomads we had come to expect.

'What a shithole', was how I voiced my first impression. We pulled up together on the other side of the city and discussed our plan. We had thought about staying in a hotel for a night but after seeing the place we decided to push on and out. I stayed with the carts while Elise and Matty ventured to a supermarket to stock up on supplies. I was tense while waiting, I hadn't been in a city environment for a long time and the overall feeling of the place had me on edge. Some locals were pushing their broken-down car up a hill nearby. I hesitated briefly before lending them a hand. They were grateful for the help and continued pushing along the road into town. The encounter summed up the city for me, broken and in need of repair.

Elise and Matty arrived back and after packing away the goods we hightailed it down the tarmac road away from town. We enjoyed the 10 kilometres of solid road before turning off east back into the dirt. I immediately felt at ease when the cart started to buck along the rough track. The security of the desert was around me again and we were away from the unknown hostilities of civilisation.

We cracked a 38-kilometre day two days after departing Dalanzadgad. We were moving fast. The carts were the lightest they had ever been, following seven weeks of food consumption, and we were disciplined when it came to rest breaks. During our one-hour break for lunch a man rode up on an ancient motorbike. He was barely four feet tall and wearing a black riding cap more suited to a fox hunt in the English countryside. He sported a long grey and black beard with legs bowed from a lifetime of riding horses. He wore clear safety glasses and sat down, saying hello in German, French, Mongolian and then English, while flashing a cheeky grin. That was the extent of his English, so we communicated via dirt drawings. He was 87 years old and lived in a ger 18 kilometres away. He warned us about the dogs protecting gers close by and asked us our ages and what we were doing. Back and forth we drew pictures in the dirt and shared our stories. We made him tea and biscuits and when we had to get moving, we shook hands and took a photo together. It was a lovely encounter with an old man who was born, bred and had lived his entire life in the desert.

> *Elise's journal: 'Day 46 and Matty's voice came from the back of the convoy this morning. "I meant to tell you guys, got an email from Guinness last night. Our crossing won't be recognised as a world record." And just like that, my dream of being a world record holder was smashed to pieces. Kidding. I never really gave a damn about the record. If I did want one, I wouldn't put my body through this to get it, I would've just gone and ate the most hotdogs in a minute or something. I was, however, stoked that we decided on Day 16 to dump some weight from our carts. If I had struggled this far with an excess load purely to salvage our chance of a record, and then got that news, it would've been a bit of a kick in the guts.'*

As we camped that night, I mulled over the email from Guinness. We absolutely made the right decision to drop down in weight and to not receive a world first record for our trip didn't bother me. Expeditions aren't for other people or for record books, they are for the participants. It's about seeing how far we can push our bodies and minds, about the people we meet along the way, and about learning. Not just learning about ourselves and what we are made of, but about the world around us and how truly insignificant we are next to the almighty Mother Nature. Expeditions are for seeing the world for yourself and not just reading about remote places in books. These adventures are not about having great stories or being the most interesting dinner guest, they are about being truly happy. The uncomfortable, harsh reality of the outdoors is where I smile, laugh and find true happiness. That is why I do it.

LUKE RICHMOND

◆◆◆

A spiral of emotion consumed me for most of Day 47. I couldn't break the cycle for longer than an hour before descending back into negativity. The wind was howling again as it had for 42 of the 47 days of the journey. There was no outright cause for my mood, it was just one of those days. A car passed by early in the afternoon packed with a family: grandma, parents, kids – the whole tribe. One of the kids spoke the best English so we had a quick, 'Hello, how are you? What's your name?' conversation before, 'Okay, bye', and they drove away. A few hours later, as I wallowed in misery, the same car appeared from behind us and pulled over at the top of a ridge further ahead. Matty was leading, followed by Elise and I was bringing up the rear. By the time I hauled myself up the incline, I wasn't prepared for what waited for me at the top. The sight instantly pulled me out of my stupor.

The family had laid out a spread of food on a blanket for us to enjoy. Grandma held centre position and like all grandmothers, she told me to sit down, wash my hands and eat. They had cooked a goat, made pots of tea and wanted nothing more than to feed us. Granny handed me a rib and a hot cup of tea and I was in heaven. The fat dripped down my chin as I bit into the meat, it was the single greatest thing I have ever eaten. My morale soared, and the negativity was swept away with the salty taste of the goat. Any time the bucket of meat was placed down on the mat, someone in the family picked it up and handed it back to us. My hunger was limitless and while I tried to keep my manners in check, I wolfed down every snippet of flesh that came my way.

We sat, talked, ate and drank for over an hour. Their generosity was overwhelming. We had no way to repay their kindness except to say thank you and share a photo together. Matty had been saving a small bottle of rum for special occasions and he produced it, passing it around between those who wanted it. When the food was gone, as quick as the family had arrived, they packed up and prepared to leave. Before they drove away, they handed us a bag of dried meat. The car departed, leaving us in the wind and dust with huge smiles on our faces. We had shared a goat with a nomad family who didn't know anything about us apart from our names.

◆◆◆

> Elise's journal: 'I could hear Matty rustling around from about 5.30am. I felt like I could've slept for another few hours but by 6am I heard Luke unzipping the tent and boiling up water, I was awake. I opened my eyes to find Luke was sitting silently, looking back at me with a smile. A herd of horses were standing at the door, not moving, just staring at us. "Good morning horses." And that's how my day started.'

We had been living in each other's pockets for so long that once again tensions had risen. In the challenging conditions it was inevitable we would get on each other's nerves. The three of us sat down and aired our frustrations, and when I look back on the issues voiced, they were so trivial it's almost embarrassing to write about. But at the time, those small issues could have caused the team to collapse. Matty was frustrated with my handling of Tumuro and Orgil. I was getting snappy with the lads about how they were navigating. I was frustrated with Matty and wanted him to break trail more often. In my mind he was always at the back when times were tough. Elise didn't want to rush every day, and was pissed at the pace Matty and I were setting.

We sat around as adults speaking our minds without personal attack, lifting the weight off our shoulders and discarding it after discussion. Once again, when it was done my mind was clear. We had a few hours of silence and then the team was back.

Elise's journal: '50 days of irritation bubbled to the surface this morning and each one of us had something we needed to get off our chest. People have blow-ups in everyday life, so naturally when you add in 35 degree temperatures, unknown territory and language barriers, personalities will clash. Some days I wanted to tear off Matty's ears and feed them to the camels. Other days I wanted to crash tackle Luke and give him three swift elbows to the ribs. And I have no doubt there are days when the boys want to throw me down a well and stomp off. So, we had it out, said what we needed to say, and communication proved to be everything once again.'

We were creatures of routine by now, and after so long dealing with Mother Nature we were able to handle anything that came our way. Eleven hours of corrugations: no worries. Wind blasting us in the face from sun up to sun down: standard. A rollercoaster of emotion as the days pass, some days short and enjoyable, others so long I felt the nightmare would continue forever. Welcome to expedition life.

The distance to Sainshand was getting shorter and shorter: 260 kilometres to go became 227 kilometres, then 191 kilometres, 170 kilometres and by the end of Day 53, we were 125 kilometres from the finish. I began to believe nothing could stop us so long as we stuck to our plan each day and put in the hours of work.

We had 87.5 kilometres to go as we passed the last village before the end. We loaded up on ice-cream, Coca-Cola and our favourite treats and carried on for the afternoon. On four separate occasions during the day, truck drivers pulled over and stopped next to us. Each time they would climb down from their big rigs and give us a bottle of water. Their concern and generosity was incredible, and we would thank them as if they were the only ones helping us that day. The people of the Gobi were showing their true colours time and time again on this trip. At one point we were given vodka shots at midday by a driver and invited in by a family for tea the next. These short encounters were the highlights for me, of real people being real humans without fear or for reward. The world needs much more of it.

Elise's journal: 'I asked Orgil if there were any trees in Mongolia and he replied confidently, "Yes, look, trees everywhere!" pointing to shrubs no higher than my knees. Our aim today was a village that sat safely within the hills. As we got nearer, we saw huge wind turbines and solar panels catching nature's energy. Before I arrived, I had created an image of Mongolia's most progressive new-age town. I was off the mark, but it was the only town in the Gobi that had figured out how to keep things cold, like actually cold, not the slightly less hot we had become accustomed to. We grabbed ice creams, Coke, beers. Not just for calories but more to curb the cravings we'd been speaking about all trip and sat outside the store in ice-cold refreshing bliss. We broke our rule of never sleeping near towns, barely making it 500 metres past the "You are now leaving" sign and calling it a day. Just before bed it all made sense as to why I felt like I'd gone five rounds with a bull and wanted to dive into a pool of Nutella. I got my period. I was really hoping my body would let it slide this month but alas, the joys of womanhood are still in full swing.'

◆◆◆

It was Day 56 and the day before my birthday. If all went well, we would arrive in Sainshand on schedule. It was also the day Matty's girlfriend, Harrie, was going to appear in the desert. She had flown to Mongolia, driven down to Sainshand with a guide and was planning to come and find us wherever we were by the end of the day. Matty was striding out like a man possessed, this was their first time apart and it had been almost two months. I knew exactly how he was feeling after going through the same emotions with Elise the year before, while I rowed the Atlantic.

There was energy in the air, the wind didn't sting as much, the weight wasn't as heavy and we were buzzing with excitement. We knew we were going to make it and even though we hadn't let success grip us, it was definitely giving us a tickle.

The day flew by and as the afternoon sun was descending, Matty was busy taking satellite phone calls and, with Tumuro's help, directing the guide driving Harrie to our location. The car appeared on the horizon kicking up dust and as it pulled alongside, Harrie lent out of the window with a big smile on her face. I hadn't smelt 'clean' for a long time and Harrie smelt incredible, highlighting how far we had slipped down the hygiene ladder. We hadn't finished our daily kilometres by this point and still had a few to go. Being disciplined machines, we pulled on the harnesses and stomped east for one more hour.

We set up camp with Harrie watching on, then it was mini-celebration time. Tomorrow we would finish, we knew, but I couldn't fully relax until we had walked every single metre. Harrie pulled out gifts of salamis, eggs, bread, tomato sauce and a frypan. With a heads-up from Matty she knew exactly what we wanted, and as I sat down to fry up the meat my mouth was watering. We devoured so much food I was bursting, sipped cold beers and Tumuro pulled out the vodka once again. With three shots of white lightning in my blood, a belly full of food and the knowledge that we only had one more day to drag, I drifted off to sleep.

Up at 4am, we wanted to start early so we could hopefully finish early and make the drive back to Ulaanbaatar before nightfall. The capital was a six-hour drive from Sainshand and would be possible if we were up before sunrise. I had forgotten what the day was until Matty produced a fruitcake with a candle shoved in the top and started singing 'Happy Birthday.' I turned 33 years old in the Gobi Desert and shared a fruitcake with my wife and mate. It was a perfect birthday and due to get even better as we packed up for the last time. We attached flags to our carts for the final kilometres: Matty had the British flag, I had the

VODKA & SANDSTORMS

Australian and Elise the Mongolian. They were flying high and flapping in the wind as we took our final steps towards the east.

Sainshand had been home to a substantial military base during the Soviet years and by midmorning we could see the city rising on the horizon. When we made it to the edge of what we thought was the city, it turned out to be the ruins of an old base and a graveyard to the former empire. Collapsed structures, wrecks of cars and rubbish were scattered across the ground. I started noticing 30 millimetre bullet casings everywhere and then piles of rusted landmines. I'm sure they were disarmed but I kept a distance from them just in case. The piles of vodka bottles signalled the start of the city and as we hauled up a short incline and reached the top, there below us was the sprawling metropolis of Sainshand.

Harrie arrived from a local hotel and we posed for photos on top of the ridge. Looking down at the city, we decided we would call the finish when we made it to the wall of homes and crossed the fence line. What we had achieved was slowly starting to sink in and, chatting like excited kids we made it to the fences and crossed the imaginary line together. We had done it. I grabbed Elise in a big hug and then gave Matty the same. We were all overwhelmed and I started to tear up.

After a few minutes I looked around. There was no media waiting for us, no fireworks exploding above our heads; it was lunchtime in a derelict city on the edge of the Gobi Desert. I watched a local man pay us no mind as he undid his fly and took a leak against his fence. I almost laughed at how insignificant we were in the grand scheme of life. As I wrote earlier, this trip wasn't for the guy taking a leak next to me, it wasn't for Tumuro, Dafka or Orgil, and it wasn't for all our sponsors at home. It was for us. And we had succeeded in what we set out to achieve, we had crossed the Gobi Desert.

Elise's journal: 'For 57 days we suffered through some of the most inhospitable terrain. Through sandstorms and snow, gale-force winds and hail. We pushed through injuries and exhaustion, through mountains, rivers and valleys. But this type of suffering was different – I chose this. And suffering by choice is very different to suffering by circumstance. Suffering by choice can be instantly educational, without having to wait for the heartache to pass. Pain becomes endurance. Mistakes become important lessons. Frustrations become personal growth, and uncomfortable becomes self-discovery. The Gobi made me hurt physically. It made me seek out different parts of my personality that don't get exposed in the daily comings and goings of western society. It made me appreciate how simple and genuine life can be when you strip it right back to water, food and shelter. How basic gestures of kindness can change a life and how privileged I am to be able to choose suffering rather than be born into it. The blisters are healing. The body is recovering. But I can still smell the camel dung, still taste the stinky cheese from the nomads and will forever have the memories of the great desert. The Gobi didn't change my life, it beautifully reaffirmed it.'

◆◆◆

It took the three of us 56 days, 17 hours and 40 minutes to walk 1805 kilometres across the Gobi Desert in Mongolia. We had dragged our carts, camped in the sand and endured everything Mother Nature threw at us. We had the support of some great local guys and met some of the most amazing nomads along the way. My body was destroyed. I had lost 9 kilograms, my joints were screaming for rest and I had grown an impeccable beard – by my own low standards. The endless hours of dragging had also given me time to think and reflect on everything that had happened in my life.

    I had remembered the good times, the wins and some incredible adventures. I remembered the relationships, friends and time spent with family. I remembered the fails, the falls and the turning points. I remembered the floor of the cell where the police hosed me down and looked at me with disgust in their eyes. I was a drug addict, covered in my own filth and I was at rock bottom.

Almost nine years later, I stood on the edge of the desert looking west from where we had come. I couldn't remember the man on the cell floor all those years ago. He was a stranger to me now. I scratched my beard and watched the flakes of skin drift away in the breeze, and I gripped my arms and felt the bones where muscles used to be. I pulled my glasses from my head and stared at the reflection in the lenses. The man staring back at me looked gaunt, beaten and broken – until he smiled. His eyes shone, and I noticed the deep blue in them before he asked me, 'What's next?'

Chapter 7

Everest Base Camp

I woke up startled a few seconds after my lungs decided to stop performing their vital basic function. As my heart pounded out of my chest, I gasped for breath and looked around at the plywood walls and handmade, rough timber bed frames.

I was inside a tiny teahouse room in the small village of Gorek Shep, located in the Upper Khumbu Valley of Nepal. I struggled to sleep and woke up every couple of hours in the same state. At an altitude of 5164 metres, while the body battles to acclimatise to the thin air, sleep does not come easy I had decided to forgo the use of Diamox, a medication widely used to help the body adjust to higher elevations. I was using the trek to Everest Base Camp to gauge how my body would handle the high mountains. With some big expeditions planned for the following year, I wanted to know what my physical limits were.

Two weeks earlier Elise and I had stared out the window trying to glimpse the snow-capped peaks as we descended towards Kathmandu on our connecting flight from Bangkok. But the clouds had obscured our view of the mountains as the plane prepared to land and touched down. 'Welcome to Nepal' announced a sign as we made our way towards the exit of the airport.

We left the semi-secure area and ventured out into the stifling heat and throng of waiting taxi drivers. I searched their handwritten signs for our names, doing a second and third sweep to no avail. Elise and our climbing buddy from Thailand, Yok, who was joining us for the trek, searched as well. The horde of taxi drivers saw the look of isolation on my face and started hustling for our business. I borrowed a phone from one of them and called our hotel. The manager answered and after a brief exchange of pleasantries he apologised for the mix-up and advised us to take any taxi available.

We drove by piles of rubbish on the sides of the road and crossed a small bridge over one of the dirtiest rivers I had ever laid eyes on. The Bagmati River winds its way through the Kathmandu valley for almost 600 kilometres, picking up a large portion of the town's wastewater, human cremations and rubbish. The level of the pollution didn't seem to bother the locals, and I would see piles of rubbish rotting in the sun right next to a table supporting the local butcher's slaughtered goat. The sight of the butcher squeezing out the lower intestines of the goat into the street affirmed Elise's choice of vegetarianism.

We checked into the Fuji Hotel and then hit the streets to stretch our legs and get a feel for the area. Ten years earlier my younger legs had walked these potholed alleys and it felt great to be back. Special care needs to be taken when on foot as the traffic is thick and pedestrians have to share the road with rickshaws, cars and cows. Kathmandu streets have an energy unlike anything I've felt in other countries. The city is a gateway to adventure in the mountains and everyone makes a living directly or indirectly off the giant peaks.

Old temples had filled the centre of town when I was here last, and I remembered sitting on their ancient steps for hours and people watching. Many, however, had been damaged or destroyed. The older timber structures were the worst affected by the earthquake, and they were still being reconstructed as we walked past. The terrible tragedy had occurred on Saturday,

25 April 2015. A 7.8 magnitude quake hit Nepal 80 kilometres north-west of Kathmandu at a depth of 11 kilometres. The worst earthquake in eight decades, it killed almost nine thousand people, displaced entire communities and devastated the infrastructure of the small nation. Eighteen climbers perished at Everest Base Camp, where tremors caused an avalanche that swept through the centre of the camp, bringing an abrupt end to the climbing season.

As I pondered these tragic events and took in the surroundings, we were targeted by a young local street guide. I knew by his friendly demeanour, clean-cut appearance and expert knowledge of the area that he had played this game before. I also knew the time would come when he would need to be paid. He protested that he was just happy to show us around his city, so we went along with the charade. We were content to have him along, and he showed us many hidden gems we would otherwise have missed. His name was Ravi, he was in his late twenties and he made his living from the tourist trade. Ravi could go weeks without earning a cent but on a single day he could earn the monthly wage of a Nepali construction worker. He had the required skill set and he was providing for his family.

As the day was coming to an end Elise and I bought a mandala painting from a local art seller. We knew it was a standard tourist thing to do, but I love the patterns of the mandalas and I appreciate the time and effort that goes into painting the higher quality pieces. Traditional Nepalese art, known commonly as thangka painting, depict deities, Buddha or mandalas from the Buddhist faith. The mandala is an image best explained as an aerial view of a Buddhist temple. It has a very intricate design with delicate detail throughout and can be finished with pure gold.

The artist must first prepare their canvas, which can take three weeks depending on the climate conditions. They draw the intricate lines onto the canvas using a pencil; the artist meditates while working and the lines themselves can take an additional four weeks depending on the size and the detail of the piece. Paints are then prepared, and paintbrushes made from scratch.

The tips of the brushes are fashioned using various animal hairs and the handles are crafted from bamboo. It can take four days to make twenty high quality brushes. The painting is finally ready to begin, first the skyline and backgrounds are painted, then shading, detail, and finally, if the artist is at a high enough level of skill, gold is applied. The painting stage can take a month and by looking at the amount of fine detail in some of the higher quality mandalas, it's very easy to see why.

We bought a middle range mandala for $140 and as we walked away with our new purchase we both laughed over where the hell we were going to put it. We had no fixed address and were living out of a backpack. The mandala was going to stay rolled up in its cardboard tube for quite some time. On the way back to the hotel we devoured some delicious roadside veggie wraps, bought a map of the Everest Base Camp trail and took in the hustle and bustle of Kathmandu.

A beggar with no legs held out his hand as we walked by. It's always hard seeing the misfortune of others. I know it's much better to support schools, hospitals and shelters for the poor rather than hand over cash, but what I have found is that the poorest countries are often devoid of that type of infrastructure. I have a soft heart for the most wretched souls and if I can give them a moment's grace with money for a hot meal, I'll do it.

The old portion of the city, the area worst affected by the earthquake because of its old timber and brick construction, still showed signs of devastation. Two years had passed since that tragic day, yet rubble filled the side roads and back alleys. Many of the temples and houses hadn't been rebuilt. I asked Ravi about the rebuilding effort and he told me the government wasn't offering much assistance to the locals. The families had to raise their own funds. It's sad to hear stories like this but it's common to hear about the greed and corruption of the Nepali government.

My good friend Vitidnan sent two 40-foot shipping containers of bottled water from Bangkok to Kathmandu a couple of days after the earthquake. He was trying to get the water to the worst affected areas. But when the containers arrived in Nepal, they were stolen, never to be seen again. These types of problems are a constant battle for the NGOs and charities that try to operate in the country. They are also a problem for people who wish to donate money to a cause, because it's hard to know who to trust or if your money will get to those in need. I advise my friends to do their homework, get references and make sure the charity or program is transparent and shows where all the money is spent.

Weaving our way through the streets back to our hotel we chanced upon the food alleys. I really love street food, it's one of my favourite things about travelling in Thailand and South-East Asia. I wandered from stand to stand and shop to shop, asking the vendors questions and trying out a variety of foods. Dozens of fruit sellers sold their produce from baskets mounted on vintage English bicycles plucked straight out of the era when the British ruled over India and Nepal. Unable to carry large amounts on their bikes, they carried one or two varieties of fruit each and filled their own section of the street. Bananas, apples, oranges and lemons were all in season.

A small band playing local wooden instruments burst to life on a street corner and sitting right next to them was a dog missing a leg. I passed shops full of spices, nuts, seeds, salt, oats and so much more. I bought bags of nuts and dried fruit for the trek and bartered for bananas from a Nepali Lance Armstrong lookalike before Ravi led us to our street and we said our goodbyes. I slipped Ravi 3000 rupees, the equivalent of $38AUD and with a beaming smile he bid us farewell.

◆◆◆

The next morning we had breakfast with Bart and Casey, our newly arrived friends from Australia. Both were lean, in supreme physical shape and raring to go. They lived and breathed health and fitness, and had owned gyms in Brisbane and Melbourne back home. They joined the trek after recently finishing the infamous Kokoda Track in Papua New Guinea. We had all signed on with my mate Dean's team from World Wide Trekking. Dean had put together a group of Stanford University alumni and I couldn't wait to meet everyone.

We made our way to the Yak and Yeti hotel just outside central Thamel, and then up to the meeting room on level two. Dean had his projector screen set up, water on the table and was ready to deliver a short seminar about the trek and what to expect. We were introduced to the rest of the team as they entered the room, and we all shook hands and acted like long-lost friends. Everyone was excited to get out into the mountains and for a few it was their first ever adventure.

There was a mixed bag of careers and life experience on the team. We had a dermatologist, a cardiologist and Biotech CEO, a computer scientist, a retired engineer and a mother and daughter tackling base camp together. We had a lady from Honduras and a retired Boeing executive. Thrown into the mix were the four Australian fitness coaches and Yok. It didn't matter where any of us had come from, what we did for a living or how much wealth we had accumulated, we were all together for the same goal and that made us equals.

Dean delivered a great presentation, he was a true professional and experienced mountaineer. He built his company from the ground up and with his growing success he developed his Human Outreach Project to give back to the local communities he works with. His outlook towards adventure and giving is summed up with his personal mission statement.

'I shall pass through this world but once. Any good that I can do or any kindness that I can show to any human being, let me do it now. Let me not defer it or neglect it. For I shall not pass this way again'.

After the presentation the team mingled and got to know each other. Elise and I had to run off early to process our visas at the Thai consulate for our return journey to Thailand. We had done the application process so many times it was like second nature to us, but we hadn't applied in Nepal before, so we wanted to give ourselves plenty of time in case anything went wrong. We found a taxi driver just off a side street next to the

Yak and Yeti. I've learnt it's always better to walk away from fancy hotels before getting taxis or you will pay a premium. He was a lovely local guy who knew exactly where we needed to go and delivered us to the front door of the consulate and told us he would wait.

We exited 30 minutes later, having submitted our paperwork with ease and been told to return in a week for collection. Our driver was sitting in the shade drinking chai, so we wandered over and joined him. He raced inside a shop and returned with two more cups. While we sat in the dusty street, drinking the delicious sweet tea, he told us about his family and how they had lived simple farming lives for generations. Everyone was always happy and had more than enough food and water, needing little else.

'The simple life was a happy life,' he said.

He went on to say that when the TVs, phones and fancy clothes arrived in Nepal, everyone wanted them. This created resentment of those who could afford them, jealousy of those who had nicer versions and caused widespread trouble in his community. There was animosity towards friends and, in his words, 'Gave them all demons.'

'Now it is hard to go back,' he said. The internet allowed young people to see the world and everything in it, and they wanted it all.

'I will remain a simple man and support them as best I can,' he said.

He took our glasses back into the shanty-roofed café and with a smile gestured towards his waiting taxi.

While we drove back through the noisy, dusty streets I reflected on what the old man had told us. When I first met Elise I was earning good money, lived in a nice apartment on the water in Sydney and drove a nice car. I had my own business, ate good food and was living a life that I thought I wanted. But I was always chasing more. Bigger, better, faster, it was always on to the next big thing, which required more money. More money meant more work, less sleep and more stress. Stress made me tired and cranky, and slowly eroded my perceived happiness. I reached breaking point and told Elise, 'I'm not happy.'

'When were you last happy?' she asked.

I remember thinking for a moment before replying, 'When I was living in a bungalow in Thailand and just training every day.'

'Well, let's do that,' she said.

Within three months we had sold the business, car, furniture and all our possessions. We moved to Thailand, away from the accumulation of things and towards experiences and happiness. It was a major turning point in our lives.

While we were on consulate business our team was sightseeing around Kathmandu and we wanted to meet up with them where the daily cremation ceremonies took place on the banks of the Bagmati River. The river's high banks were paved in stone and the locals burned the bodies of their loved ones in the traditional way and spread the ashes on the river. On arrival we saw our team down by the water. The river was extremely polluted, its dark brown colour concealing the copious amount of rubbish being swept by. We watched a body being washed before it was placed on a large timber pyre and set alight. A family member or friend would tend the fire for many hours until the wood and the remains were burnt down to an undistinguishable pile of ash.

While it was great to see traditional cultures and customs surviving through the ages, I also wanted to know how the poor afforded the expensive wood they needed to complete the ceremony. Geljin, our lead guide from the Sherpa people, explained there was a coal-fired cremation building close by that serviced the poor for a small price. They could then spread the ashes in the river with everyone else.

The following morning, when Geljin arrived to collect us from the hotel at 4am, the entire team were bright eyed and chomping at the bit with excitement. We loaded our backpacks and duffel bags into the van, everything we would need for the following two weeks, and raced through the quiet streets to the airport. Geljin was a man possessed, he wanted to beat the rush and get us onto the first flight up into the mountains. When we arrived, a few climbers and their guides had already started a queue at the glass doors leading into the departure terminal. Within an hour the place was a mass of humanity, with hundreds of multicoloured duffel bags piled high on every available patch of floor space. From what I could determine there seemed to be no orderly system, it was a matter of forcing our way to the front of the lines and, in our case, Geljin working his charm with the staff to get us in first. Geljin had completed this dance many times and we were hustled through the carnage to a waiting bus and driven out to the small plane being fuelled up on the tarmac.

Kathmandu fell away below us as we soared skyward away from the city's haze. The buildings thinned out and gave way to small clusters of homes and then lush green valleys. I could see picturesque farmlands painstakingly carved into the sides of steep hills. The roads relented to the wilderness and became yak trails, and the towns scaled back to tiny villages surrounded by scatterings of livestock.

After 30 minutes of flight time we were circling above the village of Lukla, nestled in the lower Khumbu valley. A patchy blanket of cloud had formed over the mountains, but the pilot seemed confident and was lining up for his approach. It was a visual landing and if he couldn't see the airport we would have to abort and fly back to Kathmandu. The plane began to dive at the bottom of the runway. We had a clear view out of the cockpit at our landing strip and it seemed to be too short to handle any type of aircraft. 'Here we go,' I thought, as the plane increased its speed and the passengers in the cabin became eerily quiet. A few sets of eyes were closed but most people had a look of terrified excitement on their faces.

The runway was on an incredibly steep angle and we held our breath as the plane rocketed towards the sheer drop-off at the end of the strip. At the last minute the pilot pulled on the stick and the aircraft's nose lifted parallel with the ground and the plane touched down with a small thud. Immediately the pilot was on the brakes and swinging the plane into a side bay to reduce speed. He pulled a 180-degree turn and halted in front of a small two-storey building that represented the entire airport. We all applauded the perfect landing and before we had a moment to calm our stomachs, the stewardess had the door open and was ushering us out. The crew wanted to fill up with departing climbers and get back in the air before the clouds closed in.

We had arrived at the most dangerous airport in the world and the starting point of our Everest Base Camp trek; it was all on foot from here. After finding our bags beneath the pile that had been emptied onto the tarmac, we walked over to the closest teahouse to meet the Sherpa who would be leading the way to Monjo. His name was Pasang, and he had a beaming smile as Geljin introduced him to the team. He was shy and busied himself getting cups of tea and coffee for everyone before we departed.

Pasang had a climbing résumé second to none and, like so many Sherpas in Nepal, he stayed incredibly humble. He had summited Mount Everest three times and had a long list of other successful summits as a mountain guide. If a western climber had a similar record of success, he would be called upon for speaking engagements and paid small fortunes. The Nepalese just take it all in their stride and are happy to be earning a good living doing what they love. I have the utmost respect for the guides and I enjoy spending as much time as possible with them. Their attitudes and energy are grounding and I can't get enough of it.

We departed Lukla after a warm brew and followed Pasang through the busy streets to the trailhead. The temperature was ten degrees cooler in Lukla than Kathmandu. It was October and the start of busy season, there were yaks, climbers, trekkers and porters going everywhere. Tourists were departing the village heading up looking clean and buzzing with excitement; those returning looked tired and dishevelled. The mix of cultures on the trail from Lukla included Japanese, Africans, Americans and Europeans. Trekking is an international pastime and for enthusiasts, going to the Himalaya was like going to the Olympics. The porters raced up and down while we stuck to a steadier pace perfect for acclimatising.

The valley had changed a lot since I was last there, many more tea houses had sprung up with better quality infrastructure. The Nepalese thrived on the income from the trekking and climbing seasons, and it was great to see so many locals doing well. There was even internet. I couldn't believe it was now possible to be linked up all the way to Everest Base Camp. I wouldn't need that advancement, I had decided to leave my phone and laptop in Kathmandu. I loved nature, especially the mountains, and wanted to unplug from the digital world.

The strength of the porters was evident; they were carrying supplies for the tea houses and trekking groups up and down the valley. The porters were a lifeline for the entire region, and every day we would be astonished by the weight and size of their loads. Porters could ferry enormous quantities of goods, and their pay was calculated on the amount of weight they could carry. The stronger the porter, the more they earned. Their bodies had adapted to their craft by evolving big powerful necks, strong legs, indestructible backs and an endurance level never rivalled by a European. They were in a league of their own.

We were dressed in the latest and greatest outdoor apparel made from Gore-Tex, Sympatex and every other space-aged fibre on the market. The porters wore ancient pairs of jeans, hand-me-down expedition jackets and flip-flops on their feet. I'm sure they would enjoy the comfort of the latest equipment but they didn't need it to do their job effectively. No matter what we wore to cover our fragile bodies, it was almost guaranteed not all of us would make it to our objective. One older male porter who passed us in the morning had eight cartons of beer on his back supported by a bamboo frame that connected to his forehead with a canvas strap. All the weight was held on his neck as he lent into the hill and made his way up. My back and legs were already feeling fatigue with my small pack; to have a load like his attached to me would snap me in half.

Three hours from Lukla we arrived into Phukding. It was a small village comprised mainly of guest houses and surrounded by tiered sections of farmland. We settled into a tea house with great views facing down the valley. It's vital to stay hydrated while acclimatising and sometimes drinking just water, especially in cold climates, can be a big ask. I combat this by drinking large amounts of the local teas; lemon tea, ginger tea and milk tea are readily available. A small garden next to the tea house was exploding with fresh produce. Bok choy, beans, carrots, lettuce and potatoes were picked by hand then taken inside to be washed, cooked and within 30 minutes delivered on our plates. From earth to mouth right in front of our eyes, it doesn't get any fresher than that. After lunch, while we were lying in the sun resting, I asked Elise what she thought of the place so far.

'It's magical and totally surreal. So many years of wanting to come here and I'm now blown away,' she said. 'How do you feel coming back a second time?' she asked.

I told her I loved the mountains, not just for their beauty and my desire to climb them but because they hold humans back. As a species we have spread out to every corner of the world building our homes. But the high mountain regions can never be covered by a city, they are too powerful even for us.

Hitting the trail again, we walked beside a river churning its way around boulders and down the valley. The banks were steep and surrounded with pine forest and the occasional patch of farmland. The locals would harvest the river's rocks and any dug from the ground to build walls for their tea houses and embankments for growing crops. It was amazing to see some of the places they were farming. They would build a perimeter wall on slopes that at times had a 40-degree angle. No mortar was used during construction, instead rocks were balanced one on top of the other, allowing gravity to do the rest. When the walls were complete, they would fill in soil until it was level and deep enough for their plants. Yak dung was used to fertilise the soil and grow their food. Everything was done by hand with basic tools and because the region had brutal winters, building projects needed to be started and finished in the summer months.

I reflected on my first trip to Nepal as we hiked. I'd been a different man back then; young, bullet proof, with an ego bigger than the mountains themselves. I remember telling myself trekking poles were for cheats and I didn't need them. This time poles were a valuable asset, providing efficient, safe movement into the mountains. I carried all my gear on my back during my first trip; this time we had employed smiling locals and their yaks, giving back to the community through employment and aiding the acclimatisation process through easier trekking.

The pace during my first trip was blisteringly fast, I'd charge up the trail covering big distances each day and reached base camp in record time. That speed also gave me mild pulmonary oedema and I was in bed with altitude sickness for two days after I arrived. Our pace on day one of this trip was slow and steady, never getting exhausted. We allowed ten days to arrive at our goal utilising rest days and following all the acclimatisation rules. I smiled as I reflected. If there was one thing I would say to my younger self, it would be, 'Patience, big fella, the mountains are not going anywhere.'

Patience is a virtue I had been searching for, but it wasn't until this trip to base camp that I finally found it. It had been a big year before we arrived in Nepal: we had crossed the Gobi Desert on foot and it was a brutal trip on the human body. I had picked up some tendonitis in my left knee and my joints were feeling fragile. If I tried to move too fast, pain would shoot through my knee, my hips would get wobbly and the knee would buckle with the effort. If I walked slowly though, everything would stay in alignment, there would be no pain and I wouldn't stumble. Patience was forced upon me by the weakness of human biomechanics and my pain threshold.

Moderating our pace was actually a blessing in disguise. The man who sold us our mandala painting in Kathmandu had mentioned how the artists were forced to learn patience as well. A grand master was the highest rank for an artist, and these were the ones who painted with gold. Reaching this level required a very high quality of work and years of focus; the defining component being fifteen years of time invested. If an artist was producing grandmaster quality work after only five years it didn't matter, they would not receive their title until the required time had passed. This taught them patience.

We passed a 50-metre high waterfall late in the afternoon. A pine forest lined the steep cliffs on either side and prayer flags had been strung between the trees, where they floated in the wind. We arrived in Monjo six hours after leaving Lukla. Everyone had performed well, although Casey was feeling a little sick and rundown. The team freshened up and gathered in the tea house common room where we chatted and shared cups of tea. Bart sat down next to me.

'What did you enjoy most about your first day?' I asked him.

'The people, for sure. Their patience in growing their vegetables and building those rock walls,' he said.

We ate our first dinner together in the mountains, except Casey who had retired to her room. She had nausea and vomiting and was feeling rough, common symptoms during the first few days at altitude, and I hoped she would recover quickly. I drank endless glasses of tea to hydrate and ate the local dish Dhal Bhat with a side of boiled eggs and chapatti bread. Dhal Bhat is a common meal for the Nepalese people. It's steamed rice and lentil soup with added meat when it's available. Typically the cheapest dish on the menu, I was eating it three times a day when I was travelling in my youth. Elise and I retired to our room, which was more luxurious than I was expecting, with comfortable mattresses and big blankets. I slept for nine hours straight – if there's ever one thing to guarantee a good night's sleep, it's a solid day of hiking in the mountains.

The next morning was crisp with clear skies. Our yak driver brought his animals around to the front of the tea house and loaded our packs on two per beast. They lumbered up the valley, bells sounding the advance. Our goal for the day was Namche Bazaar, the biggest village in the region. My body was stiff and sore but I was feeling great and settled into a steady hiking pace while I got to know my teammates. I started talking to Eileen, who was in her late fifties and on the surface looked like a fit librarian. She was very polite, softly spoken and lived in Honduras. She told me about her farm, where she raised a menagerie of animals including one enormous pig. I almost had her stereotyped as someone seeking excitement and adventure late in her life, when she turned to me and in a soft voice said, 'I also ride a Harley Davidson.'

'You do?' I replied with slight shock, before laughing and telling her I would never have been able to guess.

She laughed with me and began to tell me about her passion with bikes and how she took multi-day rides into the United States for biker rallies and loved motorcycles above all else. The old saying 'never judge a book by its cover' is absolutely true when it came to Eileen.

The valley opened up in front of us and we took our first break next to the river. Ahead the trail steepened as it hugged the side of a cliff before reaching a long suspension bridge. The iconic bridges were formerly erected using rope and timber but they were now made with steel cable and metal flooring. These new building materials diminished none of their beauty. I could see two long bridges from where I sat, one from an earlier era and one modern-day marvel spanning two cliffs. Prayer flags were tied from their sides and the multicoloured light fabrics were held high in the wind. A yak train loaded with duffel bags was making its way across the higher of the two bridges, completing the beautiful scene.

After resting and taking photos, we continued along the trail, climbing the steep bank and crossing the higher bridge into a pine forest on the far side. The trail became challenging as it ascended into a series of steep switchbacks that continued out of sight, and it started to become more congested as some teams slowed down to meet the required physical effort. I'm a big supporter of commercially guided trips and I think everyone should get into the outdoors and see what this beautiful world has to offer, but I'm not a big fan of standing in a line. This can be a big issue on high mountain expeditions, where waiting in minus 20 degree temperatures is not an option and could get you killed. I placed my annoyance inside a mental box of patience and decided this was just another lesson to be learned and calmed myself down.

The switchbacks finally ended and the trail topped out at a point called Everest view. There was a large gap in the pine trees, which, on a clear day, allowed views of the mountains. As I entered the clearing, I put my pack down and wandered over to a group of people taking photos. I looked over their heads and caught a glimpse of Mount Everest, with Mount Lhotse alongside. The mountains looked incredible in the clear skies and I felt like I could reach out and touch them. I took a photo and enjoyed the spectacle and the illusion, realising they were still a full week of hiking away. The rest of our team congregated at the viewing point, and Elise was blown away by Everest. She'd never seen mountains like these and the look on her face was the same one I had worn many years earlier.

The trail was mostly flat for the following hour before we arrived at Namche Bazaar, a key trading hub for the entire area. Built into steep slopes at an elevation of 3440 metres, Namche's colourful buildings and picturesque setting make it an oasis in the Khumbu. Traditionally a meeting place for Sherpa people from surrounding villages, and as far away as Tibet, to come and trade commodities, it sells everything from yak cheese and milk to the latest trekking equipment and books. The village sustained damage during the earthquake, as did much of the country, but as testament to the resilience of the trekking industry, many of the tea houses had been rebuilt, and to a higher and stronger standard.

The tea house was busy and after finding our room, dropping our bags and enjoying a hot shower, we congregated in the main dining hall. Dozens of trekkers and climbers had gathered to eat, chat and relax by the warm stove. The atmosphere was energising: people of all ages and from different countries enjoyed the simple comforts of conversation, playing cards, reading and drinking tea. While we relaxed, our porters and Sherpa staff raced around delivering meals amid the organised chaos. The prices of tea house accommodation ranged dramatically, from the most expensive at around $50 per night, granting you hot showers and a comfy bed, to $3 per night, sleeping in the common area with the porters after everyone had gone to their rooms. An entire base camp trek is also possible without a guide, but when it comes to the evening mealtime in a busy tea house, having a local with you to navigate the carnage pays dividends for hungry climbers.

Over a great dinner of Sherpa stew, boiled eggs and chapati bread, I got to talking with Afra, another member of our team. He went to school at Stanford in the United States and from my limited understanding of his field, he was a computer software engineer, mathematical-genius type guy. He was a Jewish New Yorker, wore glasses and stood close to six feet in height. He had pale skin, black hair and a wiry frame, and his camera hung from his neck. I was captivated by his stories about the Big Apple, Jewish culture and his overall nerdy outlook. One of the things I enjoy most about adventure and commercial expeditions is they pull people together from every corner of the globe to achieve a single objective. Regardless of our economic situation, race differences or class in society, our Sherpa stews were exactly the same and we shared stories as mates.

While most of the team slept through the following morning, a number of us were up early to take in the sunrise and visit the local trading markets famous in Namche. The skies were crystal clear from our dining hall windows and when we stepped outside, the views were breathtaking. Multiple 6000-metre high peaks with sharp ridgelines of exposed rock and steep angled faces dropped thousands of feet to the valley below us. One intimidating cliff face had a waterfall breaching from its middle, expelling water into the cold morning air. The momentum of the torrent lost its fight against the power of the mountain winds and was cast away, partially evaporating midair and leaving only a misty trail at the base of the mountain.

At the market, traders had laid out carpets and tarps in rows of stalls to sell their goods. Everything was on offer: tea, coffee, noodles, combs, trekking clothes, Everest beer, scotch, sauces, soaps, vegetables and eggs. It was all super cheap and mainly sold to local clientele from all over Namche and the valley. The scent of the spices mixed with cheap cigarettes smoked by the locals hung in the frigid air. The market had been trading for many generations and although the goods being sold and exchanged might have altered over time, the custom was still intact.

Namche was built into three sides of a steep coliseum-shaped hill. After breakfast we ventured out for an acclimatisation hike around the top of the village and up onto a viewing point where a large statue of Tenzing Norgay had been constructed. Tenzing was a famous Sherpa mountaineer who became a legend when he climbed with Sir Edmund Hillary and stood on top of Mount Everest in 1953. They were the first two men to reach the summit and come back down alive. Tenzing was named one of the most influential humans of the 20th century by *Time* magazine and he is a hero of the Nepali people.

In front of the museum was a large grassed area ideal for relaxing while our bodies adapted to the new altitude. The sun shone and the clouds cleared, exposing staggering views of Everest, Lhotse and Ama Dablam in the foreground. I gazed up at Ama Dablam, a 6812-metre mountain I first laid eyes on and fell in love with on my original trip to Nepal. I've had a desire to climb her since that day and it had taken me years of training to learn the skills and gain the experience needed to attempt the climb. I had recently decided that next year it was going to finally happen. The mountain intimidated me, scared me, and that made me want it even more.

An attempt on the summit would entail a full month in the mountains next season. We would need to set up multiple camps, one at the base, an advanced base camp, plus two high camps. It would mean technical climbing on rock, ice and snow at high altitude. Managing ropes and exposed camping positions and also being wary of the giant hanging serac in the centre of the upper snow face. The serac is an enormous bulge of hanging snow the size of a city that has been in place for many years. It looms above an area used for camp three, and should it let go while we are up there, I can guarantee no one would ever be found again. As lethal as the mountain could be, she was absolutely stunning, and I couldn't wait to come back and climb her.

◆◆◆

We departed Namche the following day feeling refreshed and keen to push on. The rest day we enjoyed wasn't standard for a lot of trekking companies, with some trying to get their clients up and down to base camp as quickly as possible, but an extra day to acclimatise and rest can make the difference between success and failure.

The surrounding peaks were clearly visible as we climbed the slope out of the village. The trail hugged the steep valley wall and there was energy and excitement in the team as we chatted together. The thick pine forest started to transform with the higher altitude; trees became shorter and the scrub less dense as the nutrients to sustain them diminished. High mountain goats grazed on the shrubs to the side of the trail and we stopped to take pictures of them. They were perched on tiny exposed rock formations and watched us with the same interest we had in them.

We ascended a hilltop to the Tengboche Monastery shortly after midday. The Tibetan Buddhist monastery sits at 3867 metres and is the largest of its kind in the Khumbu region. It was built in 1916 only to be destroyed by earthquake and rebuilt in 1934. It was then lost to fire in 1989 but rebuilt again by volunteers and international help. At any time of the year there could be up to 60 monks living and learning at the monastery. We spent an hour inside the temple and relaxing in its courtyard, taking in the incredible beauty of the enormous wooden structure and mountainous surroundings. The front gate is decorated with elaborate carvings of animals and mythical dragon sprits, painted in bright colours. On both sides of the entry are large prayer wheels connected to bells, sounding the arrival and departure of hundreds of visitors each month.

After the monastery we stayed the night at a remote tea house in the tiny village of Deboche. The place was full to capacity with trekkers and I overheard a number of people standing outside talking about how there was nowhere to stay in the village and they would need to trek on to the next one. It was times like these when it paid to have a local guide who could call ahead to the teahouse owners and save you a bed. The following day we ate a boiled egg breakfast and stepped onto the trail in the chilled midmorning air.

We trekked over undulating terrain and slowly gained altitude throughout the day. As we hiked I talked with Tim, another Stanford alumnus, who was one of the most interesting guys I had met so far. Tim was six feet tall, lean and strong, had the stereotypical all-America vibe about him and a humble and calming presence. He also had a knack for one-liners and we hit it off straight away. He told me about his life in the biotech world of pharmaceuticals. He loved his job and I was captivated for hours listening about drug inception and design, patenting, manufacturing and, ultimately, getting it to the consumer. I pictured big pharma as an evil entity, but Tim was honest and the real deal, trying to help people and make a living for his family along the way. The moral balance between profit and people is not always easy but he seemed to have it worked out perfectly.

Pangboche village was our resting point for the night. At 3930 metres, the tea house proved to be my favourite during our entire trip. It was timber built, managed by a lovely local lady and had a second floor dining hall that showcased 250-degree views of the surrounding peaks. Ama Dablam was basically next door and I felt right at home as I settled down to drink tea and hydrate. The owner also had some wooden cabinets containing memorabilia from the era of the pioneers: old oxygen tanks from Sir Edmund Hillary's expedition, along with goggles, ice axes and an assortment of odds and ends. My favourite piece in the collection was an old timber trunk stamped with the number 1100 and dated 1953. Sir Edmund's expedition was classic siege-style and they needed to begin their attempt from Kathmandu. From there they forged a route all the way to Everest, taking with them over 4500 kilograms of luggage carried by 362 porters. The wooden trunk I admired was one of their abandoned pieces of luggage.

Before we lost the remaining daylight, Dean wanted to take us to the top of a hill where a famous monk named Lama Geshe lived. It was a 20-minute uphill walk to a humble home, which

Dean had been visiting and bringing clients to for over fifteen years. Dean summited Everest in 2005, and it was 80-year-old Lama Geshe who had blessed him before his successful attempt. We were shown into the common area by an elderly woman who immediately started to whisper something in Dean's ear. I noticed the expression on his face change to concern at the news he was hearing. Lama Geshe was seated on a cushion on an elevated wooden bench in the corner of the room. He was a small man, dressed in flowing maroon robes with gold trimming and wore an orange beanie and glasses. Covering the walls were hundreds of pictures from climbers who had been blessed by the famous monk. I noticed the drool coming from his mouth before I focused in on the giant tumour growing from his neck. The swelling had altered the shape of his jaw and mouth, causing him to slur his speech and drool. The look on Dean's face and the tears in his eyes told me everything. He had the highest respect for this elder of the mountains, and it hurt him personally to see him this way.

Lama Geshe must have been in terrible pain but he performed a beautiful ceremony for us. One at a time we approached him and he placed a gold scarf around our necks and blessed us for a safe journey. As we hiked back down the hill, Dean told me what the lady had whispered to him. Lama Geshe had a few months to live because he was too old to have surgery to remove the tumour.

Dean's eyes betrayed his emotion. 'That will probably be the last time I ever see the old man alive,' he said.

The encounter with the Lama was something I reflected on for the remainder of the evening. In western society we are not confronted with death often enough to acknowledge it or understand it. We falsely believe that we will live forever, planning retirements and paying off mortgages for 35-plus years. This false belief, in my eyes, inhibits our day-to-day enjoyment of life and we tend to put things off for later. 'Holidays next year' or 'I'll start that on Monday', are common statements in our civilised world. As I pursue more and more extreme sports and have more encounters with death, I become very aware of its presence. It could be around the corner for any one of us at any time, and if we really acknowledge it, I guarantee we will live more fulfilled lives. If you were to die tomorrow, would you look back on your life with regret? Or would you look back and think, 'I gave that one hell of a go'? If your answer is regret, make a change today.

Since writing these words, Lama Geshi has passed away. On Wednesday 14 February 2018, the man who had blessed so many climbers for safe journeys died at the age of 87. He will be missed by all.

◆◆◆

The following morning I was up before the sun at 6am and took a walk along the quiet street through the village. There wasn't a cloud in the sky as I walked next to a stone wall that separated the paddy fields and vegetable gardens from the trail. I had an uninterrupted view of the stunning mountain range as I strolled and watched my breath freeze in the air. On the walls of the homes I noticed the flat mudlike discs that had been squashed by hand and stuck there to dry in the sun. This was yak dung, collected by the farmers, flattened, dried and then stored as a replacement of firewood. The homes and fields dwindled in the background and transformed from thick vegetation to shrubby grassland dotted with small and tough bonsai-style trees. Further away and across the river, the valley floor climbed higher, colliding with the grey scree slopes where no plants could cling to life. Above the scree the dark cliffs at the base of the mountain protruded and forced their way skyward, intimidating and cold. The ice and snow embraced the rock, forming razor-sharp ridges, steep slopes and the awe-inspiring summit of Ama Dablam.

Our goal for the day was the village of Pheriche, a tiny collection of tea houses sitting alongside the now wide, shallow and slow-moving river. On the trail I had a long conversation about life and careers with my teammate Linda. Stanford alumni, of course, she had graduated and gone to work for the airline Boeing. There she had stayed to pursue a long and successful career for 28 years before retiring. Her goal was to do everything she had ever wanted to do, hence the reason for trekking to Everest Base Camp. She was 49 years old, highly intelligent, easygoing and luckily she could understand all my bad jokes and one-liners. Her body was a little worse for wear, with knee pain causing her to move slowly, but she never complained and just got the job done. Although a corporate career would never suit me, I admired her integrity, hard work and desire to crack on with life and see as much as she could.

After a night in Pheriche, we stopped for lunch at a tiny cluster of buildings called Dughla, perched alongside a raging narrow river pouring down from the Khumbu glacier. Dughla was inhabited by locals only during the trekking season and was a rest stop for teams heading up or down the valley. During winter it became as dormant as the mountains surrounding it.

After lunch, our goal for the night was Lobuche, and along the trail during the afternoon we visited the memorials built in honour of the Sherpas and foreigners who had died on expeditions over the years. Dozens of stone structures, big and small, were scattered across the flat area at the top of a steep incline. Some stood six feet high and honoured names like Rob Hall and Scott Fisher, two incredible climbers who perished on Everest in 1996 during the disaster year that claimed twelve lives. Jon Krakauer's book, *Into Thin Air*, and Anatoli Boukreev's *The Climb* are well-written firsthand accounts of this tragedy. Some memorials were small piles of rocks carved with the names of local Sherpas. Names I didn't know but I sat with and shared a moment, while I reflected on the chances I had taken over the years in pursuit of adventure. Walking silently around the piles of stones draped in prayer flags was a solemn reminder of the risks we take to summit these giant peaks.

As we departed the memorials, we cleared the path for a trekker coming down who was ringing a bell and giving commands to a guy behind him. It wasn't until I clearly saw the guy following him that I realised he was blind. His mate in front used the bell as an auditory cue for him to follow and he relayed information vocally about what was coming up next underfoot. It was incredible to witness, and it altered my chain of thought after the earlier reflections. Yes, people die in the mountains and it's tragic, but plenty more die sitting on their couches at home. The blind guy getting out of his comfort zone to trek to base camp was what it was all about. No matter who you are, adventure is for everyone. And, yes, accidents happen, but I would rather go out doing something I loved, covered in scars from a lifetime of adventure, than die after never having lived.

We arrived in Lobuche with a cold evening setting in. This was the second last village on our trek and it had some of the most beautiful scenery so far. The tea houses were a little rough-and-ready but at this altitude, with a cold front coming, beggars couldn't be choosers. The peak of Lobuche East towered up on my right as I took a moment to gaze back down the valley. It was an oil painting of a view. The tea houses looked vulnerable and tiny compared to the massive snow-covered peaks surrounding them, their sharp ridges pushing skyward, proclaiming their dominance on the valley.

The temperature was dropping fast, and it was minus two degrees as I looked up the valley. Nuptse sat huge on the horizon and it looked so clear and pristine in detail that if I had seen it anywhere else, I would swear it had been Photoshopped. My head and heart were pounding from the altitude and my hands were numb from the cold as I stepped inside to soak up the warmth of a yak dung fire. I was given a hot butter tea and decided life in the mountains wasn't so bad after all.

◆◆◆

The next day it was rock and gravel all the way to Gorek Shep, the highest village in the Khumbu and the final tea house before Everest Base Camp. It was a freezing start to the day and I was keen to get hiking and warm up in the morning sun. The warming rays were taking longer each day to penetrate as the mountains around us towered higher. We were in their shadows for the first hour and my fingers were numb until those glorious rays of life-giving heat hit me. My blood flow and morale increased as if by the flick of a switch. It was in moments like these that I fully appreciated why the ancient civilisations worshipped the sun god.

The trail wound its way up the valley and onto the Khumbu glacier. Although it was still gravel, scree and dirt underfoot, below that was solid ice. The glacier was constantly moving and carving its way down the valley. The exposed ice sections were a multilayered deep blue. The ice dripped water as it melted to form water torrents mixed with dirt that flooded out from underneath the enormous formations we walked across. The heavily fractured glacier bottlenecked the flow of trekkers in certain places. It was a busy day, the busiest I had ever seen. Hundreds of people were moving up and down from Gorek Shep, with all their yak teams and porters in support.

Gorek Shep comprised a handful of buildings nestled into a small dip in the terrain, Dean called it the 'Trekkers Death Zone.' His clever phrase referred to the 'Death Zone' on Mount Everest, the hardest section above 8000 metres in altitude. The human body cannot exist at high altitude for long, and the number of climbers who can reach the summit without supplemental oxygen is very small. We were now in the trekkers' equivalent and depending on how well people had acclimatised, it could be hell. After dropping our bags into the rather luxurious rooms considering where we were, we had a hot lunch and I drank copious amounts of tea to combat the thumping gorilla in my head.

After lunch it was time to hike up Kala Patthar, a steep 'hill' in Himalayan terms, with its summit sitting proud at 5644 metres. The trek to the top is renowned for its incredible views of Mount Pumori and Mount Everest. Many teams chose to hike up there for dawn and departed at 4am in freezing conditions. We decided to take the afternoon option and witness the setting sun shining on the face of Everest. Casey, who after feeling sick early on the trip, had adapted to the altitude and practically led the charge. The trail formed very steep gravel switchbacks and as we trekked higher, the views became more incredible. It was tough going, but 1 hour and 47 minutes after we departed, we made it to the top.

Seen up close, Mount Everest is one of the greatest wonders of nature and should be experienced firsthand by every person on our planet. Everest towers above the other peaks and its pyramid-shaped outline was silhouetted against the light blue sky. The view was humbling and intimidating. At the base of Everest and the adjoining face of Mount Lhotse was the Khumbu icefall. A notorious part of an Everest summit climb that must be respected and appreciated for its fragile and immediate dangers. The easiest way to explain the icefall is to picture an enormous frozen river. When this frozen river slowly grinds down the face of the mountains and into the valley it fractures. Huge blocks of ice and snow tumble down, get forced skyward and split apart to reveal gaping crevasses many metres wide. The icefall is constantly moving and can shift from a few centimetres to a full metre each day.

On an Everest expedition, this jagged icefall must be crossed fourteen times on the way up and the same amount on the way down by the supporting Sherpa teams, who fix the lines and ferry loads. They play Russian roulette with the conditions every time; usually western climbers will cross only three times. This imbalance of risk has led to work reforms for the Sherpa teams in recent years, but much more needs to be done before it is fair. The icefall is considered one of the most dangerous places on earth and in 2014, thirteen Sherpas ferrying loads for climbers were killed in a deadly avalanche. Looking down on it from the top of Kalar Patthar, it visually lived up to its reputation. I still had Everest on my adventure bucket list but when I would come back and take my chances with the mighty mountain and the icefall, I didn't know.

We made it back down to the comfort of the tea house in half the time it took us to climb up. The sun was setting as I took my boots off inside the tiny space Elise and I shared; the plan was food, hydrate and rest. Tomorrow would be the final day and the culmination of our trek; Everest Base Camp was next.

◆◆◆

Gasping for a breath as my heart pounded out of my chest, I looked around at the plywood walls and handmade rough timber bed frames. Elise was fast asleep opposite me. The room was freezing and my head was pounding. I forced down a headache tablet with cold water and pulled my sleeping bag up over my head. I could hear some commotion outside with people coming and going but on checking my watch, there was still two hours before we had to be up. I dozed back to sleep.

Two hours later I was up, dressed and walking into the common room for coffee to find Dean already there. Three unknown trekkers were lying on the floor hooked up to oxygen bottles, with the Nepali staff looking on concerned. Dean told me they had succumbed to altitude sickness in the early hours and needed to be put on oxygen to bring up their blood saturation. They were stable but a helicopter had been called to take them out within the hour, back down to Lukla. That was a $2000 flight for each person, but it was better to be safe than sorry. Dean told me this was a fairly common occurrence and that their team had taken only six days to reach Gorek Shep; we had taken nine. Their fast pace had come back to bite them with altitude sickness and an expensive taxi home.

Today was our final day of ascent, and after a hearty breakfast the entire team stepped off towards base camp. I was following in the tracks of the original pioneers and even though I wasn't going for the summit, it felt incredible to be walking the same path. We paralleled the glacier for the first 30 minutes before the trail turned onto the river of ice. Steep banks on either side were a glimpse back in time to when the ice was thicker and wider. Climate change had removed some of its girth, but its size and power still baffled my mind.

VODKA & SANDSTORMS

After two hours the trail wound its way down and into the middle of the glacier; in and around huge blocks of deep blue ice, some with small lakes of meltwater forming at their base. Crevasses fractured open to reveal dark, bottomless pits to our left and right. I was studying one and imagining myself being caught inside, when I looked up from my daydream and realised we had arrived at Everest Base Camp.

The site of base camp is barren, rocky and inhospitable. Drop-offs into crevasses littered the area and this was the spot where up to 500 climbers would be camping for two months while they attempted to climb Everest. There wasn't a flat section of ground anywhere around us, it was all crumpled by the continual movement of the ice. During the two months camped here, each tent site would need to be levelled out and reorganised dozens of times. This was the end of the line. Surrounding us on all sides were the towering peaks of Mount Lhotse at 8516 metres, Mount Nuptse at 7861 metres, Mount Pumori at 7161 metres, and the biggest of them all, Mount Everest at 8848 metres. On the other side of these ancient giants was Tibet and China, and the only way up was through the icefall. Up close, the icefall was one of the most intimidating approaches to a mountain I had ever seen.

The whole team had made it and we all shared hugs and high fives, took copious amounts of photos and sat down to rest and enjoy the environment. For most of us it would be a place we would never return to and a huge achievement in getting here. We had one group photo before I took my last look up at Everest. My eyes watered from the cold and glare as I vowed to return one day and attempt the summit. If the mountain and Mother Nature let me, it would be a dream come true to stand atop the highest point on earth.

Would climbing Everest be the challenge I had been searching for my entire life? The one adventure that pushes me to breaking point and exposes what I am truly made of? I turned away and gave a thumbs-up to Dean. He smiled, turned and started to lead us back down the way we came.

I started chatting to Geljin during our return to the tea house. He was an overly cheerful guy, always smiling, and had spent his entire life in the mountains. He now taught his knowledge to the younger Sherpas rising into the guiding world. He told me a story I had never heard before, about a man from Lumbini, a town bordering India, who 2600 years ago took a journey. This man was born a prince and named Siddhartha Gautama, and he was sheltered from the ugliness of life behind high palace walls. Poverty, aging, hunger, death, suffering, everything was shielded from the young man. One day, at the age of 29, Siddhartha ventured from the palace and saw that the world wasn't what he thought it was. He departed the comfort and security of his home and took a six-year quest of discovery. He sought out spiritual healers, meditation masters and anyone with knowledge to teach him what they knew. He then began exploring his mind's true potential through meditation and after six days of cutting through the mind's subtle obstacles he reached enlightenment. He was 35 years old and became Buddha, the awakened one, spawning what would become the world's fourth largest religion, with over 520 million followers.

Life really is one big adventure and this story could be a metaphor for any one of our lives at a given time. I broke away from 'normal life' to seek adventure and happiness at a time when it was easier to stay put in comfort and security. I am in no way comparing myself to Buddha, yet the philosophy stands true. We are all on a journey.

It took us four days to return to Lukla, which gave me plenty of time to think and ponder these ideas. Was I on the right path? What was I searching for? If I was on my own road to enlightenment, would I find it in meditation, as Buddha had, or would I find it standing on top of the highest mountain on earth?

A smile crept across my face and I turned my head towards the mountains. I thought to myself, 'There's only one way to find out.'

Chapter 8
Mount Satopanth

India is a country bursting at the seams with life. With a population of around 1.35 billion, it has a diverse culture, multiple religions and the pace of London or New York. Hinduism is the most popular religion, which contains some 33 million gods in its holy texts, one for every occasion. There is rarely a time when a festival isn't blocking the streets with its bright colours, music and ceremony. India is unique among developing nations, it's a country where you can witness extreme poverty next to extreme wealth, regardless of the city or area you're travelling through.

My initial shock on seeing the dozens of beggars and shanty towns dimmed with time, and over the weeks it became normal. One day I was standing at the edge of the World Trade Centre slum in Mumbai, a place considered 'good' as far as slums were rated, and I watched a Ferrari drive by. In the same frame were women with plastic jugs lining up for water at a single tap. Water in the poorest communities was sporadic and sometimes only arrived for an hour per day. I thought, how could someone drive past in a million-dollar car and feel good about themselves? Another day, the tuktuk I was riding in stopped at some lights and the beggars arrived eager at the sight of a white face. I tried to give a little something to one or two beggars per day, but by the twentieth I shook my head, looked away and hoped they would move on and save me from my embarrassment. I was no different to the guy in the Ferrari, but looking away from the problem didn't mean I didn't care.

Elise and I had arrived in India with a plan to summit an intimidating 7000-metre peak called Mount Satopanth, a name that meant 'True Path.' We were then planning to transfer to a kayak and follow the Ganges River from its source to the sea. It was an ambitious plan we named the True Path Project. We signed on to a small team heading into the Himalaya guided by White Magic Adventure, a company with a great reputation in India. We initially wanted to climb and plan our own expedition, but the Indian Mountaineering Foundation required all climbers to hire and provision liaison officers who would go with you everywhere. This was a bigger hurdle than I was willing to leap, so we went with a local operator.

Elise and I landed in Mumbai. I cleared immigration first and looked back at Elise whose demeanour changed from tired and happy to shock as she spoke to the immigration official. She was taken to a side office where I joined her, and after ten minutes of being stared at by five men in uniform, a bosslike figure sat down in front of us. With zero pleasantries to soften the impact, he told us I could stay in India but Elise was to be placed on the next flight out. This hit me like a cricket bat to the face and initially I didn't know how to react.

'Sorry mate, what do you mean?' I asked.

He repeated his opening sentence and added, 'Do you want to stay in India or go with her?'

'Why, what's the problem?' I asked.

'We don't know. It says in the system she is banned from India forever. Her visa is fine, but she is banned,' he said. This information was an absolute shock to us. Piled on top of the 1am arrival and the jet lag, Elise broke down. We took a few minutes in a side office, away from the increasing number of guys in uniform. We had to make a decision on the spot. I had a seminar to deliver in Mumbai and I was certain the problem

Climbing in the Himalaya in India. Me on the left, Max on the right with the mighty Mt Satopanth in the background.

Tonsai wall looming over Tonsai beach, my favourite BASE jump.

Navigating our first Lock on the Murray River. Elise and me in the kayaks and Dad in the River Rat.

Our homes for 57 days across the Gobi Desert.

Elise and I dragging carts across the Gobi Desert in Mongolia.

The most incredible, exhilarating and awe inspiring thing you could do. I do not recommend it to anyone. BASE Jump - Lauterbrunnen Valley, Switzerland.

Elise and I celebrating at the mouth of the Murray River in South Australia.

I was slowly starving during our crossing of the Gobi Desert.

Me on the left, Jimmy in the middle and Elise on the right. Frenchman's Cap in the background.

BASE Jumping an antenna in an undisclosed location, a crash landing shortly followed.

Nomad boy galloping his camels across the Gobi.

Cooking dinner on the banks of Lake Mulwala.

Dad holding his 120cm Murray Cod and claiming his title as the Codfather.

Paddling past stunning red cliffs on the Murray River in South Australia.

After six weeks of trying I caught a big Carp by hand.

Lunchtime in the Gobi Desert.

Sitting with the famous 'Sadhu who clicks' in Gangotri, India.

Devouring as many Khuushuur as we could stomach.

Inside a typical Nomad Ger with a lovely family and goat meat drying on the wall.

The village of Namche Bazaar built into a valley at 3440 metres in Nepal.

Everest Base Camp in Nepal.

A porter carrying an enormous load across a suspension bridge in Nepal.

Grant and me starting our row from Australia to New Zealand. Photo by Alistair Harding.

Walking into Sainshand at the completion of our 57 day 1805 kilometre crossing of the Gobi Desert.

could be fixed when she arrived home in Sydney, so I decided to stay. Elise had no choice at all. Within 20 minutes of landing we went from being excited to getting forced apart at customs and her returning on the same plane we arrived on. The True Path Project was off to a shaky start.

The days that followed were a whirlwind of stress and anxiety, with only ten days until the expedition began the pressure was on. Elise arrived back in Sydney and turned up to the Indian embassy every day for a week. She received zero help; the embassy wanted no part in the matter and VFS Global, the company who issued the visa, said they had no control over it. Elise remembered she had an issue with her work permit when she was working in India on Bollywood music video productions ten years earlier. This could be the reason she was refused entry.

On her behalf I tried to visit the Australian embassy in Mumbai but they were useless. I then turned up at the FRRO, the work permit authority building. I was there for eight hours and given the run-around for most of the day. I knew they were going to close soon so I googled the head of the FRRO and walked up to the reception desk and said, 'I have a meeting with Madam Ananya, take me to her office.'

The guy read the fake email I'd sent myself detailing the meeting and took me upstairs. I entered the only air-conditioned room in the building and sat down opposite the boss lady. I laid on some pleasantries and then outlined the problem. She was sympathetic to our cause, gave me her email so I could send over all the relevant information and showed me the door. When I made it back to my room after one of the most stressful days of my existence, I emailed her the documents. The email bounced. That was the nail in the coffin of my day.

We hit constant blocks trying to sort the problem in India and Australia. It came to a point where no one knew why Elise was banned – it was so long ago and whoever did the paperwork was long gone. I knew the issue was with immigration on arrival and particularly the new passport scanning machines. If we could bypass the scanners at Mumbai airport, we could get lucky because Elise's visa was still valid. I remembered when I travelled through India towards Nepal overland years before that the northern borders were fairly relaxed. At some border crossings they didn't have the scanners and instead utilised the old stamps.

'Let's try Operation Northern Insertion,' I told Elise.

She laughed at first but after I explained the plan she was willing to give it one last try. We both flew to Kathmandu, Nepal, and spent two nights there organising a bus to take us over the border. We picked a border crossing town, loaded onto the local bus and went for it.

Nine hours of winding, potholed mountain roads, carsick travel companions and constant anxiety, and we arrived at the town of Sanauli. It was 9pm and the streets were bustling with travellers and locals pouring back and forth between both countries. Thumping music announcing another Hindu festival was our soundtrack as we entered the Nepal office to exit the country. In the dilapidated building, among the clutter of paper and next to an ancient computer was a single passport scanner. I had a sinking feeling and knew we were in trouble if the Indian office had the same.

We reboarded the bus, which drove us 300 metres up the road to the Indian entry. The building was dark inside and seemed to be closed. The thought crossed my mind to tell the driver to keep going but he stopped and pointed to the building. We walked to the entry and a light flicked on, as I looked through the glass door into the office my heart sank. Covered in dust, up against a wall in the back was a dreaded passport scanner. I knew we had no chance.

Elise was scanned first, and the old computer lit up like a Christmas tree. We played ignorant and tried to find out why she was banned but he couldn't tell us any more than everyone else. The bus unloaded our bags and departed for Delhi, and we were told to go back to the Nepal office to enter the country again. Elise's Visa was stamped CANCELLED and we stood outside the Indian office in no man's land between two nations. It started to rain.

'Let's just pick up the bags and walk into India,' I said. I didn't care anymore.

'We can't,' Elise replied. 'If we are caught, we go to jail.'

She was right, of course. We loaded the bags into a tuktuk, re-entered Nepal and found a local driver to take us all the way back to Kathmandu. Our mission was over and so was Elise's chances of getting to climb Mount Satopanth.

We were devastated at the outcome. We had planned to do the entire expedition together and now we were weighing up whether to do it at all. After long conversations, tears and analysing our remaining funds, it seemed silly to waist the money we had spent and not one of us try the climb. We decided I would continue to India and carry on with our trip.

We spent a few days together in Kathmandu before I flew out to Delhi and Elise flew to Bali for work. This was the last time we would be seeing each other for a few months.

I was anxious going through Delhi immigration after everything that had happened. I imagined the officer knew who I was and what I had said to Elise while standing in no man's land in the rain. But I breezed through without a hitch and was picked up and dropped to my hotel by a member of White Magic Adventure. I tried to clear my mind of the drama from the previous two weeks and set myself to task, getting ready to climb.

I unpacked all my duffel bags and laid out the climbing gear. I unpacked the shipment from Australian Sports Nutrition, enough supplements to last me three months but I needed to break it down into small ziplock bags. I also needed to have the sponsors' patches sewn onto my jackets, vests and baggage. So that's what I set out to do first.

Outside the hotel the foot traffic was thick and the road traffic thicker, and stalls were selling everything from chai to deep-fried samosas and barbecue corn. I found an old man sitting in the street with his sewing machine on a small table. It was an ancient pedal-powered model common in India. I played charades until he understood what I was wanting and then he set to work.

I'm fortunate in my adventure career that I can get sponsorship for my crazy ideas, in exchange for marketing, brand awareness and keynote talks. I try to limit my sponsors to three per expedition to give each of them a good return on investment. I'm often asked, 'Who sponsors you, sports companies?' The answer is always, 'Anyone.' I have found mutually beneficial relationships with companies of all varieties: investment firms, supplement companies, real estate, coffee, plumbing and even hotels. What matters is whether I can deliver, how much brand recognition they receive and whether the lessons and stories I share can benefit their people. One of the best aspects about adventure is it's for everyone, no matter your race, religion or bank balance. It's the ultimate leveller that intrigues plumbers and bankers alike, and the lessons I have learned over the years have been shared with all of them.

I turned back to my local friend and he had finished sewing on the three major sponsors: Stamford Capital, Belle Property Parramatta and Australian Sports Nutrition. He got to work trimming my flags and when he was done he wanted the equivalent of two dollars for his efforts. I gave him ten, shook his hand and said farewell with a smile.

I stopped off at a small pharmacy to buy some headache tablets and spied a shop selling biscuits. After paying the miniscule price for the drugs I turned away from the pharmacy, took a big step towards the biscuit seller and fell knee deep into a huge hole full of liquid human shit. My knee took a hit on the broken pavement and my shoes were soaked through with the black sludge. My shorts were covered, my shirt took a splashing and the stench from the water was absolutely horrific. I gagged as I pulled myself out of the hole and shook off as much of the slop as I could. All I could do was laugh and return to the hotel.

The little Indian man, whose job it was to open the hotel door, saw me coming and his smile turned to concern as he noticed the state of me. He took me to the side and started washing me from a barrel of water. Once he was satisfied I wouldn't soil the floors too much, he let me pass. I made my way upstairs, leaving a light brown trail of footprints behind me. I took a shower and scrubbed myself clean, followed by a Dettol wash of the open scratches on my legs. I realised that in India, Darwin's theory of natural selection was in full effect. Unlike Australia, where ten layers of occupational health and safety would have been guarding that exposed sewer, here the risk was back on you. I had to adapt to my new environment quickly if I was to make it through unscathed.

I went down to reception in the late afternoon and met two of my teammates. Alex and Nitya were both doctors, a skill always helpful on big expeditions, and were from Tasmania. The couple had recently summited Aconcagua in Argentina and Satopanth would be their first 7000 metre peak. Alex was well over six foot tall, had the build of a basketball player and sported a huge black beard. Nitya was around five foot, slim build with short black hair. They were on a one-year sabbatical and Alex had vowed not to cut his hair or beard the entire time.

I then ran into Uli and Karin, a German couple who had also signed onto the expedition. They were both in their sixties and had completed a long list of adventures together. They fell in love with India in their youth and had visited the country a dozen times. They were both slim builds, and I could tell they would have trekking endurance. They spoke great English and we all got to know each other while we travelled to the Indian Mountaineering Foundation (IMF) building.

Every expedition in India must have official approval and be allocated a liaison officer (LO) from the IMF. If you have never been to India before, the level of bureaucracy and paperwork can be mind-boggling, and being forced to have a LO is just another layer of it. The LO must be provided with climbing equipment, transport and all food and accommodation on the trip. It's a big ask if you're trying to put together an expedition on a budget. Luckily for us, White Magic had been in business for a long time and had a good relationship with the IMF. Our LO was named Druv, and he had been employed by White Magic in the past as a guide, so they knew him well.

When climbing in Nepal, helicopter rescue is as easy as buying tea but in India there are no rescue agencies. This made climbing and high altitude mountaineering a much riskier undertaking. One of the main roles of the LO was to coordinate with the military in case of a big emergency and to keep foreigners away from border regions and military bases. Satellite phones were also banned in India, cutting off all communication with the outside world for the duration of the climb. This crazy rule made expeditions much more dangerous, as most teams would get no weather forecasts and have no way to call for help. To remedy this problem, we had a small GPS device that had the ability to email, skirting the grey area of the rules.

We had to receive a briefing from the IMF director before we could leave, so we sat down for chai and waited. When he finally arrived his speech was full of long pauses punctuated with a loud hacking cough and there were moments when I was holding back laughter. But he was deadly serious. 'You will go to the mountains happy and healthy, and come back happier and healthier,' he said. This was a true statement but the way it was delivered, with extreme pomposity, was pure comedy. The briefing ended, we shook hands with the director and returned to the hotel. We had a few hours to pack and sleep before our scheduled train departure at midnight.

At 11pm we drove through the now quieter streets en route to the train. We passed countless men, women and children setting up cardboard sleeping mats out in the open. There were many more already curled up asleep under every overpass and sheltered piece of pavement available. If you are ever in doubt about how lucky we are in our 'developed world,' drive around Mumbai or Delhi late at night.

At the train station, porters scrambled over themselves to carry our packs and duffel bags to the platform. We bustled our way on board the sleeper carriages and found our bunks. I was separated from the rest of the team and shared my room with a local family. The bottom bunk on one side was mine and I made my bed with the sheets and blanket provided. The air-conditioning was a welcome relief from the humid heat and the vibration of the train's engine was soothing when I lay down. The train pulled out at midnight and I fell asleep to the rocking and grinding of the ancient carriages.

VODKA & SANDSTORMS

◆◆◆

I woke at 5.20am and remembered we were due to arrive at our destination of Dehradun around 5.40am. My stomach was bloated and rumbling, the spicy Indian cuisine from the night before wasn't sitting well, so I decided to take care of business in the squat toilets while the rest of the train slept. Afterwards I found the side door of the carriage wide open with the cool morning air coming through. Back home a door wide open on a moving train would be a serious breach of safety, but in India it was a place to stand and watch the sunrise.

The platforms were organised chaos as we shouldered our bags and left the station. Out the front we were met by a van and our climbing team. Avilash, our head guide, greeted us with a big smile. I had corresponded with him at length before signing on to the expedition. He had many years of experience in the Himalayas and I couldn't wait to pick his brain on the climb. He had a slim frame, a slightly hunched posture and a warm, friendly demeanour. Our climbing Sherpas were Namgyal, Mingma, Mingdempa and Nima, all incredible climbers with a bulging résumé of successful summits. These guys were our insurance. If something went wrong high on the mountain, the strength of the Sherpa team was critical.

What followed was a nine-hour drive up and down mountainous terrain on derelict roads. We had enough near misses with oncoming trucks to make me want to walk. The most riveting moments were when the driver of our van overtook at the same time as a truck overtook a vehicle up ahead coming our way. The moments when four large vehicles play chicken at high speed on a dodgy road are terrifying at first, but after a few hours it seemed normal to pass within inches of the other trucks and buses with horns blasting. It was almost like they were two magnets repelling each other before the moment of impact. When we pulled up in the small village of Dharasu, nestled high on the banks of the Bhagirathi River, I was well and truly ready for a break.

The next day the roads were less busy as we drove higher into the mountain range and away from civilisation. The traffic thinned and the roads narrowed during the four-hour drive to a village called Gangotri. The village was named after the mighty Gangotri Glacier, which we would see in a few days, and was considered a holy place and the source of the Ganges. This was the final stop for vehicles and our staging area before departing on foot. We were at 3000 metres in elevation and needed to take a rest day to aid with acclimatisation. I was pumped and ready to get going but I had to calm myself and prepare for the slow safe pace of mountaineering.

We met our final team member in Gangotri. Max was from Italy and looked to be a hardened mountain man with a grey beard and cigarette in his mouth at all times. He was 50 years old and had been waiting a few days for us to arrive. He had kept himself busy by trekking in the surrounding valleys and visiting the local temples. He was a lovely guy and had plenty of stories from his sailing past to entertain us. Our team was now complete, the porters were scheduled to arrive in two days and then we would be ready to depart.

Rest days were part of mountaineering but we didn't want to be lying in bed all day, active rest was key to speeding up acclimatisation. On our rest day we took a three-hour hike up a small valley to gain some altitude and get used to walking as a full team. Another team from Germany was also in Gangotri preparing for Mount Satopanth, and during our hike they came rushing past setting a cracking pace. I took one look at them and shook my head. The ability to move fast comes in handy on summit day, but the start of a climb is the time to move slow and enjoy the process.

After lunch we went in search of a famous 92-year-old Sadhu. Sadhus are Hindu holy men who have renounced the worldly life and survive off donations from the many pilgrims making their way up into the valley to the source of the Ganges. There were plenty of them scattered around the village near the small shops frequented by tourists. I'm not a religious person, I struggle to believe in a higher power governing everything we do and experience, but when I'm about to enter the mountains I will go along with any ritual the local villagers or holy men want to bestow on us. Sometimes while mountaineering a climber could die of exposure one day, and three days later a team could ascend all the way to the summit in perfect conditions. Sometimes an avalanche will snatch a climber from the mountain, and other times it will slide by for the perfect photo opportunity. Sometimes it's all about luck and when luck is involved, I'll take every blessing thrown my way.

The following morning the porters had arrived, and it was chaos at the hotel as our Sherpa team separated all the expedition kit and supplies into loads for them to carry. Each porter received the same weight unless they wanted to carry double or triple loads for extra money. It was typically the older and stronger porters who chose to double up and lead the way. While we were watching the work, Avilash told us one of the females on the German team fell and broke her shoulder on the acclimatisation hike the day before. Given that they'd been rushing up the valley when they passed us, I wasn't surprised by the news. Such a shame for her after months of training to be going home before the trip had even begun.

We took our first steps into the Himalaya and started the long slow trek towards base camp. I carried my pack and handed off my duffel bag to the porters. I've found it best to carry some weight while acclimatising to get my body prepared for the load to come. We followed the river up into the valley along a well-trodden pilgrim trail. The roar of the white water was ever present, and I was buzzing to be finally hiking towards Satopanth. We took regular breaks, shared stories and bonded as a team during the five-hour hike to Cherbasa, our first camp.

Cherbasa means 'Home of Pines' and when we arrived it was easy to understand why. The lush pine forest, although small, was a little haven nestled next to the river. It was busy with trekkers and pilgrims but there was plenty of room for us to set up our tents under the trees. Cherbasa sits at 3520 metres and I wasn't feeling any ill effects from the altitude. As I walked down to the bank of the river to watch the sunset, I could see snow-capped peaks in the distance. Bhagirathi one, two and three stood at 6856 metres, 6512 metres and 6454 metres, respectively, and they looked incredible in the dying light. Their sheer rock faces were intimidating.

I could feel my body adapting to the 20 kilograms I carried on my back, the boots on my feet and the terrain we were crossing. The body is a complex adaptive system, and I was sensing all of the little changes taking place. The team came together for dinner and then we were in bed early to write in journals, read books and be alone with our thoughts. The simple life in the mountains had begun.

For breakfast I devoured bowls of cornflakes, toast, eggs and coffee, all prepared by our team cook, Dawa. He was our master chef up here and the luxury of not having to boil water and prepare my own meals was huge. During the Gobi Desert expedition we had to do everything ourselves, and the extra work of meal prep, water purification and monitoring gas levels cannot be overstated. On this trip all we had to worry about was sleeping, hiking and acclimatising. We departed camp by midmorning for an easy three-hour hike to Bhojwasa, gaining 250 metres in altitude.

Bhojwasa is a collection of derelict and newly built buildings bunched together on the bank of the river. Apparently the entire area was covered in birch forest many years ago but over the years the trees were logged for fuel and construction, leaving only boulders and shrubs. It was also home to a small contingent of police and the military, who were playing a boisterous game of cricket as we arrived. The British gave the Indians many long-lasting habits and behaviours but I don't think anything has penetrated the culture like the sport of cricket, which is like a religion in India. And whether it's an international match against Australia or a backyard tussle like the one we were watching, they play to win.

Alex went off to join the match and I took a walk down and along the bank of the river. The sound of the white water was relaxing and the sudden chill in the air as the sun disappeared was a reminder of where I was. This remote outstation was the last sign of humanity, from now on it would be tent life and dealing with everything Mother Nature could throw at us. Due to the lack of infrastructure and the sheer volume of tourists, I had to be cautious of where I placed my feet. The sandy riverbank became the go-to area for human waste. The smell at certain spots brought back the memories of my army days deployed in East Timor. We would always know when a village was up ahead in the jungle by the smell of human shit. The aroma is unmistakable and unforgettable.

A nine-hour sleep delivered my mind and body into a new day refreshed and ready to hike. We stepped onto the trail as the sun broke over the ridgeline, its warming rays a blessing in the below freezing start. We hiked for three hours before arriving at one of the holiest places in the Himalaya, the source of the River Ganges. Known as Gomukh, water bursts out from under the snout of the Gangotri Glacier, a place thousands of pilgrims come to every year to wash their sins away. The wall of ice was partially covered in dirt and rock, and in places we could see the enormous blue-ice face of the frozen river. The rumbling and fracturing of the ice pierced the air and every so often fragments and debris fell into the frigid water pooling at its base. The meltwater would travel over 2500 kilometres to the Bay of Bengal near Calcutta, on India's north-western shores. It's a journey I was hoping to replicate, but first I had to climb.

After a break for lunch we shouldered our loads and continued on. The trail began to disappear as it wound its way up onto the glacier. For three hours we had to pick our way through the mass of boulders, scree and ice. I took multiple slides on my backside as I adjusted to the new terrain and had to work on my balance as we crossed newly formed rock bridges. I could hear the groaning of the ice and the trickle of meltwater below my feet. To the west, two incredible peaks came into view: Mount Shivling and Meru.

Shivling is one of the most iconic peaks in the Himalaya. Nicknamed the 'Matterhorn Peak' by Europeans because of its similar appearance to its famous namesake in the Alps, it's a dramatic rock feature impossible to miss. To Hindus, Mount Shivling was named after Shiva, one of the 33 million Hindu gods. Apparently it was Shiva's long hair that formed the mighty Ganges River. Standing at 6543 metres, the peak was first climbed in 1974. Since then it has seen a number of successful and unsuccessful attempts. Every route to its summit is a serious undertaking due to its exposed faces and serac dangers. It's a mountain I would love to climb but, in reality, with my current skill and experience, it's one to be left for true specialists of mountaineering.

Meru Peak, at 6660 metres, is a famous mountain made more so in 2012 by Jimmy Chin, Conrad Anker and Renan Ozturk, when they made the first ascent of the 'Shark's Fin' ridge. A line that only a handful of elite climbers could ever attempt, it took these three professionals two attempts to claim it. The documentary about their climb, *Meru*, is a masterpiece and inspiration for me. I stared up at these intimidating features of rock, ice and snow and was truly humbled. The journey of acquiring the skills to attempt mountains like these is a long one and most of us will never get there, but a mountain like Satopanth is a perfect training ground. It's the next step up for me, higher than I had ever climbed, had a greater skill level and higher risk.

We pushed on and upwards to 4450 metres. The last hour of the day was a steep incline as we climbed out and away from the glacier. We camped at Nandanvan, a flat area of tough grass and boulders where we would take a rest day. I hadn't seen the German team since we departed Gangotri, they must have skipped rest days and made haste for base camp. My head was pounding as I entered camp and I could only imagine how they felt from moving on without breaks.

◆◆◆

During the following day of active rest, we wanted to gain some altitude to help acclimatisation. We hiked up the valley towards Satopanth, with Mount Bhagirathi looming large off to my right.

The trail hugged the high eastern edge of Satopanth glacier, and at certain points a step too far to the left would ensure a life-ending 30-metre fall onto the ice below. We peeled off from the trail and made a steep ascent towards the sheer face of Bhagirathi. After four hours we had ascended to 4820 metres. When I first lay eyes on Bhagirathi a few days before I had been intimidated, but up close I could start to pick apart her vertical rock wall and see lines that could possibly be climbed. Bhagirathi had lost her inhibiting power over me. We rested and enjoyed the view before turning around and heading back down to camp.

I sat in my tent for the afternoon and thought over my up-close encounter with the mountain. In life we aspire to achieve things that can often seem intimidating, impossible or unattainable. More often than not this would halt us before we even started. What if we continued towards those objectives anyway, would the same thing occur that happened with Bhagirathi? Would the intimidating objective slowly become achievable as it was broken down, showing the cracks in its veneer?

It was the coldest night so far and I bundled myself up in my sleeping bag. Simply trying to read a book by headlamp made my exposed fingers go numb. I had also mistakenly packed my pee bottle into my duffel bag, which was en route to base camp with a porter. This left me with two options: I could get out of my tent during the frigid night to pee or I could repurpose one of my water bottles. Of course, I used my water bottle. The small issue I had was all of my bottles looked the same, so I would have to get used to a urine-flavoured tinge in my water until base camp. It's incredible what becomes 'okay' while on expedition.

We were up early, breaking camp and getting ready to move. The surrounding peaks blocked the sun and it was freezing. In our normal lives the sun is often a hindrance causing sunburn, drought for farmers and general discomfort in cities. But up in the mountains at dawn, in below-zero temperatures, the flow of heat and energy through my system from the sun's rays was incredible.

I shouldered my full pack and we moved off from Nandanvan and along the same trail as our acclimatisation hike the day before. This time we didn't peel off to Bhagirathi but continued along the glacier, crossing it after lunch and coming up against a wall of scree and rock. The 30-metre near vertical climb wasn't overly technical, and a fixed line was in place for porters to use while carrying their huge loads. Climbing with a pack on was never easy and as soon as I started up my heart rate jacked, my breathing became heavy, and I felt unfit. I had a flash of panic as I thought, 'I'm not ready for Satopanth.' I realised I was being ridiculous. It was my first actual climb at near 5000 metres, so of course I was puffing.

I made it to the top and dropped my pack on what turned out to be a ridge. The ground gently fell away in front of me and I looked down below at a valley with a tranquil lake at its centre; this was Vasuki Tal and our base camp, at 4900 metres. Next to it was a cluster of tents, which Avilash told us were ours. As we rested on the ridge the porters who had carried our duffels were on their way up towards us. We flagged them over long enough to thank them and hand over a tip before they bolted off down the valley. They would be back to Gangotri in a day and most likely loading up again with another team's equipment. They were some of the hardest working men in the mountains and an essential part of big expeditions.

During our first dinner at base camp, Avilash congratulated us on completing stage one and arriving fit and healthy. He then unloaded some information he had been holding back. The mountain had seen a lot of change in the last two years and camp three was currently too risky to set up as a camp during our summit push. The small flat area that had been utilised in the past was no longer viable due to avalanches. He told us we would need to make our summit bid from Camp Two. This would mean a huge 15 to 20 hour day at high altitude on a semi-technical route. This wasn't ideal information to receive but at least we could start preparing ourselves for it.

Then he dropped the next bombshell: the weather report. A large storm system was due to hit us in four days and lots of snow was forecast. He said we would need to be back at base camp when it hit to avoid getting stuck up high without an exit route. This was bad news. Heavy snow before a summit attempt would increase the risk of avalanche, it would also mean tough climbing conditions depending on the snow depth. He wanted us to complete a load carry to Camp One, and ideally have Camp Two set up before we pulled back for the storm. We would be heading up the following day with a full load. The climb had just gotten real and it was time to work.

◆◆◆

Mountaineering is about the balance between rest, acclimatisation and very hard work. Day Nine was a workday and one of the toughest I had endured in the mountains for many years. I shouldered my pack, the heaviest of the expedition, and as a team we started up shortly after sunrise. I felt the weight of my climbing kit and extra food burying into my shoulders. I drowned out the discomfort with conversations and podcasts during the five-hour slog through the moraine. Halfway up, we could see the mighty Satopanth in all its glory.

It was a mountain unique in appearance, with the centre of its northern face gouged out from avalanches. Directly below the fractured scar was the icefall. The tonnes of snow falling from the mountain became the next layer of ice that would slowly make its way down the valley over the coming years. Satopanth had a large summit plateau and a snowdrift was blasting off the summit ridge. The ridge was razor sharp and to get on top meant a steep ascent across another razor ridge from Camp Two. I couldn't wait to get up there, but the route was difficult and it wasn't going to be a walk in the park. I was excited thinking about a night ascent of the razor ridge.

Camp One was situated at 5330 metres and sat on top of an uneven boulder field right next to the glacier. Our first job on arrival was to even out a section of rocks and erect one tent that would store all our team gear. Our Sherpas had completed a load carry and dropped off a pile of equipment they needed to fix ropes to Camp Two. I thought I was adapting to the altitude well, but during lunch my head started to pound in time with my heartbeat. A few headache tablets did nothing to stifle the drum and as I shouldered my empty pack to start heading back to base camp it was sounding my retreat.

I was quiet all the way back. Alex, being the doctor, would ask me at every rest stop, 'How are you feeling now, mate?' and the answer was the same each time, 'Pretty rough, bro.' I couldn't complain, however, because I had been watching our 60-year-old teammate Karen soldier on all day. She must have taken 20 tumbles, slides and falls throughout the climb, and every time she picked herself up, dusted herself off, and carried on like nothing happened. She was a true machine and watching her gave me strength; if not actual physical strength, at least the strength not to complain.

Eight hours after departing we walked back into camp. Hot tea and biscuits were waiting for us and I felt like a pioneering British explorer. I gulped the fluids and devoured the biscuits. Over a hot dinner, Avilash said, 'Well done today, we will move up to Camp One tomorrow.' My head was bothering me but I knew sleep would help me adapt. I inhaled a handful of tablets and crawled into my sleeping bag. I drifted off to sleep with the image of Satopanth's razor-sharp ridges and gouged out northern features on my mind. I'm not sure if it was a dream or a nightmare.

What a difference a good night's sleep can make. I woke up a new man. The headache was gone and I was ready to move up. We repeated the process from the day before, loading our packs and stepping off shortly after sunrise. The ascent took five hours and I fell over just as many times as before. I hung back with Karen who was moving a bit slower than normal but I didn't mind moving slower on carry days. I kept her company as the others pushed on at their own pace.

We arrived and set up camp among the rocks. Five tents were squeezed together and I was lucky to find a spot with flatish rocks. Some of the team were not so lucky. I was headache free as we worked, when a sudden crack had us frozen silent and staring up at the north face. An avalanche thundered down, sending up an enormous cloud of snow as it impacted the glacier. Its power humbled us and we didn't mention it, instead choosing to keep working and pretending it wasn't likely to happen again.

Two more let go during the afternoon and by sunset I was starting to have my doubts about our summit attempt. Just as I was having these thoughts, snow started to fall, a light dusting at first and then much heavier. By the time we ate a hot meal, a white blanket covered the tents and buried the rocks. The storm wasn't forecast to arrive for another day and I hoped it hadn't come early. I zipped up my sleeping bag and tried to sleep.

The snow lasted a few hours and by dawn the skies were clear. I crawled out of my tent into the frigid morning and pulled on my big down jacket for the first time on the expedition. The plan for the day was to move halfway to Camp Two for acclimatisation and to get comfortable with the climbing. Our three strongest Sherpas would lead the climb all the way to Camp Two and fix lines on the exposed sections. Afterwards we would descend the mountain and move back down to base camp to wait out the storm. The fixed lines would be left in place for when we made our summit attempt later in the week.

After breakfast and coffee, I geared up and attached my crampons to my boots. I was carrying no weight, just food and water. We stepped onto the glacier's exposed surface and started moving up towards the north face. This close to the mountain, the glacier was free of rocks and in their place was fractured blue ice, crevasses and a veneer of snow. The icefall barred our way ahead. Its enormous jumbled ice blocks, dozens of metres in height and weighing hundreds of tonnes, were something we did not want to climb. It was constantly moving and as we rested at its base the groans and cracks from deep below were unnerving.

Our route detoured to the east, across the glacier to the base of a cliff. We would need to climb off the ice onto the rock and traverse it until we reached a wide snow slope leading to Camp Two. The Sherpas were out of sight up ahead and had left a fixed line in place. I clipped onto it with my ascender and started climbing. My heart rate jacked immediately, and I tried to settle into a smooth pace keeping a sharp eye on my foot and hand placements. Even though the fixed line made exposed sections much safer, taking a fall on the line was still a risk. The anchors attaching the line to the mountain were snow stakes, ice screws and pitons. Some were new and some were from many seasons prior; I didn't trust any of it with my life.

The traverse was a mix of rock climbing, snow ledges and ice climbing. The crampons stuck well on the snow and ice but with the rocks, I needed to find specific places to plant my toe spikes and ice axe. After an hour of climbing, the icefall was directly underneath me, a short 40-metre fall away. The exposure added to the excitement and when I paused at an anchor for a rest, I wished Elise was with me to enjoy it. She loved climbing and had never done anything like this before. I was missing her terribly.

Two hours after leaving the glacier I inched my way up over an overhanging rock ledge and saw the snow slope stretching away. This was the halfway point. I located a safe place to sit down and wait for the rest of the team. Below me the icefall looked fierce with its jagged surface and gaping crevasses. Satopanth towered over it all on my left, its gouged north face much closer and bathed in the midday sun. I felt so privileged to be sitting in the snow at 5540 metres, seeing something not many people would ever get to see. The team trickled in one by one, and we had a good rest before turning around and making our way back down. The next time we would come up to this altitude would be on our summit attempt.

I set off first behind Max. Our comfortable pace was a little faster than the rest of the team so we took the lead. The snow was melting under the sun and turning the route into slush. Special care needed to be taken to avoid dislodging the loose rocks on the face. I have always enjoyed abseiling, and coming down on the exposed traverse was awesome fun. I could grip the fixed line with one hand and almost jog down the route. I took extra care on the exposed sections and was loving every second of it. By the time my feet hit the glacier I was high on adrenaline but exhausted all the same. I sat down in the shade of a huge block of ice and watched the others descend the line.

Nitya and Alex were coming down with the Sherpas who had reached Camp Two. They had dropped gear and come all the way back at an incredible pace. As I was watching, a loud crack rang out across the valley. I looked up above our team and saw a shower of rocks plummeting down the face directly towards them on the fixed line. A chorus of voices yelled out 'ROCKS!' and those on the face hugged the wall and braced for impact. Some of the falling rocks ricocheted off other rocks and some exploded into pieces as they struck ledges. It was an intense 20 seconds before silence returned and amazingly, no one had been hit. Nitya started moving again, albeit a little faster, and when everyone was safely back on the glacier we gave a collective sigh of relief.

We were back at Camp One 30 minutes later, pulling off crampons and enjoying a hot soup with chapati bread. It had been a big morning and I was tired. We still had to break down camp and descend to base camp before we could relax. As I finished my coffee I noticed dark clouds forming behind Satopanth – it was time to move. We piled all our tents, climbing equipment and supplies into one tent and then collapsed it. If heavy snow built up, we didn't want the tent poles being snapped under the weight. We moved onto the glacier and into the moraine as a light sprinkle of snow started to fall and the temperature began to drop.

The storm followed us down for three hours, gaining in intensity every hour. Swirling snow blocked out views of Satopanth and the surrounding peaks, and as we walked into base camp it was near whiteout conditions. I was exhausted but on a natural high; this is what I loved most about mountaineering. A perfect morning of climbing, a tough hike out and Mother Nature opening up and showing us her power once we were safely back in our tents. The weather forecast was spot-on, the snow increased and by the time I crawled into my sleeping bag, a layer of snow had built up on the ground. The scenery had changed from a green, rocky, summer valley to pure white and freezing cold.

The snowfall was the heaviest I had ever experienced, it came down in thick white sheets, non-stop all night. Snow collected on the tent until it reached a tipping point, when it broke off and slid to the ground. Anytime I was awake I shook the tent to help it stay clear, and twice during the night one of our incredible Sherpas dug away the mounting snow; a tireless effort to prevent the tents collapsing under the deluge. By morning a wall of snow surrounded us and the entire valley was under 30 centimetres of fresh powder. The snow didn't let up over breakfast as Avilash delivered the latest weather report.

'The snow will fall for three more days,' he told us as I shoved a hot fried egg into my mouth. While I cuddled my coffee to warm my hands he added, 'Then we must wait two days to let it melt and avalanche.' This meant we were tent-bound for the foreseeable future. Being tent-bound might sound fairly comfortable at first, time to rest, recover and prepare for the summit push. But it also means countless hours to think. What could go wrong? Do I have what it takes? Am I strong enough? Too much time inside your own head is never a good thing as it can chip away at your resolve, dissolve your confidence and, if you aren't ready for it, make you want to quit.

I have two habits that help me endure long days inside a tent with no ill effects. The first was keeping a detailed journal, which not only gives me an in-depth account of the expedition but is also therapy. Writing down my fears and emotions helps to keep them at manageable levels, never allowing them to build up and affect my actions. The second habit is reading. I had brought with me five books from George R.R. Martin's epic series, Game of Thrones. Other climbers always laugh at me when I hump up extra weight in paperback novels. But when it comes to mental health during a week-long storm, the investment pays dividends.

We settled into Groundhog Day: sleeping and resting, eating three hot meals, digging out the tents and watching the weather. Through the whiteout conditions I could hear avalanches breaking off from surrounding peaks and was happy in our decision to wait out the storm at Base Camp.

Before leaving Delhi, I had given my teammates a copy of my first book, *One Life One Chance*, and Karen was reading her copy in the tent next to mine. Every so often she would yell out a question, 'Luke, what is a wait-a-while vine? Is it an animal or a plant?' I explained to her and Uli about the demon plant that caused havoc during jungle patrols in my army days. It was good feedback for me. Other cultures would interpret my words differently and I needed to be able to bridge the gap.

For three days we were tent-bound and the snow didn't quit falling. It felt like I'd been in the tent my entire life. During the fourth night the temperature dropped significantly and I had to zip up my sleeping bag around my face. The sudden drop meant the cloud cover had moved away and the snowfall had stopped. I woke to clear skies, and the morale boost I received from the first rays of sun touching my face in over 72 hours cannot be overstated. The sun was going to shine all day and the snow would begin to melt instead of piling higher.

Over breakfast, Avilash told us, 'The storm has moved on. We will go for a walk today to get the legs going.' The scene was a thick blanket of white, contrasted occasionally by steep sections of black rock. The moraine was tough to travel across at first and with a couple of feet of fresh snow on top it was treacherous. The holes, cracks and rocks were hidden and when I broke through the snow I sank up to my waist.

The sun blazed away during our three-hour 'get moving again' hike. The reflection from the snow increased the sun's force and I needed to coat myself in 50 plus sunscreen to avoid getting scorched. The valley was coming to life after three days of hibernation and I noticed animal tracks of all shapes and sizes in the snow, as they too had started moving again.

We turned around and made our way back to camp as our Sherpas carried on up. They wanted to assess the mountain, check the condition of the climbing route and locate our buried supplies. We spent the rest of the day watching avalanches come off the surrounding peaks during the afternoon heat. This was exactly what we needed to happen before we could move up safely. The Sherpas made Camp One and radioed a report down to Avilash. Over dinner he told us, 'It was waist-deep snow and very tough going. The heat during the afternoon made the snow very soft and much more dangerous.' He added, 'After a rest day tomorrow we will leave for Camp One at 5am, when the snow and ice are still frozen.'

◆◆◆

The snow was melting rapidly the following day, and the more it melted the faster the remaining snow would melt too. The small stream feeding into the lake was flowing again and at least 30 centimetres of snow had disappeared in 24 hours. I took the day to rest, trim down all unnecessary weight out of my pack and prepare myself for the summit push. The weather was predicted to hold clear for the next five days, which gave us our window. The head guide from the German team visited Avilash during the day and asked to team up. They had brought very little equipment, no extra rope and wanted to use our fixed lines on their summit push. In exchange they offered to help in any way they could. Avilash agreed. It was better to have both teams on the same page than working against each other.

In the afternoon I read a book about Buddhism, as you do when in a country surrounded by holy men. One of the book's characters, Vinod, had an epiphany and decided Gandhi had it wrong. Gandhi told the people to be humble, frugal, peaceful and everything would be okay. Vinod thought opposingly people should embrace life fully, make money, be successful and then give it all up to gain enlightenment. Upon reading his opinion and reflecting on my own life experiences, I agreed with Vinod. Through excessive drinking, becoming a drug addict and hitting rock bottom, I decided to turn my life around. In business, I had to open my second gym in Sydney, reach a point where I was a 'success' and making money, to realise it didn't make me any happier. Personally, I needed to feed my ego to realise it didn't gain me any more real friends. Only then did I gain some semblance of enlightenment.

The challenge to this theory, however, is in applying it to our way of life in the western world. When we have made money, how do we break the cycle, and reach a stage of not wanting more? When we're living with luxuries and excess, how do we resist wanting more when everyone around us is seeking it? With the constant enforcement of these ideals through marketing, celebrity endorsement and idolising of the rich, how do we stop the spiral? What would make you step back and say, 'Okay, that's enough, it's time for something else?'

A change of environment can help. Travelling to places like India, Africa or Asia and laying eyes on extreme poverty might confirm to us 'I have enough.' But if we holiday in five-star luxury and surround ourselves with people wealthier than us, it can have the opposite effect. Environment can be the key, but in the dog-eat-dog, bigger, stronger, faster western world, will enough ever be enough? I don't believe Gandhi was wrong; reaching peace, enlightenment and happiness is the ultimate goal. But to bypass everything that a full life has to offer, the good and the bad, in order to attain it, seems, to me, to be missing out on a lot of life's lessons.

We were up at 4am and it was minus seven degrees. I dressed in multiple layers and after downing a few cups of hot tea, we stepped onto the solid snow at 5.15am. Avilash wanted us at Camp One before the afternoon melt started, so with solid snow underfoot, we set a cracking pace with few breaks. The clear sky faded from dark blue to amber as the sun slowly rose. The sunlight touched the summits of the peaks then slowly descended into the valleys and onto the glacier. Our Sherpas had broken trail for eight hours to reach the camp, and it took us five hours, following in their footsteps. I was sinking up to my knees by the time we arrived just before 10.30am. To make the same journey in the afternoon would be absolute hell. Our old camp was buried under a couple of metres of snow. The change to the mountain after the storm was dramatic and we set ourselves to digging and flattening out places to erect our tents. In the distance, high up on the mountain, I could see our formidable Sherpas trying to reach Camp Two.

I was able to watch their progress for the afternoon, and seeing their tiny figures clear the glacier and traverse three-quarters of the rock wall gave me hope. They stopped before reaching the snow slope, turned around and slowly made their way back down. We watched them descend, not knowing why they had turned back, and it wasn't until they had arrived safely to camp that we received the news. Over a hot chai, Avilash interpreted Mingma's words: 'The fixed lines are either buried or torn away by avalanche. The snow is very thick and avalanche danger is high.'

This wasn't the report we were hoping for. In closing, Namgyal, one of our strongest Sherpas said, 'We will try again tomorrow.'

The loss of the fixed lines was a big hit to the expedition. Thousands of feet of rope and protection had been buried or torn out completely. Avilash didn't have enough rope to do it all again and he wouldn't risk climbing the vertical traverse without safety. He gathered up all our remaining rope and combined it with the small amount the German team had carried. It was just enough to get us to Camp Two, where there was more rope cached from the week before. His altered plan was to fix rope across the knife ridge and leave the summit slope exposed with no protection. The highest section of climbing, the summit slope was the least technical. This new plan was our last hope. If the Sherpas could break through to Camp Two the following day, we still had a chance at the summit.

◆◆◆

It was Day 18 of the expedition and I watched our Sherpa team set off just after dawn; they were determined to break through and I wished them every bit of luck. This was going to be a long day of waiting for the rest of us. Sherpas who support big expeditions are some of the strongest climbers in the world. They are born and bred in the mountains and have a level of endurance that very few climbers outside the Himalaya can match. They also have a commitment to doing everything in their ability to help teams succeed, often to their own detriment. Sherpas have died trying to get clients to the top of mountains, knowing the client shouldn't have been there in the first place. They are the backbone of Himalayan expeditions and I was in awe watching them inch up Mount Satopanth.

They made their way up to the point where they had turned around the day before and this time climbed higher. Their tiny figures reached the snow slope and then were out of sight, ascending even further. Over the following hours the heat began to rise, and small avalanches broke off, sliding down the north face. Avilash was communicating with the Sherpas via the VHF radio and every time he received a call I hung on his every word. Speaking Hindi, I had no idea what he was saying, so I would grab hold of a smile or nod of his head as a sign of success. He received a call just after lunch and his facial expression changed; he held the radio at arm's length by his side and stared up at the mountain. He spoke into the mouthpiece and I could tell by his slumped shoulders and the moisture forming in his eyes that it wasn't good news.

The Sherpas had battled through waist-deep snow for as long as they physically could before calling Avilash. They had run out of rope just before Camp Two. The conditions were very tough and avalanche danger high. Avilash told us, 'They wanted to keep pushing but I told them to turn back, I won't risk them in these conditions.'

Mother Nature dictates everything in the outdoors. She can let you climb in perfect conditions or snatch your life away in the blink of an eye. Namgyal, Mingma and Nima returned to camp looking defeated and emotional; they felt they had let us down. Namgyal looked the most upset. I pulled him aside and told him something a Russian climber named Valentine told me while we sheltered behind a rock in terrible conditions on Mount Elbrus. 'It's better to come to the mountains ten times and go home, than to come once and never go home.' We turned around and I failed to summit Europe's highest peak, one of the 'seven summits', yet lived to try again.

Over dinner Avilash told us something we already knew, the expedition was officially over. To be a day away from the summit and have to turn back after three weeks of work was gut wrenching, especially with clear skies overhead. With a day up our sleeves he said we were welcome to climb up towards high camp the following day before descending back to base camp. I was up for a day of climbing, every minute spent up on Satopanth before our retreat was a privilege.

The climbing in the morning sun was incredible, the route was solid snow and I ascended the traverse in half the time it had previously taken. I rested at the snow slope before moving higher. I wanted to finish my expedition at the highest possible altitude. The sky was clear, the mountain was open and begging to be climbed. This made the decision to turn back much harder. The snow was softening, and I stopped under a cliff to rest at the top of the snow slope. Avilash, Nitya, Alex, Karen and Namgyal joined me there and we had a few moments of silence. I took some photos and video for my sponsors before taking one last look up to the summit from where I stood at 5800 metres. We turned away and started to head down. It was all over.

As we descended I reflected on my climbing history. Out of my seven big mountain expeditions this was my second failure, the second time I'd had to turn back due to weather and unsafe conditions. As far as mountaineering goes, it was a good strike rate; I was still alive to try again.

We descended the fixed line quickly, crossed the glacier, which was covered in a slushy veneer of snow melting under the midday sun, and arrived back at camp. We packed up knowing the descent to base camp through the afternoon heat wasn't going to be easy. I loaded up my pack with all my gear, totalling around 30 kilograms and set off behind the rest of our team. I was going to move slowly and methodically down the glacier, as I didn't want to risk a twisted ankle or broken leg carrying a heavy load. I still had phase two of the expedition to get through and as we descended my mind started to shift towards the Ganges.

The descent to Gangotri took three days. I suffered physically for the first day and a half, but as the air thickened in the lower altitude my strength returned. We were side by side with porters carrying up to 75 kilograms of expedition kit. I was in awe watching these stick-thin men descend the sheer rock wall section to Nandanvan in flip flops. We arrived into Gangotri to our waiting bus 22 days after departing. It felt like a lifetime since I'd spoken to Elise and I couldn't wait to get back into a place with phone reception to call her.

We tipped our porters, loaded the bus and travelled four hours down to Uttarkashi, where we were greeted with soft beds, hot showers and a cold beer. I immediately phoned Elise and downloaded all my thoughts and emotions from the last few weeks onto her. I missed her terribly and knew she was missing me. The lack of contact for the last three weeks had been very tough for both of us.

Over dinner and drinks that night a report came through about a climbing team attempting a similar size mountain to Satopanth in an area of the Himalaya not far from where we were. Nine members of a South Korean team in Nepal had attempted to climb Mount Gurja, a 7193 metre peak. They were led by the famous mountaineer Kim Chang-ho, who had climbed the world's fourteen 8000-metre mountains, a feat shared by only a handful of professional climbers. As they waited at base camp in bad conditions an avalanche struck, killing the entire team.

This story was a wake-up call and confirmation of our decision to turn back. In my opinion, no mountains or adventures were worth dying for. It doesn't matter who you are, your experience level or which god you believe in, Mother Nature could be ferocious and unforgiving.

'It's better to come to the mountains ten times and go home, than to come once and never go home.' –Valentine

Chapter 9

The Ganges

The snow high on Satopanth eventually ends up on the glacier we had traversed. Over the years, the snow will be compressed into solid blue ice and make its way down the valley as part of the glacier. It will pass Nandanvan and the towering peaks of Shivling and Meru to arrive at Gomukh. There it melts and fractures away into icy pools and becomes the source. The pools feed into a brown stream and begin to flow. The stream grows and becomes a river as it descends from altitude and is fed by countless smaller streams from the surrounding valleys. The river becomes a force to be reckoned with in Gangotri, where its roaring power carves its way through the granite cliffs. Here it is worshipped by sadhus and pilgrims, and as it descends further its volume grows and becomes a lifeline for farms and villages built along its bank. The first large community the river nourishes is Rishikesh. And by this stage the white water has calmed and the river is wide and flat and is known to everyone as the Ganges.

After dropping my teammates at the train station in Dehradun to travel overnight back to Delhi, I stayed with the driver who lived in Rishikesh and who was more than happy to take me with him. It was a short afternoon drive and I was on a natural high as I started the second phase of the True Path Project. As the sun set, the driver dropped me off at a small hotel in the middle of town. I hadn't seen the river during the drive but knew it wasn't far away.

I had previously arranged to buy a kayak from a local seller and wanted to leave first thing in the morning, so I gave him a call. There was no answer. I followed up with a text message and an email, already thinking about the possible delay to my departure. I received an email back an hour later and my heart sank. Apologising profusely, the seller told me the kayak was sold. After dealing with Indian bureaucracy for weeks I should have known better, especially with the debacle of Elise entering the country.

I immediately started working the problem and phoned every kayak company in town, googled every seller and sent dozens of emails. By 10pm I had a sinking feeling. Everyone who answered and replied to my emails gave me the same response – there was nothing available. Apparently it was high season for tourism and pleasure kayaking was the main business in town. I decided to get to bed and work out what to do the following morning. One thing was certain: I would be getting down this river.

Over street chai the next morning, I realised paddling the river wasn't the only way I could get to Kolkata. There were multiple roads following the general path of the Ganges, so I could cycle. As this fresh idea marinated in my mind, I looked across the road from the chai stall, and directly opposite me on the corner of an intersecting street was, you guessed it, a bicycle shop. I took this as a sign of fate and sat back with another cup of chai to wait for the shop to open.

I hadn't ridden a bike since my youth in the military and had no idea what I was getting myself into, but I'd always wanted to do a big tour on a bike. The freedom and self-reliance appealed to me. An older man walked to the front of the bike shop around 8am, unlocked a padlock and pulled the roller door open. I gave him ten minutes to organise the shop and swallowing the last of my chai, walked across the street wearing a big smile to say hello.

The shop owner greeted me warmly as I pointed towards the bikes and asked, 'Can I buy?' He nodded his head and set to work digging out two of them for me to try. The first one was an old model which I had seen everywhere on the streets, it looked like something left over from the days of the British colony. I mounted up and gave it a test ride. It was brutal. The steel frame sat on thin solid wheels, had no shock absorption at all, the steering was all over the place and my legs were way too long for the frame. I rode it back to the shop. The second one was a modern mountain bike and much closer to what I was looking for. It was a bit small for me but it had a decent seat, gears and was semi-comfortable to ride.

'How much?' I asked.

After the standard back and forth of negotiation that started at $200, I ended up with the bike, pump, spare tubes and a wheel spanner for $180. I put on my climbing helmet as some form of protection and shouldered my daypack. I had trimmed down my supplies into the one small pack, consisting of a change of clothes, water, snacks and film gear. It would have been about 12 kilograms in weight but when I mounted up, I could feel the extra pressure on my backside. I brushed the feeling aside and hit the road, with 2000 kilometres to go.

The roads were chaotic in the midmorning traffic, and my head was on a swivel as I tried to watch all the trucks, buses, cars, cows and people rushing through the streets. After the first hour, the pain in my bum forced me to stop. It was a numb, burning and stabbing sensation all at once, which would have been familiar to any cyclist but was totally new to me. I refilled my water at a local store and bought some Vaseline for my bum and inner thighs. I wore small running shorts and realised why all those riders I made fun of at home wore Lycra. I would have given anything for some bike shorts at that moment.

My first sighting of the main flow of the Ganges gave me a boost of energy. It was incredible. I can't say it's the most beautiful river I'd ever seen, but it's the lifeblood for the people of northern India and seeing thousands of them washing, drinking and praying to this brown body of water was a special sight. The pollution level down on the flat lands was tough to understand. I had been among pristine mountains for weeks and here I was witnessing poverty and pollution on an enormous scale.

The holiest of rivers that was supposedly a sacred representation of God, also acted as a toilet and rubbish dump. I couldn't rationalise this in my own mind. If the locals really did believe in the text and all the millions of Gods I had learned about, surely something would be done to keep the river clean and stop the holy cows from feasting on rubbish. Perhaps I shouldn't judge. I couldn't fathom the scale of infrastructure and resource management that comes along with 1.3 billion people living together, but as I rode the streets hour after hour all I saw was a lack of education in the common people and an overwhelming hypocrisy in the government.

I stopped and devoured five bananas at a roadside stand after nearly getting side-swiped by a truck. I hadn't heard the overloaded ancient lorry coming until it was centimetres from my elbow. I was trying to keep an eye on so much that close calls with vehicles were becoming common. I rested for lunch in front of a shaded temple three hours after departure. Physically I was hurting but I was also making great time. I had picked a small town on the map called Bijnor, which I thought I could reach in my first day. I'd covered almost 50 kilometres and believed I would be resting in the hotel air-conditioning in a few more hours.

Shortly after lunch I turned onto the back roads. I wanted to follow the river as close as I could and also avoid the jam-packed highway. For some reason I assumed the smaller roads would be in a fair condition but I was very wrong. The road quickly turned to dirt, potholes and washouts, and I was down to first gear and pumping my legs to stay at walking pace. To make matters worse, the afternoon heat kicked in and I was pouring sweat in the humidity. Up ahead 15 kilometres, I was due to cross the Ganges again, so I thought I'd take a big rest on the river for the afternoon and get out of the sun.

I pushed on through the heat, aiming for the river. I don't know why I didn't stop and rest earlier, I guess I became disorientated and just kept pushing. I was dehydrated and started to lose my focus. My bum was in agony and my clothes were soaked through from sweat. When I stopped sweating, an early sign of heat exhaustion, I knew I was in trouble. At this critical moment I saw the river and close by to it a bridge with a police checkpoint. I pulled up to their building, which had its own water pump and was shaded by a tree. The officers came out to greet me and I gestured to their pump.

'Can I drink?' I asked. They smiled, nodded and gave their approval, so I dismounted my torture machine and sat down.

I was dizzy and didn't have a good grasp on reality, I took off all my clothes except my shorts and put my head under the water. It must have looked hysterical, this pasty white foreigner cycling up saturated on his little bike, diving under the pump and trying to pull the ancient handle up and down, while soaking his head at the same time. After a few minutes of cooling off, I filled my water bottles and threw in some purifying tablets. I smiled and waved at the officers who were now sitting under the tree. It was a stupid error on my behalf to push on in the hot conditions, I had seen heatstroke send guys to hospital in the military and kill tourists in the outback where I grew up.

I chastised myself for the following hour, while I rehydrated and shovelled in food. I had to recharge and recover if I was going to finish my day to Bijnor. After a short nap I pulled my wet clothes back on, stretched my aching body and remounted my bike. I waved to the police thanking them for putting up with me and set off down the bumpy road and across the bridge. The road improved on the opposite bank and I could settle into a good rhythm for the afternoon. During the last two hours of the day I was almost hit by a bus, a tractor and, at one point, nearly collided with a buffalo pulling a wagon full of rocks.

My last close call came when two buses tried to overtake each other, and I ended up on the outside at a critical moment. I almost had a heart attack as the bus roared past at top speed millimetres from me. I tore off the road, stopped in the gravel and shook my head. Never had I wanted to get to the end of a day more in my life. I rode into Bijnor eight hours after leaving

Rishikesh and entered the first hotel I saw. I was soaking wet, couldn't speak properly and don't remember checking in. I came out of my haze half undressed and under a cold shower in an air-conditioned room.

I drank three bottles of water, lay down and thought back over the day's event. I had travelled 105 kilometres on my first day, and while it was physically brutal, I knew I could handle the suffering day after day. It's what I had come to enjoy about big expeditions. What I had trouble rationalising was the close calls with the traffic. Any of those buses, trucks or cars could have wiped me out. To be killed or injured on the side of a road in rural India wasn't a reality I enjoyed thinking about.

I began to look at it with the climber's mindset; if I was climbing for eight hours and was almost wiped out by an avalanche five times, would I continue the climb? What made it worse was that I was at the mercy of human ability. At least Mother Nature was predictable to a point but humans, on the other hand, were fallible, and Indian drivers added a wholly unacceptable level of risk for me.

I reflected on the issue while devouring naan bread and masala in the hotel restaurant, then called Elise and raised my concerns with her. We talked for an hour and by the end of our chat I had decided to call off the expedition.

From the beginning the True Path Project had problems, starting with Elise being kicked out of the country then the failed summit due to weather, the non-existent kayak, and finally the close calls with traffic. To push on in the face of it all would be resilient but also foolish, and driven by ego. Failure is a tough pill to swallow, especially when so many people support you to succeed. But sometimes you have to know when to throw in the towel.

I called my sponsors and told them my decision. I was overwhelmed by their support in backing my choice. I told them I would make up their investment on another expedition, but for now I was coming home. The following morning, after a great sleep, I woke up stiff, sore but confident in my decision. I loaded my bike into the back of a taxi and was driven four hours to Delhi by a lovely old man who chatted with me the whole way, and when we detoured off the highway into sugarcane plantations, I got to see more of the real India.

Women with bent backs working the cane fields, buffalos pulling wooden carts full of mud bricks, women and children carrying huge bundles of grass on their backs, a dead horse and some cows eating rubbish. As we reached the outskirts of Delhi there were whole families on scooters, women living in poverty yet wearing the most beautifully coloured Saris, kids caked in mud and kids in immaculate uniforms on their way to school. I noticed malnourished street dogs everywhere and saw old men sitting alone under trees in front of their homes.

The traffic was absolutely insane as we entered the city. The farms were gone and in their place were street hustlers, men with a set of scales on the footpath to check your weight for a fee, shoe repair men in a shop that was literally a cardboard box, a barber with a wooden crate as a chair, and shops of all shapes and sizes selling everything you would ever need. My last afternoon was a cultural tour. The following morning I donated my bike to a member of staff from White Magic Adventure, picked up the duffel bags they'd kept for me and made my way to the airport.

I've been going on expeditions for the better part of a decade, some have been a smashing success, some I have just scraped through with my life, and some have failed miserably. Knowing when to pull the plug on a trip you've been planning for years comes with experience. The weighing up of risk, analysing your ability and putting your ego, money and sponsorship obligations to the side is always tough.

I leaned over to the window of the 737 jet bound for home and my waiting wife and took a last look down at the sprawling cities, the immense agriculture and the holy land of a billion people. India is a unique and special place. She'd handed me a beating this time but I was alive. And I would be back.

Chapter 10

Rowing the Tasman

My mind snapped back to reality. I had ingested too much cocaine over the previous 24 hours, mixed with the constant flow of alcohol, and had just spent half a night and day in what I called my blackout period. My body would carry on with the party but my mind had checked out, preserving its cells against the onslaught of chemicals.

As my vision cleared and the connection between mind and body calibrated, I had no idea where I was. I was sitting in a poorly lit room that felt like a basement. I had no shirt on, only board shorts and flip flops. Sitting next to me was a young skinny guy wearing similar clothes and looking shit scared but I didn't yet realise why. In front of me, across the small table between us sat a middle-aged Mexican man. He was fully dressed and looked serious, if not slightly agitated. On the table were countless packets of cocaine, a pile of cash and a gun.

My mouth was moving and I had to gain control of the reality I found myself in. I was negotiating a purchase of drugs from this guy and he was getting more and more irate, I didn't know why. My full awareness returned and I was in control again.

'Okay, done,' I said to the last price he suggested to finish the deal.

It was then I noticed the six other guys in the room behind us. All Mexican, dressed in street clothes and not looking pleased with me. I counted out the cash and handed it across the table. I gathered up all the packets and stuffed them into the small pocket on the side of my shorts.

As I stood up with my skinny friend, whom I had yet to meet, the negotiator stood too and slammed his hand on the table, picking up the pistol. The tension in the room was palpable. He gestured with the gun and with broken English said, 'You give us all a line.' I hesitated for a split second before digging out two of the packets, pouring them onto the surface of the table and racking up nine lines. Giving lines back to a drug dealer wasn't the norm but I was in a precarious position and didn't argue. One by one we inhaled the fine white powder and as the rolled-up note was passed around, the immediate change in the faces of the men was comforting. I was last to bend down and sniff up the white demon that had come to consume my life.

I stood up, and shoved the note away. 'Thanks lads, have a great night,' I said, with as much chemical confidence as I could muster.

My friend and I turned and exited past the men, up a flight of stairs and down a long corridor. The light of day burst around us, and we were back among the busy streets of Cancun, Mexico. It was stifling hot and I guessed around lunchtime. I hadn't slept in a couple of days, but with a pocket full of fun, sleep was a way off.

I turned to my mate. 'That was interesting,' I said.

'Fuck that. I'm out of here. You're on your own,' he replied in an English accent. He turned and walked away and I never even got to know his name. I looked around at the hustle and bustle of the busy holiday destination and smiled. I thought to my deluded self, 'How good is life.'

Flash forward ten years and I'm sitting in a coffee shop reminiscing about this other life. I don't remember the guy I used to be, those were the days during the addiction and before the fall that would alter my life forever. The hot coffee delivered by the Balinese waiter brought me back to the present.

'Terima kasih,' I said, thanking him in my newfound Indonesian.

I had landed in Bali after the True Path Project. Elise was working as a coach at CrossFit Wanderlust in an area called Canggu. I was licking my wounds after failing to reach the summit of Mount Satopanth and had lost a tonne of weight. A solid month of training and eating was in order.

The gym was an incredible facility to train in, full of world-class athletes, beginners and everyone in between. People from all over the world, of all ages, trained hard there, ate clean and enjoyed the beach life. Over the years my body had become a fast adaptive system. When on adventures I lost weight quickly as my body adjusted to the limited calories and intense workload. But when I put myself back in an environment where I could eat nutritious food, slept well and lift weights, I gained it back just as quick. Putting on a kilogram per week of body weight is fairly normal for me post-adventure. In my younger years I would get back and crush myself with training to recover and prepare for the next one. Through experience, I've learned that light, slow and focused training delivers much better results.

The coffee was hot and strong. I had been living on chai for over a month in India and I was missing this perfect start to the day. Lost in my cup of black gold, a clean-cut fit guy with a big smile on his face approached me.

'Luke Richmond,' he said, more a statement than a question.

'That's me,' I replied, trying hard to remember if I'd met him before.

He pulled up a chair like we were long-lost mates and sat down.

'You won't remember me, I'm sure, but you changed my life.'

His name was Jon-Olaf Hendricks, and after ordering a cup of coffee and apologising for the intrusion, he told me his story. We had met briefly at the bar on Tonsai Beach two years earlier. Elise and I were drinking coconuts and watching the sunset after a day of climbing. Jon-Olaf was there with a few friends and was knocking back local whisky straight from the bottle. He had dreadlocks back then, scrubby facial hair and looked like the standard gypsy traveller drifting around the world.

'I offered you a drink' he said, remembering in detail our brief encounter. 'But you said no thanks, you were going BASE jumping the next morning and needed to be sharp. Then you told me your story, about all your adventures, about overcoming your addiction and it stopped me in my tracks. You were living my dream. That was the moment I decided to change my life. I was the party guy, an alcoholic and it wasn't who I wanted to be.'

'That is so amazing to hear,' I said with sincerity. 'How has the transition been, how is life now?'

'I'm two years sober,' he replied with pride and confidence. 'I'm a new man and on the right path.'

'Good on you, mate,' I said and shook his hand.

I knew how hard the transition was to make. As he got up to leave he turned to me with a smile.

'Anyway, I have to go to training now. I just wanted to tell you how much our short conversation had meant to me, keep doing what you're doing.'

I waved him off as he tore away on his scooter.

I sat back to enjoy another cup of coffee.

The encounter with Jon-Olaf gave me a moment of clarity. It was refreshing to hear how a simple conversation had such a huge impact on him. We are living in a world where everyone is a life coach, where self-help books are the biggest sellers and everyone wants to be an inspiration. In reality just follow your own dream, be successful in your endeavours and share your story honestly. It can change lives.

◆◆◆

I developed a perfect routine in Bali over the following month. Writing every morning before Elise woke up, training together twice daily, and devouring all the delicious food Canggu was famous for. I had no expeditions planned and was content to have a break from extreme adventure for a while. I certainly wasn't expecting to hear from Grant Rawlinson, a Kiwi mate of mine. He'd found out I was free and sent me a message: 'Can we grab a quick Skype call?'

I knew something was up straightaway.

Grant was an experienced outdoorsman, he had climbed Everest, among many other achievements, and his most recent adventure was to row a boat from Singapore all the way to his home in New Zealand. He had succeeded in rowing from Singapore to northern Australia, then rode his bike across my vast arid home and met up with his boat again on the southeast corner of New South Wales. He had tried to row to New Zealand twice in the last two years but the formidable Tasman Sea had forced him back both times. During the first attempt he rowed for 2100 kilometres and ended up back at his start point. In his second attempt he was hit by huge swell, broke his parachute anchor attachment and had to be rescued. The boat was recovered at a later date once it drifted back closer to Australia. I knew he was planning a third attempt so when he asked for a chat I had a feeling.

We connected online and had a few minutes of idle chat and banter before he cut to the chase. 'Would you be willing to attempt the Tasman Row with me?'

'Yes,' was my immediate response. But I knew more time away from Elise, this soon after an expedition, would be very tough.

'When are you looking to start?' I asked.

'In ten days. There's a weather window and we have to go for it.'

To join his expedition, which had cost him hundreds of thousands of dollars already, I needed to purchase 50 days of food and buy my own survival suit, lifejacket and emergency locator beacon. The survival suit was critical. If we ended up in the Tasman without a suit on, we would succumb to hypothermia within the hour. I was borderline broke and needed to call on my sponsors again for support.

I emailed and called my backers from the True Path Project and gave them the details of the expedition. Stamford Capital and Belle Property Parramatta didn't hesitate in supporting me again. I was fortunate to have such an amazing group of companies and friends around me, without them this stuff would never be possible. They transferred funds and I paid it straight back out for equipment and booked my flight to Australia.

I had mixed emotions before I flew out. Elise always supported me, but it was hard on both of us to be apart for so long. But I was glad to have a shot at redemption after Mount Satopanth, and to be able to deliver some extra publicity to my sponsors. I boarded the plane for home and as it gained altitude above the island paradise, my mind was in overdrive creating lists of tasks I had to complete to be ready to row another ocean.

◆◆◆

I landed in Sydney on a Tuesday morning and had a message waiting from Grant, saying the weather window was holding and we were going to launch from Eden in New South Wales. I had three days in Sydney to sort out all my gear and be on a train heading south by Thursday lunchtime. We would need the weekend to prep the boat and then we would be off. I called Mum and Dad to give them the latest expedition plan. My poor mum had gone grey over the years dealing with my expeditions. When I was held captive in Papua she was the one behind the scenes hounding the embassies to help get us rescued. When I told her, 'I'm off to row to New Zealand,' she replied, 'Okay love, where are you leaving from?' After telling her Eden, she said they would load up the caravan and drive over to meet me. They were travelling around Australia so the detour wasn't a problem.

VODKA & SANDSTORMS

My first stop was Beecroft in Sydney's north-west. Elise's grandma, Dawn, lived alone and her ancient home had become our base camp in recent years. When I arrived, she answered the door and welcomed me in. She was 93 years old, still self-sufficient and when I told her I was off to row to New Zealand she replied, 'What the hell do you want to do that for?'

'I just love it,' I answered.

'Fair enough. Well, the house is yours, there's food in the fridge, I'm off to bed,' she said as she shuffled away to her room. It was only lunchtime, but if I made it to 93 I would be going to bed early as well.

I got busy sorting out my equipment. My climbing gear from the last expedition had arrived back. I'd sent it from Delhi in two new duffel bags and it arrived in three busted cardboard boxes with rope holding it together. Nothing in India was ever done the way you wanted it to be. I started calling all the dehydrated food suppliers and telling them my story, begging for a discount and quick delivery. I found Sea to Summit, in Sydney, and they were able to give me wholesale prices and next-day delivery on 50 days supply of Back Country Cuisine meals.

I changed from my Bali clothes into jeans and a clean T-shirt. I had to start making the rounds to see sponsors and pick up equipment. My first stop was the inner-city suburb of Surry Hills and a restaurant called Chin Chin. It was Melbourne Cup Day in Australia, the horse race that stops the nation. A huge portion of the workforce finished early and squeezed into pubs, clubs and restaurants to watch the race, gamble and drink. I had been invited by Jerry, a good friend of mine, to his company's function. He was sponsoring me with funds for my survival suit and wanted me to swing by and meet his team. I arrived underdressed and famished just as the food was being brought out, which looked incredible.

Jerry and his entourage were taking up half the restaurant and they were well on their way to enjoying the afternoon. He called me over to a seat beside him, shoved a glass of Dom Perignon into my hand and toasted the success of the next expedition. The plates of food were constant and even though many of his staff weren't eating, I was making up for them. Kingfish sashimi, fried squid, sticky tamarind chilli duck, pork belly, chargrilled swordfish and sirloin steak, it was one of the best lunches I have ever devoured. The party around me was escalating, Jerry was shooting one of his staff in the mouth with Dom Perignon out of a gold Tommy gun replica and I knew it was time for me to leave.

'How much will this lunch cost you?' I asked him.

'Probably $30,000,' he replied.

I almost choked on a mouthful of barbecued king salmon. That was enough money to fund three expeditions.

'Why do you do it when it costs so much?' I asked.

'If my staff have a great day and go on to perform well, I'll make it back. Also, if I get one deal out of all these big wigs I've invited, I make it back tenfold. It's all business.' He slipped me $800 cash for the survival suit and wished me the best of luck.

I spent the remainder of the afternoon and all the next day bouncing around Sydney collecting equipment I would need on the ocean: lifejacket, locator beacon, waterproof jacket and pants, diving knife and the dehydrated food. Thursday morning I was dragging two big duffel bags through the streets towards Central railway station. The train was delayed until 1pm but eventually I was being rocked to sleep in the comfy chairs on the way to Canberra.

Once in Australia's capital, I needed to change to a bus and travel over the mountains through the Namadgi National Park to arrive at Eden. This quiet and picturesque South Coast fishing town was where Grant's boat ended up after his second failed attempt. I stepped off the bus at 11pm to meet my waiting parents, who I hadn't seen in almost a year. We went to the caravan park where they were staying, and I was allocated a tiny two-person seat inside their caravan's kitchen to sleep on. Compared to what I would be sleeping on in a few days, it was luxury.

Grant flew in the next day and we set ourselves to work preparing the boat. We had to go over every inch of it checking for breakages or deterioration. Boats are renowned for constant maintenance, and I remember meeting a sailor who told me, 'Before buying a boat, remember what it stands for: break out another thousand.' Grant had named his boat *Simpson's Donkey* after the famous First World War soldier John (Jack) Simpson Kirkpatrick. John served as a stretcher-bearer with the 1st Australian Division in 1915, during the Gallipoli campaign. Simpson used donkeys to help rescue and evacuate the wounded men from the battlefield before he was killed in the third attack on Anzac Cove. His story became part of the Anzac legend (Australian and New Zealand Army Corps). With this connection to our history, and with Grant and I being from New Zealand and Australia, we had the spirit of the Anzacs on our side.

The boat was in good shape. It had a few small issues with the electrics, which Grant repaired easily. The vessel was smaller than the boat I had rowed across the Atlantic, it only had one small cab at one end for us to share. That one tiny space was our safe warm haven from the cold, wind and waves. It was vital to keep the cabin dry, not just for our own comfort, but to protect radios, emergency equipment and the water maker.

The cabin door was air and water tight when sealed correctly and had a hardened glass window for watching the rowing deck and checking the weather. We climbed inside to check the space and we were literally spooning each other when we both lay down. Ideally one person would always be rowing to give the other some room, but in bad weather we would both be battened down inside. We loaded all the dehydrated food into compartments, triple checked the radios and emergency beacons, and by Sunday afternoon we were raring to go.

◆◆◆

Grant and I had cleared immigration and were given 24 hours to be out of the country. We watched the weather on our computers. We'd employed a weather forecaster nicknamed Clouds, who would send us updated information every 24 hours while at sea. As we sat drinking coffee and refreshing the screens, I said to Grant, 'How long are we going to take to cross?'

'To be home for Christmas would be ideal, so 43 days to get the job done,' he replied.

'Sounds good to me,' I said, as his phone rang and he talked to Clouds again. I was keen to get going. I wanted to see where my mind would go being out in the exposure of the ocean again. I just hoped Mother Nature would be kind to us.

Grant really wanted to do it solo but he was constantly getting capsized while sleeping at night. The boat he'd built in the UK was originally designed for the Atlantic. It was a fast boat and when in predictable, steady winds, it was a perfect vessel. In the Tasman, however, where winds constantly varied and wave direction fluctuated, the *Donkey* became, in Grant's words, 'tippy.' He'd asked me to join him to mitigate the risk of capsizing. He believed constant rowing shifts of two hours on, two hours off, would get us through unscathed.

He finished his call and looked at me with a grin on his face. 'Clouds said it's looking good. Let's go for it.'

'Hell yeah,' I said, standing up and heading for the door.

I asked Mum to grab us some Chinese takeaway food for dinner and meet us at the boat ramp. It was 6pm when we backed the boat down into the calm waters of Eden harbour.

'I'll see you both at Christmas,' I said to Mum and Dad as I gave them big hugs.

'You just stay safe, and you'll owe me a new box of hair dye after this one,' Mum replied, with tears in her eyes.

I stood on the tiny deck centimetres above the water and waved goodbye. Grant was at the oars and guiding us through the moored boats and around the pier. We were heading towards the mouth of the harbour with a setting sun and a small swell bumping us along. When I took my first two-hour shift on the oars, it had been just under two weeks since I answered the phone call from Grant inviting me to row.

The sun disappeared and we crept further and further out to sea, where the lights of the town lost the battle against the stars.

Their sheer number and brilliance were wondrous, I'd forgotten how incredible a clear night sky could be. It was only while on the Atlantic or in the middle of the Gobi Desert that I really appreciated their abundance and beauty.

I often forget the pain and discomfort from past expeditions, focusing on the overall grandness of the achievement. But in that first rowing shift it came flooding back. The queasiness of seasickness, the ache in my unseasoned hands and back, and the ever-increasing exposure. Grant and I completed three shifts each the first night and sleep was hard to come by in between. Compared to the larger four person boat I lived in on the Atlantic, this one was much smaller. The sleeping cabin was crammed and doubled as the kitchen. The small hatch at the other end of the boat was purely for storage of equipment. The deck was exposed to the elements and privacy was non-existent. On the Atlantic we could use our toilet bucket behind the rowers line of sight, offering at least a turned head of privacy. On the Donkey the only spare space was half a metre in front of the rowing seat. Eye contact and conversation while using the bucket was awkward at first but after a while became the new normal.

At dawn I had a visit from a great white shark. The enormous grey predator paused to inspect the vessel and swam alongside. At about half the length of the *Donkey*, the thought of ending up in the freezing water with him gave me the shivers. Dolphins and seabirds also appeared as the sun rose, the marine life in the Tasman seemed to be much more abundant than the Atlantic. We started our first day shifts and swung south towards Bass Strait. Clouds gave us our daily bearing and told us to avoid a large eddy offshore that could give us trouble. We needed to row south to get around it before turning east towards New Zealand. My bum was giving me grief after the first few rowing shifts, the pressure sores and boils wouldn't be far away.

It was an eventful first day on the ocean. We saw the tail of a whale breach on the horizon and later a smaller whale breach entirely, crashing down and causing a huge eruption of white water. Jellyfish and seaweed speckled the surface as we kept our eyes peeled while crossing the shipping lanes. The enormous container ships were our biggest threat in the first few days. They couldn't see us due to our size, so we had to monitor our AIS detection system and make radio contact if they were heading towards us. I pumped water through our desalination machine to fill our bottles but it wasn't working the way it should. We would need to be gentle and care for it, as the machine was our lifeline. If it failed, we had a backup hand pump to make water but we would need to spend four to six hours per day hand pumping.

We lost sight of the Australian coastline just before sunset and began our second night. Sleep deprivation finally caught up with me and after my second two-hour shift, I passed out and slept for 90 solid minutes. During my Atlantic crossing, the best sleep I could manage after being out there for over a month was three 90-minute blocks during a night. If I could get back to that, I knew my body could survive. The water was covered in bioluminescent algae and during the darkest hours their brilliant colour display when disturbed was incredible. I was missing Elise already and thought about her constantly. Listening to my Dad's playlist, which contained mostly love songs, didn't help the situation.

It was nearing 2am and fifteen minutes before I could stop rowing, hand over to Grant and close my eyes in the warm cabin. For some unknown reason it was always at this precise moment that a wave would break over the deck and soak me with freezing water. I yelled in frustration, as it meant a wet sleeping bag and a cold cabin for me. It was a very tough night at the oars, my body was hurting and trying to adapt to the new schedule. I couldn't eat much due to mild seasickness, I was sleep deprived and my mind was having 'What the fuck?' moments already. I had a beautiful wife on a beach in Bali and here I was, once again, miserably pushing myself through the dangerous ocean and enduring the mental ups and downs that came with such a venture. Always at the end of these negative spirals I came to the same question: 'Why?' To which my answer was always the same: 'Because I love it.'

Just before dawn a large orange moon brightened the water as well as my mood. However, the sea was angry during the second day, rearing up in big swells that broke across the deck in random formations. Rowing became more of a hindrance when the waves approached from behind us. We would be picked up and thrown forward down the face of the swell, increasing in speed, surfing down into the trough between sets. We lashed the oars to the deck and guided the boat using two steering ropes. Surfing was exhilarating and terrifying, feeling the power of the waves easily throw us around and shove us along was humbling. We were at the whim of Mother Nature.

While not on deck our tiny cabin became our sanctuary and only place of safety. And in the big swells, we had to keep the single hatch closed at all times. This was an air and watertight seal that caused the tiny space to heat up quickly. The cabin filled with condensation and would become very uncomfortable during the day. So it was a tough call between fresh air, freezing waves and exposure, or the stuffy cabin, condensation and safety. Crawling out for my shift at the end of our second full day, I was greeted with 30-knot winds, huge seas and a container ship cutting our path a kilometre to our east. We made contact via the VHF radio and the ship altered its bearing slightly to avoid us, most likely thinking we were utterly insane to be out in these conditions.

Our bilge pump on deck decided to stop working during our third night. Whenever a wave swept the deck it filled up our footwell and the forward storage compartment, where we housed our ropes and parachute anchor. The added water weighed us down and our buoyancy altered. This setback meant I would now get to enjoy using a bucket to bail out in between rowing and getting soaked by the swell. The joys of ocean rowing were many.

We had been rowing for three days and about to start our fourth night shift. I'd been having the usual mental battle as my body adjusted to the new environment, and I was also feeling something I had never felt before. I thought at first that it was seasickness or maybe I was missing my wife, who I wouldn't see for possibly eight weeks. But as the days passed and we rowed further and further away from Australia, I realised what it was: a feeling of impending doom. This was accompanied by the gut-wrenching thought that I would never see Elise again. I didn't share this with Grant at first, I pushed it aside and got on with the job, but it was always there. If I had been new to the adventure world I would not have worried, putting it down to nerves and general fear. But this wasn't my first rodeo, I had a career full of dangerous expeditions behind me, including 55 days rowing the Atlantic and regular BASE jumping, a sport that will bring you closer to death than any other. Yet through everything, I'd never experienced what I was feeling now.

Gut feelings arise from intuition and are built from all of our past experiences. Perhaps it stemmed from our rushed departure, the less than ideal weather conditions or the reality of two failed attempts in a boat with a design unsuited for the Tasman. Whatever it was, I couldn't shake it, and when Grant asked how I was feeling, I told him the truth. Being an emotionally aware character with a lifetime of adventures under his belt, Grant wasn't shocked by what I told him, and we calmly discussed it in detail. We broke down the trip and weighed up all that was going right and what wasn't. At the end of our chat we agreed to acknowledge how I was feeling but push on. I felt better after unloading it onto Grant and breaking it apart. But as we carried on through the following two days, I couldn't shake the feeling.

In fact, it grew.

◆◆◆

The seas during Day Five were very big, but I had grown accustomed to their size. We were battling through gale-force winds on the eastern edge of Bass Strait, a notorious stretch of water between mainland Australia and Tasmania. As the waves rolled through I sat on deck eating some fruitcake with peanut butter. The boat sank deep into troughs and was lifted high on the summits of the swells. I began my rowing shift, but once again I was alternating between trying to row and using the steering lines to guide the boat down the face of the monsters. Over the course of my shift, the waves got bigger and more erratic. I double checked the metal safety line and carabiner hanging from my waist tethering me to the boat in case the unthinkable happened and I was thrown overboard into the frigid waters. The waves came at us from the left and the right, and it was hard to predict their pattern.

Halfway through my shift a rogue wave rose up on our left and I turned the boat to line up with it. The wave was huge and doubled in size before we made its crest. The lip of the wave started to break above me.

A guttural growl escaped my lips as the boat's stern lifted and we were carried skyward. We were going to be pitch-poled, flipping end over end, but at the last second the bow dug in and with violent speed we were capsized down the face of the monster. I was upside down and underwater with the roar of the ocean all around me. I tried to push free but something was wrong, my foot was trapped, I felt ropes around me and my first panicked thought was, 'I'm going to be tangled up.' I yanked my leg hard and felt the foot plate give way. Desperate for air I spun around and pushed upwards to the surface underneath our upside-down rowboat.

I was connected to the boat by the safety line, which was the only thing that stopped me being pulled away by the current. Grant was in the cabin with the door tightly sealed. He would have gone from dozing to being thrown around and upside down. As I was assessing the chaos, my lifejacket self-inflated and almost tore my head off. I'd forgotten to tie the crotch straps and now it was riding high and choking me.

Inside the cabin, Grants head collided with the handle of the hatch breaking the seal. This allowed a flood of water to enter the cabin and saturate our sleeping bags and electrical equipment. He realised what had happened and looked out through the half-submerged window to see me in the water.

'You okay, bro?' I yelled to Grant.

'Yeah,' he replied.

We were in a bad situation and we had to get the boat upright before the next set of waves came down on us. The boat was supposed to self-right but it was struggling to do so. My body weight on my safety line seemed to be inhibiting the process. I had to get my weight off the line and help the boat turn. Knowing that if I screwed up my next move I was a dead man but seeing no other remedy to our problem, I reached over to my safety line and tentatively undid the screw gate on the carabiner, then paused. Was I making the biggest mistake of my life in the middle of the Tasman Sea?

I unclipped my line and started swimming.

I held onto the side ropes with white knuckles as I worked my way around the side to the back of the boat, where I clipped back on. I grabbed hold of the rudder, which pointed up towards the heavens, and brought my full weight to bear. What moments ago had nearly been our downfall was now helping us survive. My muscles, all 92 kilograms of them, strained in the twilight. The rudder went below the water and I pushed it down with all my strength until the momentum and weight of the *Donkey* continued the roll and she popped upright.

Grant opened the cabin hatch and came out on deck. His first thought was to get me out of the water. I swam around to the side and he helped haul me on board and to relative safety.

'Get inside, quick. And get warm, mate,' he said.

'Roger that,' I replied, shivering.

We looked out at the angry surface of the ocean and the debris that littered it. We watched our rowing seat, water bottle, and plenty more that wasn't lashed down float away on the current. Retrieval wasn't an option, Bass Strait owned them now. Grant deployed our parachute anchor, while I crawled into the cabin out of the cutting wind. I ditched my wet clothes, slipped on some thermals and crawled into my sleeping bag. The adrenaline subsided and my jaw started chattering violently.

Grant joined me inside; the para anchor would keep us connected to the current and hold us relatively straight into the big swell. It was a rough ride when waves picked us up to carry us away, only to be snapped back straight when the anchor tightened. Grant got a hot brew on and we stayed quiet for a while taking our own personal stock of what had happened. The warm liquid worked its magic and I stopped shivering.

'How do you feel now, bro?' Grant asked.

'That was crazy out there, mate. We went over so quick,' I said.

'Yeah. I swore last time that I wouldn't attempt a crossing in this boat again, but I thought with two of us rowing continuously we could avoid problems.'

A moment's silence hung between us.

'So, what's your gut saying now?' he asked me.

'The feelings I shared with you are still there, mate, and today's incident could be a warning sign or just another day of ocean rowing. What do you think?' I asked.

He outlined that we were 200 kilometres offshore and at the limit of helicopter rescue if we did have a serious problem. The weather forecast wasn't looking great for the following week and it would mean many more chances of going over again.

'If we have a big problem in another week, it could be very serious. We have a responsibility to make the right decision here, mate, not just to ourselves but to our families as well,' he said.

'I can't make the call but you know how I'm feeling. What do you think we should do?' I said.

'I think we should turn around and I'll need to rethink this crossing,' he replied.

I was relieved to hear the words.

'I agree with you. Let's get back safe and fight again another day.'

Together we made the decision to abort. Trust me when I say that abandoning an attempt is never an easy decision to make, whether it is ocean rowing or mountain climbing. We had to weigh up our dreams and ambitions against the risks and our personal responsibilities. We do these adventures because we want to get the most out of life, not have it cut short through a mistake. We made a satellite phone call to Clouds to start looking at getting us back to land, then we let our families know what had happened and that we were turning around.

Getting all the way back to Eden wasn't going to happen, the ocean currents wouldn't allow that. If we could make landfall anywhere on the south-east coast then that would be good enough. Clouds sent us a plan first thing the next morning; our new bearing was turning east to get out of the southerly currents. We were no longer turning towards New Zealand, we had to complete a big circle and start inching our way back to Australia.

We dug out the spare rowing seat, settled into our two hour shifts and over the following three days we fought the currents, the swell and the winds, to slowly make our way towards home. Our destination was the Victorian coastal town of Mallacoota, which harboured a boat ramp. It was 50 kilometres south of Eden and my parents had agreed to meet us there with the boat trailer.

We were 55 nautical miles off the coast when the weather changed and we were hit with cross-currents and a headwind. We had to cease rowing and sit on the parachute anchor again for 12 hours, losing valuable distance to the west the entire time. To be a day away from safety and not able to get there was frustrating. Bass Strait wasn't done with us yet.

During our forced drift, while Grant was asleep beside me, I opened my phone to my list of adventures. This was a hit list of expeditions I would love to do if I had an unlimited budget. I scanned the list and even after I'd been beaten by Mother Nature once again, I confirmed my desire to achieve them. At the top of the list was 'Rowing the Tasman.' I pulled up the keypad and typed 'to be continued.' I read through the others and asked myself a question, 'What if I only had five years to live?' I reshuffled the list in answer to this question and underlined my top five. I made a silent decision that as soon as my feet touched dry land, I would put the wheels in motion to complete these top five in the next five years. If being tangled upside down in the freezing water of the Tasman had taught me anything, it was to not waste a single moment of this life. I put my phone away and slept.

Around midday and 28 nautical miles out, we saw land. The sight was energising and if we could put in some solid rowing, we would be home in half a day. The Tasman, however, wasn't going to let us go that easily. The currents shifted and we dropped to barely one knot. Our projected half-day of rowing could easily turn into two more days if things didn't change. We decided to row in one-hour shifts to get us moving along. If we could keep up the effort and not sleep for the night, we had a chance of making it by dawn.

Eight miles out the wind picked up and slammed us head on, pushing the bow of the boat around. It was impossible to maintain a heading while rowing, and I cracked it. Like a little kid, I threw my toys out of the pram and tossed the oars onto the deck. Grant took over and gave me a rest in the cabin. He chugged away like the veteran he was at half a knot of speed until I'd calmed down and scolded myself for letting my frustration boil over. I returned to the deck but instead of taking over, we joined forces. We decided to add a second set of oars in the water but we had no second rowing seat. I made myself a seat out of ropes in front of Grant and began to row with him as best as I could without full use of my legs. At that stage I didn't care if my back blew out, we were getting off the water at dawn.

My hands were blistered and throbbed with pain, forcing me to stop and rest every hundred strokes. But even with my struggles, our combined effort increased our speed; we were making almost two knots when we rowed together. For six hours we battled, stopping every mile to inhale water and chocolates as a reward. We were sleep deprived and exhausted, but as the sun rose over the horizon and the seas calmed, we entered the sheltered harbour of Mallacoota. The red and green channel lights guided us in and we phoned the coast guard to let them know we'd made it safely. We called customs to organise an official to come down to meet us and stamp our passports into Australia. Mum and Dad were en route and I could see the rock wall of the boat ramp up ahead.

Grant took us in solo through the headland and sandbars with absolute skill. He drifted us in right alongside the wooden pontoon and I jumped out to secure us to the first solid structure we'd touched in over a week. My legs were wobbling all over the place, I'd adapted to life on the ocean and I could no longer walk straight. Grant secured the other end of the *Donkey* and climbed out as well. We gave each other a hug and congratulated ourselves for self-rescuing and making it home in one piece.

A guy from the coast guard arrived first to welcome us. He had a huge beard and looked like an extra out of *Sons of Anarchy*. He shook our hands and offered us tea and biscuits. The customs official arrived shortly after and sorted our passports. He was very welcoming and congratulated us on our attempt and the smart decision in turning around. It's always a guess as to what people's reaction will be. Some would say we were stupid to even attempt it, while others gave us full credit for trying.

Mum and Dad arrived with the trailer and I wobbled over to give Mum a big hug. She had tears in her eyes and I fought back mine.

'Never do anything like that again, okay?' she said.

'I'm done with the ocean…for a while,' I said to her.

I shook Dad's hand and thanked him for helping out again.

'Back the trailer in, mate,' I told him. 'We're ready to go for a shower and eat some bacon and eggs.'

He jumped in the truck and reversed the big trailer down the ramp. We winched on *Simpsons Donkey* and strapped it down safely for the drive up to Eden. I was staring out at the open ocean and lost in thought when Dad pulled the truck up beside me. He wound down the window and looked at me with a grin and a raised eyebrow.

'Where are you off to next?' he asked.

I turned back from the ocean and took a second to pause as feelings of success and failure churned inside me. I smiled and looked him straight in the eye.

'I have a list.'

Chapter 11
Thumb and a Book Tour

It was 2001 and I was standing in the hallway of an old brick four-level building at Kapooka military training base in Wagga Wagga. I was 17 years old, had just signed up to the Australian infantry, and was beginning six weeks of indoctrination into the military machine. I was in a group of fresh recruits being yelled at as we stood up straight and sweat poured from our pale faces. We were being crucified for folding our socks incorrectly. After the verbal abuse was over, I was pulled aside by one of the training staff and given advice that was pivotal to both my emotional development and future as a writer.

He told me to go to the shop on the base and buy a notebook and pen. I was to keep it hidden and inside its pages he told me to write down everything. He said, 'You're gonna go through a whole lot of shit here, get all your thoughts down on paper each day and it will help you deal with it.' I took his advice and started a journal. The first line I ever wrote begins 'I'm sitting at my tables personnel…' The military couldn't let a desk be called a desk. I also wrote about my fears, goals, hardships and triumphs. Putting all those words down each day, in detail and with brutal honesty, was a form of counselling, and it helped me deal with the adversities over the following months and years.

I continued to write journals into my adult life, including during my years of drug addiction as well as my life of adventure. Once I had accomplished enough crazy expeditions to make me the world's most annoying dinner guest, the thought of writing a book took hold. It marinated until one day I collected all my old journals and started reading. I had kept so much detail that a book was a real possibility. If I didn't have the journals to go back to and help me remember, I don't think *One Life One Chance* would have ever been a reality. Over the two years I wrote that manuscript, I dished it out to selected family and friends for feedback, and when I finally had something worth publishing, I was ready to share it with the world.

I sent the manuscript to every publisher I could find online. Some had tight submitting windows that I had missed, while others wanted the whole thing printed out and mailed in like it was the 1950s. I'm sure a large portion of my submissions fell into the junk folders of cyber space. I received rejection emails from dozens of publishing houses until I opened an email from Ventura Press in Sydney. They believed my manuscript had potential and wanted to publish my book. The following weeks of back and forth emails with the lovely girls in the office educated me about the new world of books, publishing and being a writer.

I signed my contract and it took nine months to produce the book and get it to market. I was told by Simon & Schuster, our distributor, that it would be on the shelves by the middle of March 2018. I was travelling to Bali for a training camp at the beginning of March and after my holiday I intended to hit the ground running, promoting my masterpiece. While browsing the shelves of a WHSmith store inside Sydney International Airport, my heart skipped a beat.

'No way!' I yelled out loud.

There on the centre shelf in all its glossy mountain glory was my book, *One Life One Chance*. The picture we'd chosen for the cover was of me climbing Denali in Alaska, and here it was, stacked four deep and three wide for everyone to see. Like an overexcited teenager, I started taking selfies with my books behind me. The customers looked at me like I was crazy until I told them, 'This is my new book guys, just out now.' I chatted to a few of them about my adventures and after getting the green light from the store manager, I signed all the copies on the shelves. I thought I had 'made it,' and took off to search the other bookshops in the airport to sign their copies as well.

My book was distributed to hundreds of stores in Australia and New Zealand, it went everywhere, and while I was training in Bali and enjoying time with Elise, I was putting together a plan of how best to promote it. The girls at Ventura told me that if I visited bookshops and signed their copies, not only was it great promotion but it also meant the stores couldn't return the unsold copies. The bookshops ordered copies based on what they thought they would sell, on a sale or return policy, so if the books had been signed, they couldn't be returned. Essentially I was locking in the sale with the stroke of the pen.

I had just finished reading a great book titled *The Long Hitch Home*, by Jamie Maslin. Jamie had an incredible adventure hitchhiking from Hobart, in Tasmania, to his home in England. Inspired by his method of travel I came up with the Thumb and a Book Tour. I was given a list of the stores stocking my book and put together a route that would visit most of them in New South Wales, Victoria and Queensland. I decided I would hitchhike the entire journey to help me gain some publicity. Taking it a step further, I would do the tour starting with no money and would drag a big suitcase full of books along with me. I would need to sell one book per day to survive. I would take along a hammock for camping and document the entire adventure.

The publisher loved the idea and through their PR contacts arranged radio interviews with the ABC en route to help share my story with the Australian public. Before leaving Bali, I made a video for my social media about the upcoming tour and the towns I would be visiting. In the video I told my followers I would come and deliver a talk about my adventures to anyone along my route who was interested. Schools, businesses or backyard barbecues, I would talk to them all for free. All I asked in return was to be able to sell my books to those who attended. My social media blew up. I was inundated with requests to talk and offers of accommodation – the true power of social media hit home. Over the following few days I had a huge spreadsheet of stores to visit and talks to deliver. I had my plan set and when I landed back in Sydney I was ready to put it into action.

I spent three days in Sydney visiting dozens of stores. Initially I was nervous approaching the staff and introducing myself as a new author, but after the first day it became second nature. Most stores were excited to have me drop by and were happy to let me sign all the copies they had in stock. Others seemed to have played the game before and only allowed me to sign two or three copies, knowing full well if they didn't sell, they would be stuck with the signed ones. I also had some ABC interviews to do before I got ready for the road.

I borrowed my mother-in-law's large suitcase for the tour, the type on wheels that can be dragged along. I have avoided these bags my entire life, always preferring a practical backpack, but here I was loading it up to capacity. I managed to squeeze in 50 copies of my book protected in plastic and bubble wrap in case it rained. I also carried my backpack, which contained clothes, camping gear and a laminated A3 piece of paper that would be my sign. I was ready to depart. I ditched the cash out of my wallet and with my last three dollars bought a double espresso at the train station. I had just enough money on my travel card to get a train to the edge of Sydney, where I planned to head onto the highway. My first planned stop was the coastal city of Wollongong, 90 kilometres south-east of Sydney.

I was on the train heading for Heathcote Station, situated right alongside the Princes Highway, heading south. An elderly lady started chatting to me.

'Off on holiday?' she asked.

'No, actually I'm just starting my book tour,' I replied in an overexcited manner, and detailed my plan to her.

'Well, I'll buy a copy. How much?' she asked.

'Twenty-three dollars,' I told her, as I fumbled around trying to undo the bubble wrap.

As we arrived at her station I was still digging one out. She held the door open to the annoyance of the platform attendant, who was surely thinking I was some unorganised tourist. I hadn't even left the city and I had enough money in my pocket for the day's food. The early signs were looking good.

I got off at Heathcote, swiped my travel card, watching it flash into negative two dollars, and walked to the highway. To improve my chances of getting rides from drivers, I had a number of commonsense rules to follow. Rule number one was to find a place next to the highway that had a pull-over area for vehicles. If a car cannot stop safely after noticing you, they won't bother. I walked about 500 metres up the highway until I found a suitable spot.

Rule number two was to use a sign. Most drivers will be hesitant to pick you up, so you have to give them reasons to relate to you in the few seconds it takes them to pass. A well-written sign showing your destination is a great tool. Ensure that the location is spelt correctly and use thick black letters so the drivers can read it easily. A trick with the sign is to write the name of the next town. Even if I was hoping to get to a city much further along, I'd write the next closest place. Doing this will give you a better chance of drivers stopping, and nine times out of ten they will be going further.

Rule number three is to look presentable and use deodorant right before you put your thumb out. Living on the road is going to roughen up your appearance, but a quick dash of spray for the convenience of the driver is a big benefit to the hitchhiking community. If the driver has a pleasant experience, the more likely they will be to pick up another hitchhiker next time. If you abuse their sense of smell with a pungent, unwashed aroma, they won't stop for the next person.

Rule number four is to smile and put out your thumb. Don't use a finger and point at the ground in a half-hearted attempt, be clear in your intentions. Hold your thumb out proudly and smile. Try to limit the 'crazy face' overexcited smile. Think about a soft smile you would give a friend if you met them randomly in the street. Follow these simple rules and you will be travelling free around Australia for as long as you wish.

It was time for me to put all the rules into action and I set a timer to see how long each ride was going to take. I set up with my sign showing 'Wollongong,' put out my thumb and smiled.

I waited four minutes exactly before a small white sedan pulled up. I packed my sign away, grabbed my bags and hustled over, hoping the driver didn't suddenly become tired of waiting and drive off. I opened the door.

'G'day mate, thanks for stopping.'

'No worries at all, jump in.'

I threw my bags in the back and hopped in the front. After shutting the door, I held out my hand for a firm handshake.

'I'm Luke.'

'I'm Joseph,' he replied.

Joseph was finishing his nightshift as a commercial property manager and was on his way home to Wollongong.

We started chatting and as Joseph realised I wasn't a crazy person, he relaxed and became flamboyant in his storytelling. I shared a few of my adventure stories but it was mostly Joseph telling me about himself. What tends to happen as a hitcher is you fall into the role of a temporary friend/councillor. It always amazes me how quickly people will open up and tell me their life stories, not holding back on any dark details. I was more than happy to play this role and if there was a lull in the conversation, I'd fill it with my adventures.

I'd arranged to meet a girl named Susannah in Wollongong who had reached out via social media. She wanted to buy a copy of my book and get me to visit the gym where she worked. Joseph dropped me off in 'The Gong,' as he called it, and Susannah picked me up ten minutes later. She was of Italian descent and worked as a fitness coach.

'You made it. Welcome,' she said.

'Thanks for letting me drop by. What's the plan?' I replied.

'It's time to head to work, let's go.'

She took me to her gym, where I was able to squeeze in a training session before the clients and coaches arrived for the evening classes. I became a novelty for a few hours and chatted to members about my adventures, sold five books and shared some of my training tips. Susannah finished her last class and invited me to a barbecue at her parents' house for dinner. I was low on food for the day and a big juicy steak was just what the doctor ordered.

Susannah's parents were lovely, and I was spoilt with one of the best meat feasts I'd enjoyed in a very long time. They were hardworking Italians who owned a Caltex service station close to the highway on the edge of town. I entertained them with some climbing stories and when it got late, Susannah said she'd booked me a hotel room for the night.

'Thanks so much, but you're not wasting money on hotels. What's wrong with that?' I said, pointing to the couch in the lounge room.

'Are you sure you'll be comfortable?' she replied.

'That is more comfortable than any mountain,' I said with a grin.

She cancelled the hotel and I settled in on the soft couch. Eight books sold on my first day, I was off to a flying start.

◆◆◆

Susannah was up at 6am for work at the service station, so I said I would tag along. A service station on a highway is one of the best places to score a ride. I'd sold two copies of my book through my website overnight and using the postage bags I'd brought with me, dropped them into a post box on the way. I was hoping to reach Canberra by nightfall, which at 248 kilometres away was a long shot but I had an ABC interview booked and a friend to stay with. En route I needed to stop at a bookshop in Nowra, 80 kilometres south, however the next closest town was

Kiama, just 40 kilometres down the road, so that's what I wrote on my sign.

I grabbed a coffee from inside the station and asked Susannah if I could stand at the front door. 'Go for it,' she said.

I had my sign out and smiled at the customers fuelling up and walking inside to pay. After five minutes a tradesman yelled out, 'Jump in mate, I'm going all the way to Nowra.' I quickly packed up, waved to Susannah and climbed aboard.

The driver was John, a builder who started early to go and quote for a new job. He was interested in what I was up to and over our coffees I told him all about ocean rowing and the jungles of West Papua. The 80 kilometres whipped by and he dropped me off in front of Dean Swift Bookshop at 8am. There was an hour to kill before they opened, and with a growling belly I found a café on a nearby corner.

After an enormous feed of bacon and eggs I went and introduced myself to the girls at the store. They were very receptive and couldn't believe I was hitching everywhere. I signed all of their copies and we took some pictures together for social media.

The next closest town was Moss Vale, 59 kilometres away up a winding mountain road. Trying to hitch through towns is a waste of time, as cars are heading to a hundred different directions and rarely stop. I needed to set up on a road that went in the direction of Moss Vale, which meant a 30-minute walk through town. I had my pack on and was dragging my overloaded suitcase behind me. The morning heat was intense, and I was soaked in sweat by the time I made it to a good spot. Remembering rule number three, I changed out of my grubby shirt, put on a fresh blast of deodorant and set up with my sign. Five minutes and fifty seconds later a red car pulled over. I packed up and opened the back door.

'Thanks so much for stopping,' I said to a woman wearing a high-visibility work shirt.

'No worries, mate. Get in,' she replied.

I hopped in the front and shook hands with Bec, who was going to Moss Vale, where she worked at a book distribution warehouse for HarperCollins. That was a good starting point for our conversation and I told her all about my book. Bec was a working-class legend and her stories about her life really got to me. She had completed ten years of IVF with no success, and had been diagnosed with liver tumours shortly after.

'From all those treatments and drugs,' she told me in an upbeat manner.

She had to cease her IVF but was determined to try again when the cancer was dealt with.

Bec had a sister in a similar position. She had tried two years of IVF and fell pregnant but was also diagnosed with stage four cancer. Her brave sister carried the child full term and gave birth to a healthy baby, but she passed away six months later from her cancer. It was a tragic story.

'You've just got to have a go at life,' said Bec, the eternal optimist.

Bec dropped me off in the tiny town of Moss Vale. After a quick hug she was on her way to work, and I was walking to the other side of town. I set up with Goulburn written on my sign, as it was the next town along and about halfway to Canberra. My ride took six minutes to arrive. A white four-wheel drive with a lovely lady named Tracey behind the wheel. She looked about my mum's age and when I said I was hoping to get to Canberra by nightfall, she passed on very good news.

'Well, I'm going all the way to Jindabyne, love. Past Canberra. I'll take you all the way.'

I started to bring her up to date on my hitchhike and when I mentioned Susannah in Wollongong she burst out, 'That's my ex-daughter-in-law.' Tracey's son had married Susannah a few years ago but it didn't work out. She became a little emotional while telling me the details.

With that mutual connection, we chatted like old friends. Tracey told me how she'd recently beaten breast cancer. She had multiple tumours that were shrunk with radiation and during her therapy she took up knitting to keep her mind occupied. Knitting had changed her life and I was curious to find out more. After she recovered her life goals shifted, as you would expect, and she wanted to travel and see more of the world. Through knitting she'd met groups of people online who held knitting gatherings all around the world.

'I'm going to Scotland next,' she told me with excitement.

The knitting gang planned to get together to discuss all things wool related and then explore the outdoors. I was so happy for her.

Tracey drove me all the way into Canberra, and to the area of Belconnen, where I needed to visit the next bookshop. Before leaving Sydney, a friend of mine, Vincent, paid double for a book and told me to pass one on during my travels. As Tracey dropped me off, she said she wanted to buy a book, and I told her I wanted to give her one instead. We hugged like departing family on the sidewalk before she drove away.

Canberra is Australia's largest inland city, with a population of 390,000. It's home to our parliament, the Australian War Memorial and before the explosion of the internet, was also the porn shop capital. It was Friday afternoon and I dropped in to visit a Dymocks Bookshop. They had great staff, who quickly tracked down a stack of my books and let me sign them. A friend of mine, Rohan, worked in a cushy government job close by and offered to put a roof over my head for the night. I headed over to his building and met him and his colleagues as they were winding down for the week. They all wanted signed copies of my book, which guaranteed I was going to eat a big dinner.

My publishers were pushing the PR campaign for me and I was receiving constant emails about stores to visit and interviews to do. They had arranged an ABC radio interview for Saturday morning, but then asked if I could be in Melbourne for another one on Monday morning. This was a distance of 652 kilometres in two days. I would need a few big lifts to make it there in time, but I backed my chances and locked it in.

Rohan drove me to the ABC the following morning. I had been telling my stories for so many years that it had become second nature to me. Greg, the host of the morning show, asked great questions and we had a solid conversation about adventure and my mode of travel during the book tour. Once we wrapped up, I asked Rohan to drop me at the highway. He said he could do one better. He drove me 50 kilometres north to the main highway leading to Melbourne, where the volume of cars heading my way would increase my chances.

While driving we saw two hitchhikers on the side of the road who were not following my hitching rules. They were in an average spot, we couldn't read their sign and the two young guys looked like they had just woken up after sleeping behind a dumpster. We picked them up anyway. I hinted to Rohan not to drop them off with me, as getting a ride with three people, especially two looking rough, was a big challenge. We dropped them in the town of Yass before we drove to the highway intersection and found a good spot for me to set up. I bade farewell to Rohan, made my sign for Gundagai, the next town heading west, and put out my thumb.

Five minutes later a four-wheel drive towing a trailer pulled up. I jogged to the door.

'G'day, mate. Thanks for stopping,' I said.

'No worries. Get in, mate. I'm heading to Gundagai.'

I shook hands with Michael and closed the door. He was in his forties, in good shape and had an assortment of health food snacks across the seat between us.

'Eat whatever you like, mate. The wife makes all of the vegan stuff herself,' he offered.

Michael worked for the fire brigade and was heading to Gundagai to collect a car for a friend. We were chatting along like old mates and sharing stories when he cut me off.

'See that,' he said, pointing out the window. 'It's an apple tree.' I looked out and there on the side of the highway stood a solo apple tree in full fruit.

'They grow from cores people throw out of their car windows,' he said. 'Me and the kids stop and pick them all the time.'

During the drive he shared some stories with me about his dad, who had served in Vietnam. He said he was a strong-willed no-bullshit soldier who brazenly ferried ammunition and stores up the Mekong Delta on his boat, resupplying the

Americans. When he returned home after the war, he worked for the Australian War Memorial in Canberra for 20 years. Michael choked up when he told me how his dad was fit and had a sharp mind, but recently slipped on the stairs, hit his head and developed an aneurysm. Michael had found him at the bottom of the stairs with no signs of life. He resuscitated him and got him to hospital. His dad recovered and was released and brought back home, where he died the same day, in his sleep, on Anzac Day, at the age of 85.

'Not a day goes by I don't think about the old man. He was a sharp, honest Aussie bloke and I miss him,' he said with watery eyes.

'Your dad was a legend, mate,' I told him.

Michael pulled over at the turn-off to Gundagai and bought a book from me. He also gave me some of his wife's vegan Bundt cake and plums. I waved him off and assessed my hitching options. I was on a busy motorway in a 110 kilometre an hour zone, which was not ideal for people to stop. The pullover area was also too small to make it safe. I consulted Google Maps and could see a good area near a service station about four kilometres down the road. I set off wearing my backpack and dragging my bag.

The rough surface of the highway and the weight of books was destroying the soft rubber wheels on the bag. It was a hot day and I must have looked quite the spectacle walking along with cars rocketing past. I saw the station in the distance and started crossing a long bridge to get to it. When I was halfway across, a blue ute pulled up next to me, stopping in the middle of the road.

'Need a ride, mate?' the young guy behind the wheel asked.

I was caught off guard but quickly assessed the risk of what he was doing. 'Yes please, mate,' I yelled and threw my bags in the back, climbing in before any traffic backed up behind us.

I shook hands with Brendan, who told me he was heading home to Albury, 179 kilometres away. I thanked him for stopping.

'You looked like you needed a ride, bro,' he replied.

Brendan was in his early thirties, obviously gay and said he was heading home after the Sydney Mardi Gras weekend.

'How was the party?' I asked him.

'It was big,' he said with a smile.

I noticed his blackened teeth when he smiled. The signs of drug abuse are crystal clear when you know what to look for. From Brendan's slightly malnourished appearance and his fidgeting, I guessed he was using amphetamines of some description.

'How does Albury compare to Sydney?' I asked.

'Full of ice, and too small. I have to get out,' he replied in a matter-of-fact way.

'Wow, ice in a small country town,' I said, slightly shocked.

'Yeah mate, rampant. It's everywhere.'

We chatted for a few more minutes before he turned up the dance music and zoned out. I was happy to stare out the window and watch the countryside whip by. Brendan's comment about the spread of drugs and especially the drug Ice through the smaller rural communities was a shock to me. I hadn't realised it was that widespread in Australia.

I was dropped off at the train station in Albury and thanked Brendan for the ride. With the music still blaring from the car stereo he yelled, 'No worries mate,' and drove away. I contemplated jumping on a train to Melbourne. It was late afternoon, hot as hell and it was the easy way to my destination now that I had money from my book sales. Then I saw a sign for a Subway restaurant down the road and my stomach led me there instead. I ordered three footlongs, lounged in their air-conditioning and drank copious amounts of free ice water. I also grabbed a handful of cookies to fortify myself before walking back towards the motorway.

I waited in a bad spot under the scorching afternoon sun for sixteen minutes until a guy pulled up. 'Thanks for stopping' I said, as I opened the door.

A middle-aged man in corporate uniform replied, 'I'm only going to Wodonga mate, but I'll get you off the motorway.'

'Sounds great,' I replied, and we were away.

Albury and Wodonga are two small towns sitting either side of the Murray River, which is Australia's longest river and acts as the border between New South Wales and Victoria. Five kilometres from where he picked me up, we drove across a bridge over the river. The water looked beautiful.

'Could you drop me down there, mate?' I asked.

'Sure can.' He pulled off onto an exit ramp and onto a gravel road. We stopped at a park and he pointed to a track that would take me to the river.

It had been a long day, I'd made it halfway to Melbourne and a cool swim was too good to pass up. I found a secluded spot on the bank, dove into the cold water and swam out into the flow. After my swim I located some big trees perfect for my hammock and decided to camp for the night. I had a Subway footlong in my bag for dinner and some cookies for dessert. My equipment was all military grade and once I was set up in the trees I was nearly invisible.

I crawled inside and read a book, while getting rocked by the cool evening breeze. I was exhausted from a big day on the road and fell asleep with the book on my chest.

◆◆◆

At dawn I dove into the icy water to get my blood pumping then packed up my hammock, brushed my teeth and walked towards the gravel road and up onto the highway. My phone was constantly vibrating as messages came through at a rapid rate. I stopped to check what was happening and the first message I read was from a good friend: 'Great article, mate.' The next message: '*Sunday Telegraph* bro, top work.'

I clicked through the link and there was a picture of me on the cover of the Sunday newspaper. I remembered doing the interviews and sending photos off to a journalist earlier in the week but didn't think it would lead to much. I was wrong. The main photo they chose was my before and after weight-loss picture from the Atlantic Ocean row. I'd lost 14 kilograms in the 55-day crossing. The news story had been shared across multiple sites and was six pages long. I was also getting email notifications and when I checked, they were book orders coming through from my website. There had been ten orders since I woke up. I was making headline news online, while sleeping in the bush and eating a Subway sandwich.

I was 316 kilometres from Melbourne and had to get there by nightfall, the ABC interview was first thing on Monday morning. I was in a bad spot again, but I had no choice other than to try my luck in the 110 kilometre per hour zone. After fifteen minutes I decided to write 'Melbourne' on the other side of my sign in the hope of picking up someone going all the way through. I rotated between the two destinations every five minutes. Twenty-three minutes passed before a big white van pulled up with two young Chinese guys sitting in the front. Wangaratta was showing when they stopped but the first thing they said was, 'We are going all the way to Melbourne, but we can drop you on the way.'

'Actually, Melbourne is great for me, lads. If that's okay?'

'Get in,' they said in unison, as the side door slid open.

Their names were Benny and Funghy, and they looked like they'd been driving all night.

'So, what are you boys up to?' I asked.

Funghy was dozing off so Benny replied.

'We have a production company and a big problem to fix in Melbourne. We left Sydney last night in a rush. We have 40 people flying in for the production today, so we have to get there and get everything ready.'

'Sounds like a hectic day ahead, mate,' I replied.

I gave them a quick rundown of what I was up to but Funghy was asleep and I could tell Benny had his mind in a million places. I trailed off saying, 'If you want me to drive so you can crash out just ask, mate.' Benny nodded his thanks.

My phone was still blowing up in my pocket and when I checked I had received 25 online orders and was gaining a tonne of new followers. The story was getting shared across all of our domestic news platforms and while the Australian countryside passed by, I read the article in full. The journalist had done a great job. He'd opened with my rockbottom years of drug addiction in London and then went into the adventures. He'd used all the pictures I sent through, and at the end of the story was a link to buy my book. I couldn't be happier with how it came out. As the orders kept coming, I realised I could sell out of the books I was carrying. I drafted an email to the publishers to have a shipment of books ready to send to Melbourne after I had found a place to stay.

The van slowed and we pulled off at a service station and towards the big golden arches of McDonald's. It was breakfast time for the boys, and I was starving as well. There was no way I was going to put most of what Maccas made into my body, but there were two things they did well, and over the years I have been one of their best customers. After Benny had ordered, I stepped forward.

'Five eggs and a long black coffee please.'

The young girl looked at me cross-eyed.

'Just five eggs?' she said.

'Yes please, in one small box and no bag.'

I paid and stepped back. At $1 per egg it was the healthiest item on the menu, and a breakfast for $5 was a bargain.

Back in the van, Funghy took over the driving and Benny was much more animated, explaining the latest script he was working on. It was about the first Chinese settlers coming to Australia during the gold rush years. I knew a little bit about this side of Australian history from spending time in North Queensland and reading about the Palmer River gold rush in the late 18th century. He told me some of the history I didn't know involving the Aboriginal community and we got into a back and forth discussion. During those early pioneering years, interbreeding and marriage between the Chinese settlers and Indigenous communities had been common. Benny wanted to write a love story dating to that period for the big screen.

I checked my phone as we entered the outskirts of Melbourne and after tallying the online orders, I calculated I only had eleven books remaining. I also received a message from Andrew, an old friend, who offered me a place to stay. His timing couldn't have been better, and I inserted his address into the email to my publishers. A shipment of books would be on its way. The boys pulled up at Crown Casino in the city.

'Thanks again for the ride, and let me know when the movie comes out,' I said. They waved me off and I headed towards the trams. I'd arrived in Melbourne after hitching over 900 kilometres and was ready to stop in one place for a few days. I had about 20 bookshops to visit, two ABC interviews to do and three talks to deliver.

◆◆◆

The following week was a blur and I became semi-professional at navigating public transport throughout Melbourne. I visited every bookshop. Whether they were stocking 30 copies of my book or just one, I would make the effort to visit. While inside the stores I would reshuffle my books to a centre shelf and give them a more prominent position. Every little bit helped with sales. Another small hustle I developed was to go into any bookshops not selling my book and ask, 'Have you got this great adventure book by Luke Richmond?' 'No, sorry, we could order it in,' they would reply. To which I would respond, 'Okay great. I'll pop back next week.'

My first ever public talk was to four personal trainers at a Fitness First, and they all bought a copy of the book afterwards. The next one was organised by an army buddy, Ross. It was held at his local café and 26 people turned up to hear me speak. I delivered my stories with no slides or video, just sharing my adventures vocally and from the heart. In the beginning I found it hard to read the crowd, one lady kept checking her phone and I thought she must have been bored. Then at the end, after I'd spoken for 45 minutes, she came up to me crying, saying she loved it and was inspired. I sold 20 copies and one guy gave me a $100 donation and said, 'Keep doing what you're doing, mate.'

I loved giving talks. It was so rewarding to share my stories and see people getting excited and wanting to plan their own adventures. During the week I was booked last-minute by Stamford Capital for an event back in Sydney. This meant an early morning flight from Melbourne to deliver a lunchtime presentation at Rockpool, one of Sydney's top restaurants. Knowing I would be back in my hammock eating Subway sandwiches very soon, I didn't hold back on the quality food. I was bursting at the seams afterwards as I made my way to the airport and back to Melbourne.

The original plan was to sell one book per day to survive. With the overwhelming support from the community and the media, the target was surpassed tenfold. I had sold 91 books in 13 days. I was still living on sandwiches as I didn't want to jinx myself, but I would also splash out on bacon and eggs with hot coffee on occasion. I had 22 books left from the second supply as I started to plan my route out of Melbourne. My next interview was scheduled in Wagga Wagga, so on a perfect Saturday morning I said goodbye to the city and was driven by Andrew to a service station situated on the main highway heading north. Wagga Wagga was over 400 kilometres away but I had a couple of days up my sleeve and I was confident I'd make it. I had a new system to help me get rides from busy service stations. First, I'd go in and walk around, make a coffee and say 'g'day' to the customers inside. A guy was at the coffee machine with me and we had a brief exchange of pleasantries. As he reached for a glazed donut I said, 'Nice nutritious breakfast, mate.' We both laughed before I moved over to the counter to pay for my coffee. There was a line of people behind me and as I approached the counter, I asked the cashier in a louder than normal voice, 'What's the best road to hitch to Shepparton from here?' The cashier was a little thrown by my question but he regained his composure and pointed to an exit road through the window.

'Thanks, I'll get out there and try to hitch a lift,' I said.

From behind me in the line, the guy holding the glazed donut said, 'I'll give you a ride, mate. I'm heading that way.'

Paul was a middle-aged, slightly overweight guy who drove with one hand on the wheel and the other around his donut. He was a driver in Melbourne, owned his own small fleet of cars and was racing to get to his son's rowing competition on Lake Nagambie, 100 kilometres away. His wife was a teacher at one of the best private schools in Melbourne, and because of this Paul proudly boasted, 'We get a 40 percent discount on the kids' tuition fees. We'd be stuffed without that.' We discussed my ocean row and he shared with me countless stories from the taxi-driving world. We rolled into the small town of Nagambie by 8.45am. While shaking Paul's hand he asked, 'Did you know I was going to give you a ride from the service station before I offered?'

'I was just trying my luck and then a good bloke helped me out,' I replied with a smile.

'Cheeky bugger,' he laughed. 'Have a good trip.'

Shepparton was my next destination and I found a perfect spot in a 60 kilometre zone to stand with my sign. Fourteen minutes later, Adam from Albania pulled up in his Commodore and said, 'Jump in.' As Nagambie disappeared behind me, I said, 'Thanks for the ride, mate,' then gave him a quick rundown on what I was up to. He was excited for me and told me his story in return. He was 22 years old and had immigrated to Australia with his family when he was eleven. He loved it here and was chasing the Australian dream. He said, 'I have one house already and will buy my second one very soon.' He worked as a plasterer and in response to all of my travel stories he said, 'I will work hard now and travel later in life.'

I could have replied about the bonds of too much debt and the illusion of freedom in the current structure of society but instead said, 'It's great you're having a good crack at life.' Adam seemed to acknowledge my reply and then the conversation took a turn.

'I hate refugees,' he said out of nowhere, with some deep-rooted animosity. 'They come here the wrong way for a free ride.'

I nodded my head in acknowledgement of him speaking, rather than agreement with what he was saying.

'The Abos need to get over it and move on with their lives too,' he added.

He was referring to the Aboriginal population of Australia, our indigenous people. Most people would agree they have received the raw end of a brutal deal since the British landed in Australia in 1788. Not Adam, he thought they were lazy. I didn't bite at his racist comments, not wanting to risk my ride for a conversation that would yield very little. I changed the subject and we rolled on through the countryside.

Adam dropped me outside the local McDonald's in Shepparton, and I walked across the road to make my next sign. I had a cousin who lived in Corowa, which was on the way to Wagga Wagga. I sent him a message to see if he was home in the hope of a bed for the night. I then followed my hitching rules and set up. I didn't know which town to write on my sign, I was off the main highway and it was a grid of country roads linking all the smaller towns. I decided on Yarrawonga, mainly because I liked the sound of it. Twenty-one minutes later a middle-aged lady pulled up in a red sedan. 'I'm going to Strathmerton, that's on your way,' she said, then introduced herself as Kylie.

'Sounds great, thanks so much,' I replied and hopped in.

Kylie was a big lady, super friendly and very talkative. I briefly told her my story and she told me hers before moving quickly onto her brother who was the current world champion pistol shooter. She was very proud of him and told me how he travelled all over the world with his sport.

'Do you travel much yourself?' I asked.

She took a gulp of her McDonald's cola and said, 'No I don't travel. I have adrenal fatigue, so I get sick a lot.' I looked around the car, noticing the fast food wrappers filling up the back seat. I'd worked in the fitness industry most of my life after leaving the military, and had conversations like this countless times. In my experience there was never a receptive ear when I started talking about habits, behaviour, nutrition and lifestyle being the major contributors to illness. I left the topic alone, paid a sympathetic ear to her ailments and told stories about my adventures. We pulled up at the local bakery in Strathmerton.

'They have the best cake you've ever eaten!' Kylie announced enthusiastically. I thanked her for the ride and made my way to the roadside.

It was early afternoon by the time I set up again and changed my sign to 'Corowa.' The sun was scorching so I found a shady place to wait and stuck out my thumb. Twenty-four minutes later a big four-wheel drive pulled up.

'We can get you very close to Corowa, if that's good enough,' said the smiling lady in the front passenger seat with a British accent.

'Absolutely, thanks so much,' I said and jumped in.

This was Katie from England. Her Australian husband, Lance, sat in the driver's seat and their twelve-year-old son, Johnathan, shared the back with me. They were a lovely family and were out for the day looking at caravans to buy. They asked me what I was up to and I gave them my spiel about the book tour and travels.

They dropped me on the New South Wales border just east of Yarrawonga, near Bundalong. I wasn't far from Corowa and while I was reshuffling my bags, I received a call from my cousin Mathew. When I told him where I was, he said, 'Wait there I'll come get you, I'm just down the road.' This was a relief to hear, as it had been a long hot day and I was ready for a break. I noticed a pub across the street and thought an ice-cold drink and air conditioning would be ideal. As I was about to cross the street, Lance and Katie pulled up.

'We forgot to buy your book,' they said with beaming smiles. 'Can we have two copies?'

I signed the copies for them and off they drove again, waving out the window.

The air-conditioning in the pub was glorious, as was the massive jug of ice water placed on the bar. I stood in front of it and drank cup after cup as the barman watched on. I then bought a ginger beer and found a table with the locals to relax. The hardened tradesmen drinking their beers eyed me suspiciously until I said, 'Bloody hot one out there today.'

They nodded in agreement and asked me, 'Where you off to then?'

I delivered my well-rehearsed book tour and adventure life pitch. They seemed to relax and we chatted about fishing and a working man's life. My cousin arrived to collect me so I bade farewell to my fellow working men and was driven to my final destination of the day, Corowa. I had hitched 305 kilometres in a day and decided I could rest for Sunday with my family before aiming for Wagga Wagga.

◆◆◆

On Monday morning I went to the gym in Corowa with my cousin's wife, Megan, who was a personal trainer. While I was working out in the weights room, I met a guy named Dean who owned the local chocolate and whisky factory. I told him about my tour and the next destination.

'My mum is driving down from Junee and back today. She goes through Wagga Wagga and could easily give you a lift,' he said.

'That would be awesome if she could. Thanks, mate.'

'No worries. Come by the factory in an hour to meet her,' he said.

After finishing my training, I carried my bags to the Corowa Whisky and Chocolate factory. The place was huge, and Dean gave me a tour of the new whisky section before I settled into his café for coffee and breakfast. He said the place was basically given to him derelict and he'd spent A$600,000 to make it into what it was today. His mum, Coral, arrived delivering supplies. She must have been in her late fifties but had the energy of a twenty year old, bouncing around smiling and talking to the staff. She had short grey hair and a lean physique, and joined us for coffee. Coral couldn't be tamed for long. As soon as she'd emptied her cup she sprang up and said, 'Okay Luke, let's get going. I want to hear your story in the car.'

VODKA & SANDSTORMS

The conversation started as she turned the key in the ignition. Coral was a really interesting person and had lived a very diverse life. She owned the Junee Chocolate Factory with her husband Neil, whom she had travelled the world with on humanitarian missions. We swapped stories for almost two hours and the time simply vanished. We pulled up in Wagga Wagga's main street and before we parted, Coral said she wanted six copies of my book for her family and staff. She was a true Aussie legend.

'I'll come visit the factory when I hitch through,' I told her before we parted.

'You better,' she said with a smile then drove away.

I'd been invited to visit Crossfit Victus, a local strength and conditioning gym operated by two guys: Mark and Brett. The gym wasn't far away, so I towed my roller bag behind me and set off. The day was another scorcher and by the time I arrived I was soaked in sweat. As I walked in, Mark yelled out, 'You must be Luke, welcome.'

'Thanks, it's great to be here,' I replied.

I was given water, protein bars and a T-shirt. Their hospitality was amazing and even though they had no time in their class schedule to let me talk, I was asked to stay and chat to the members between classes. I trained with them and hung out sharing stories with their members for the afternoon and evening. In the process, I sold all my books and needed another resupply. I was hoping to sleep inside their gym, on my hammock, but in a final act of generosity the guys booked me into a hotel for the night and they wouldn't take no for an answer. I was blown away by the kindness and professionalism of these CrossFit legends, and I cannot thank them enough.

I woke up fresh and ready to go. I wanted to cover the 305 kilometres to the town of Orange by nightfall where I had a friend who I could stay with, but first I had one media appointment and a bookshop to visit. I had an interview with Wagga Wagga TV, an online news-streaming program that had grown exponentially over the years. The show was hosted by Adam Drummond and Jimmy Smithson, and they'd arranged to meet me in the memorial park at 8am.

We had a three-part conversation over 45 minutes for their online viewers. We spoke about my early years in the military, completing my basic training at the Kapooka army base just outside of town. They dug deep into my drug addiction years and into my life of adventure after hitting rock bottom. Jimmy was a character and he offered to drive me down the road to Junee after our talk.

He dropped me at the Junee Licorice & Chocolate factory and I walked in and asked if Coral was around. She came out smiling and embraced me like one of her sons, then gave me a tour of their factory and home. The place was amazing, bustling with tourists and the factory section was enclosed behind glass walls so customers could watch the chocolates being made. I was allowed inside, given a hairnet and shown how to make rocky road and giant freckles, which I could take on the road with me for later. Coral also loaded me up with all sorts of chocolate treats from their store. As she was giving me the tour, she tried to secure me a lift at the same time by asking every customer and staff member if they were heading to Orange. With no luck, Coral dropped me off at the highway with a bag full of chocolates and a hug. She was such a generous and caring person and one of my favourite people I have met on the road.

I caught a lift to Cootamundra with a lovely middle-aged lady named Annette. She worked for Toyota, was a vegetarian, loved pasta and was considering a move to Papua with her husband for work.

'Do it, it will be a great adventure for you,' I advised.

From 'Coota', as the locals call it, I hopped a ride with an elderly couple, Shell and Mary, to the town of Young. They loved travelling and went on organised tours every year. They were very conservative, complained about the speed of the other drivers and I wouldn't have picked them for people who offered rides to strangers. Shell couldn't talk much as he'd recently had a mouth operation, but Mary made up for it, giving me some advice about keeping safe, before they dropped me off at the train station in Young. I walked to the other side of town and now had 161 kilometres to go to reach Orange.

I waited four minutes before an old four-wheel drive stopped. Out jumped a guy in a big cowboy hat, blue long-sleeved shirt, jeans and glasses, who introduced himself as Graham. He looked to be in his late fifties and had a truck loaded with canola seed and dog food for his farm. He was the 'True Blue' Australian farmer, and even though his truck was fully loaded, he grabbed some rope and tied my bag to the top of the seed pile.

'Climb aboard, mate,' he said, and we were off.

It was a hot day and he turned the air conditioning on full blast for me, before asking for my story. After telling him mine, he told me his. He had farmed his whole life and was a one-man band most of the year, only hiring help for mustering or shearing once a season. He had 5000 sheep, and produced lamb and wool. When I asked him how business was doing, he replied, 'I'm surviving, mate.' I enquired about the meat industry and whether he gave cheap deals to locals for meat. His reply shocked me.

'I used to sell to locals at a cheap price and made a better profit than selling to the big companies. But then the government changed the laws to make it illegal to do that, we could only sell to the big blokes at their set price. I kept selling to friends but then the government sent out investigators pretending to be locals. If you were fooled and sold to them, they would charge you and it was big fines. We can't do it anymore, we have to toe the line of the corporations.'

I shook Graham's hand as he dropped me at the turn-off to his farm. 'You're a top bloke, mate,' I told him. 'Keep doing what you love.'

It was the middle of the afternoon and the heat was belting down. I still had a fair distance to travel before nightfall and the spot I was in wasn't the best. But luck was on my side. A work truck pulled up with two guys inside wearing orange high-visibility shirts. This was Matt and Emar. They were heading back to Cowra after a full day of trimming trees next to powerlines. They told me about their jobs, which sounded like tough work at times but it paid extremely well. The biggest downside according to Matt was, 'Being away from home for three weeks at a time, but it will be worth it in the long run.' Remembering my shift work in the coal mines and spending twelve hours per day underground, I knew what he was going through. The money was great, of course, but long term it could be very tough on family and relationships. Emar, on the other hand, was single, travelled the world on his weeks off and raved about Ecuador. 'It's the best place in the world, bro. I love it there.'

They dropped me off with 70 kilometres to go to Orange and two hours till sunset. A car drove past, slowed down and circled around to pick me up. It was an old car in a poor state of repair, containing three smiling youngsters.

'We felt sorry for you so came back. Get in,' said a female up front, who introduced herself as Sarah.

They were only heading 25 kilometres down the road to Canowindra, but I was happy for the ride.

Sarah gestured towards the back seat. 'That's my son and his girlfriend. He busted his shoulder, so we're coming back from the doctor's.'

They were a lovely bunch and obviously didn't have much money, but were kind enough to help me out. Sarah explained that she worked at a small local dairy and loved what she did. She gave me a run-down on the milk industry during our short ride together and as they dropped me off, I asked them a question that could have only one answer: 'Do you guys like chocolate?'

'Hell yeah,' said the girlfriend, speaking for the first time.

I handed over some of the chocolate Coral had given me, which was rapidly melting in my bag and needed a new home.

I was on the edge of town and it was close to dark, and I'd started to think about where I would camp for the night when a big delivery truck rolled up with a Maori couple inside. A lady wearing glasses and a big smile leaned out the window and said, 'We're going to Orange, get in.'

They had very little room in the cab but were happy to cram my bags into their sleeping quarters behind the seats and squeeze me into the middle. Ray welcomed me aboard with a strong handshake, Tanya was his wife and passenger. They were both smiling as I told them my story and Tanya replied, 'We love travelling as well, we move every two years with work.' Ray chimed in, 'Always close to the sea, though. We have to be able to fish and be near the ocean, it's in our blood.'

Ray had a very important job in Australian culture – he was the beer delivery driver. He serviced all the small towns in the area and loved being on the road and having freedom. 'We always stop for people, some just need a little help to get where they're going,' he told me. They were genuine, lovely people, and we bounced along and rolled into Orange together. They gave me their phone number as they dropped me off and said, 'If you need any help, you just call us.'

I had travelled over 300 kilometres that day, met a bunch of characters along the way and I was seeing Australian culture up close. I gave my friend a call and she drove over to pick me up. Sonya was Italian and grew up in North Queensland. She had two older brothers who I had played rugby league with during our high school years. She had a fiancé named Jared, who I met after we arrived at their house. Jared was working in the mining sector but had recently been made redundant. He seemed like a great guy and after Sonya went to bed he told me his story from the last few years.

'I was in jail a year ago, bro. Eight months for drug trafficking,' he told me with blunt honesty. He used to be in the military, and while he was enlisted he sold party pills on the side to make money. His small business got bigger and evolved into a small ring of dealers, servicing the bustling nightlife of Sydney. Eventually one of the dealers was caught and unlike what you might believe after watching *The Godfather*, 'There was no loyalty, everyone rolled,' he said. They were all discharged from the military yet escaped any serious charges through lack of evidence. He changed his life, matured and moved on to start again in North Queensland. Years later a friend contacted him out of the blue and asked for his help with a deal. He said he wanted nothing to do with it but passed on a phone number of a friend who was still prevalent in the underworld. His friends were busted, and he was hauled down with them.

'I had to plead guilty,' he told me, shaking his head. 'In Queensland, if you fight it, they throw the book at you and you'll get years. I pleaded guilty and got eight months.' He went to Townsville Correctional Centre to serve his time. He was an intelligent guy and told me he stayed out of all the violence, gang drama and drugs while inside.

'It was wild, mate. Lots of bikies, blackfellas and not many white guys. I gave everyone respect and was left alone,' he said before adding with a laugh, 'The biggest, toughest bikies were all gay, bro. They loved the queenies. I'd watch them sneak away to shag guys all the time. Totally different to how they behave on the outside.

'I kept to myself, read books and took advantage of the free education. I did back-to-back courses and got an engineering certificate. When I was released, I was able to get a job in mining straight away.'

He'd paid his dues and started his life anew. He met Sonya, and according to him, 'I will never go back.'

◆◆◆

The next morning was cold and rainy. I had no books left to sell and the publishers told me the warehouse was out of stock and they needed to do another print run. I planned to head back to Sydney and rest for a day before reloading from my own supply of books and heading north into Queensland. Jared offered to drive me 100 kilometres east to Lithgow, where I could catch a short and direct train into Sydney. Looking at the cold rain falling, I gladly accepted. I visited two bookshops in town who were stocking my book before we hit the road. The conversation picked up from the night before and the drive flew by as we discussed adventures, politics and life.

When the train pulled away from Lithgow station I relaxed into the comfy seats. It felt great not to be hitching for a few hours. The rain fell on the Blue Mountains and the national parks bordering Sydney's west, and as they rolled passed I thought over the previous two weeks. The first half of the book tour was completed. I'd hitched over 2000 kilometres so far, with the Queensland leg up to Brisbane still to come.

I spent two days in town stocking up on books, visiting sponsors who were coming on board for the next expedition and planning my journey. Then out of the blue I received a call from my mother-in-law, Pam.

'I haven't seen you in forever,' she told me. 'Let me give you your first ride north.' I accepted and at 6am the following morning we were driving up the Pacific Motorway. Caves Beach was my first stop, a small coastal community with two gyms, the owners of which had both invited me to drop by. Pam delivered me to the front door of CrossFit Caves Beach and in I walked with a spring in my step, dragging a newly loaded bag of books.

CrossFit gyms or 'boxes', as they're known, were similar the world over. The gyms are a basic set-up and always welcoming. They attract a certain type of person and create a tight-knit community of people striving to be the fittest they can be. I was welcomed by James, who was one of the owners. He was a young guy, clean cut and polite. He was also a missionary and was running programs supporting orphanages in India and the developing world. I met some of the members and hung around telling stories and selling books throughout the afternoon classes.

At 6.30pm I said farewell and was picked up by Tracy from CrossFit Motive, who took me over to her box where I repeated the routine for their night classes. Tracy and her husband Scotty operated the gym, as well as raising their three kids and working separate jobs. They both loved fitness and had built a solid client base that, according to Tracy, were just like family. We sat around eating pizza after the classes and shared stories late into the night. I once again avoided camping and was invited to stay in a spare room at their home.

In the morning I wasn't allowed to continue my journey until I'd joined the CrossFit Motive team in an obstacle course race called the Raw Challenge. I'd completed some challenging obstacle courses during my time in the army, and I wasn't worried about the physical aspect of this one. What blew me away, however, were the thousands of civilian participants who voluntarily put themselves through the pain of completing the course. There were people everywhere, with wave after wave being set loose on the enormous course every few minutes.

I lined up with 20 members of the CrossFit Motive team and was set free with a horn blast. The course contained dozens of structures to negotiate, countless mud pits and dams to wade through, monkey bars of varying designs to climb, ice baths to swim, tyres to drag and kilometres of running to do in-between. Getting everyone to the end was a team effort but we all made it. We crossed the finish line almost two hours after we'd started. The event gave me flashbacks of the military days, but it was much more fun with Tracy and her fitness family.

That night we all gathered at the local bar for dinner where Tracey had organised a private room. While the team enjoyed a well-earned beer, I delivered my 45-minute talk about adventure and lessons learned. Whether it was alcohol lubricating the process or because we had shared physical hardship together, the questions at the end of my talk carried on for a further half an hour. After the talk concluded, a lovely lady named Jillian asked me a question she'd been too afraid to ask earlier. 'Are you searching for the thing that kills you?' I was stumped. During my talk while recalling several near-death experiences I said, 'I don't know what I'm searching for in this adventure life…' I wasn't sure what to say to Jillian. I thanked her for asking the question and said I would think about it and come back with an answer very soon.

The following morning, I had to say goodbye. I was booked to give a talk in Woolgoolga at another CrossFit gym at 6pm. It was 430 kilometres of highways to get there and because I had used up a day with the Motive team, I made the call to catch a train. I didn't want to cancel a talk if I failed to hitch the distance, so for the second time on the tour I settled into a comfy seat and was bounced along by a slow-moving Australian locomotive. Talking and telling stories for days on end was tiring, and to have a few hours of silence to myself was exactly what I needed to charge up again.

I arrived late afternoon and was picked up at the station by Lisa. She was in her late fifties, in great shape and was a dedicated member of the gym. I was taken to Crossfit Woolgoolga, a great box with a tight-knit bunch of members who all hung around after the evening class to hear me talk. I sold a bunch of books and even squeezed in a cheeky training session afterwards. Lisa took me for a pub feed and gave me her spare bedroom for the night.

◆◆◆

I was up early on Day 22 of the tour and primed to get back on the highway. I had to hitch inland away from the coast to a small country town called Glenn Innes. I'd been invited to talk at the high school assembly at 2pm and I had five hours to get 217 kilometres. I was confident I could make it in time.

Lisa gave me my first lift on her way to work, dropping me 54 kilometres down the road in Grafton. I set up on the other side of town close to a big intersection where cars moved slower. I held up my sign to Glenn Innes and stuck out my thumb. I waited 40 minutes and was getting nervous I wasn't going to get a lift when a car drove past, slowed down and then circled back to pull up beside me.

The window rolled down and a smiling couple in their forties said together, 'Jump in.' I didn't hesitate. 'Thanks so much,' I replied, as I piled my bags and myself in the back. They introduced themselves as April and Andrew and said, 'We're going through Glenn Innes on our way home to Victoria. What brings you out this way?' I told them my story and about the high school talk in a few hours. 'We will get you there for it,' said Andrew as I felt the car accelerate.

Once underway I asked them, 'What about you two? What's the story?' April told me about their love of travel and how they had downsized their work lives to accommodate it. Then, after remembering my army connection, she said, 'Our house in Beach Grove was built by a German prisoner of war, you know.' I was intrigued so she continued. 'A German battleship had sunk one of our ships and then been sunk herself. One of the German sailors survived in the sea for days and was rescued by the Australians. He was put into a prisoner-of-war camp outside our town and he fell in love with the country. He was shipped back to Germany but after the war he returned and built a house in 1968. He became an outstanding member of the community and lived the rest of his life in Australia. We now own that house.'

They dropped me in Glenn Innes with two hours to spare before the talk. April wanted a signed copy of my book, which I gladly provided before saying farewell. I found some lunch and coffee then made my way to Glenn Innes High School, where I met Joanne, a librarian and teacher. She gave me a tour of the school before the assembly. I sat on the stage inside a big hall, watching 200 kids from grades 10, 11 and 12 file in. I was introduced to three students who were going to be my photographers, and Joanne gave me a lovely introduction.

As the kids clapped a welcome to her prompting, I had a flashback to my own high school days. I remembered sitting exactly how they were sitting and listening to a speaker named John Coutis. He gave an incredible talk that had a big impact on me as a teenager. The power one talk can have on a kid's future cannot be overstated, and it felt like I'd come full circle standing on stage to deliver my story.

The students sat and listened for 45 minutes while I told them my life's journey. I didn't hold back about the years of drug addiction and didn't shy away from deaths in the mountains. In the world they lived in, they needed real-life lessons, not sugar-coated versions of society. Question time followed, and the kids didn't hold back on what they asked about. 'How did you go to the toilet on the boat?' was the first question. Joanne eventually called an end to assembly and thanked me while the kids clapped. I stayed for photos and afterwards, when the last student had departed Joanne said to me, 'I haven't seen the kids quiet for an hour like that before, well done.'

I walked out of the school on a high. Being able to share my story and see the effect it had was truly rewarding. I was invited through social media to stay with a young couple, Mark and Felicity, who also wanted me to deliver a talk at their local gym. I agreed, of course, never being one to pass on a free bed and a hot meal.

Four hours later I was on stage again but this time talking to a group of adults in the back of a gym. They were just as receptive as the kids and I sold a bunch of books. Mark cooked a fantastic barbecue afterwards and I slept like a baby.

The next day I needed to turn back towards the coast and head north to my final destination, Brisbane. I travelled with Mark on his way to work and he dropped me on the outskirts of town. It was 7am when I held up my sign for Grafton and stuck out my thumb. The first hour went by with nobody stopping and it was the longest I'd waited on my entire tour. During the second hour the only person who came near me was a dishevelled guy offering to smoke drugs with me. I declined. During the third hour of waiting I just couldn't figure out what the problem was. It was a good spot, I was following all of my rules, but I was having no luck.

An older guy came out the front door of his house and walked over to me.

'You won't get a lift, mate,' he said.

'Really, why is that?' I asked.

'Oh, mainly because there's a prison 40 kilometres outside of town and sometimes they let the prisoners out for the day,' he told me. 'I'm sorry to say it, but you look like a prisoner. Maybe take your beanie off.'

'Thanks for the info,' I said.

As he went back inside I took my beanie off. With honest reflection I did fit the stereotype of a prisoner waiting for a lift back to jail. I'd been waiting for three hours and decided to call Mark.

After laughing at my situation, he said, 'I'll be there in five minutes. Just need to tell the boss I'm off for a couple of hours.'

He turned up in his truck and drove me the 150 kilometres back to the coastal highway near Grafton. Without his help I would still be standing there looking like a smiling criminal.

I was starving after the morning's travels and found a Subway restaurant. After downing two footlongs, I walked to the road and set up. Much to my relief, a car pulled over after just five minutes. Inside were a smiling elderly couple, Phil and Ally, a couple of retirees who lived in Maclean, 54 kilometres away, and were happy to take me there. Both had matching heads of silver hair, wore glasses and seemed delighted with retirement on the coast.

As I waved off Ally and Phil, another car pulled over 100 metres in front of me. A tall skinny guy with long hair got out of his car and waved. I had that awkward second of hesitation before diverting my wave from the departing car toward this new guy. He gestured for me to come over.

'Where you headed, bro?' he asked as we shook hands.

'Byron Bay, mate,' I replied.

'Jump in. I'm driving to the Blues and Roots festival near Byron.'

Just 30 seconds of waiting, the shortest wait of the tour, and I was off again. My new driver was Josh, who was in his midforties, wore a floral shirt and was a throwback to the seventies. He was a lovely guy and we dissected the state of the world, politics and life in general. It was early afternoon and the sun was shining when he dropped me off at the turn-off to Byron Bay. There was only three kilometres to go to one of Australia's most famous beaches, so I decided to walk and enjoy the remainder of the day.

The traffic heading into Byron was thick and the festival atmosphere infectious. Cars full of young people were arriving to enjoy the weekend and listen to their favourite blues bands. I'd travelled 320 kilometres and on my arrival into Byron I stepped onto the pristine sandy beach. The water was too inviting, so I stripped down to shorts and jogged into the surf. While drying on the beach afterwards, I messaged Alex, an old army buddy, who lived close by. He called me straight back.

'I have a bed for you, bro,' he said.

It was the end to another great day on the road.

◆◆◆

I woke the following day to a Facebook message from Bec, the lady who'd given me a ride in my first week and worked at a book distribution warehouse. The message read, 'I have been packing your book to send out every day this week, looks like your tour is going well.' It was nice to hear the book was selling. Before moving on from Byron I had a podcast interview to do with a local named Guy Lawrence.

I turned up at his house at 8am and knocked on the door. Guy answered dressed in a towel and said, 'Luke, great to meet you, mate. You're just in time for an ice bath.' I looked up at the overcast sky and noted the chill in the air before replying, 'Absolutely, why not.'

Guy led me to the side of his house where two men were waiting in their swim shorts. They were both staring at a large deep-freezer that had been filled with ice and water. The younger guy climbed in and submerged himself up to his neck. Guy held the stopwatch and didn't let him out for four minutes. They were taking it fairly seriously and began telling me about an ice bath course they'd recently taken with Wim Hof, aka The Iceman. I'd heard about Wim's exploits in mountaineering. Wearing only shorts and shoes, he'd climbed 7000 metres up Everest. He was an extreme character. In my opinion, the jury is still out as to whether there are any scientific benefits of ice baths for the human body, but I do use them to help recover after big training sessions, bouncing between ice and sauna to get the blood flowing. Placebo effect could play a big role in this as well.

When it was my turn I stripped down and climbed in. The bath was so cold it felt like fire on my skin, and when I dropped down up to my neck I could barely breath.

'Two minutes for your first time,' said Guy.

'Sounds good to me,' I replied in a whisper.

I zoned out to control my breathing and just as I was sure the bath was getting warmer, Guy called out, 'Time's up.' I climbed out glowing red and shivering, and wrapped myself in a towel as Guy climbed in for his turn.

Once we were all done, Guy and I grabbed a cup of tea and shut ourselves off in a quiet room for the podcast. He was a great interviewer and the conversation flowed for over an hour. Guy has a big following online and I thanked him for the chat, the ice bath and for helping me promote the tour.

I visited two bookshops in Byron before Alex offered to drive me to the Gold Coast, where I would be taking a rest day with another great friend of mine. The Gold Coast is one of Australia's most famous locations. With its pristine beaches and bustling nightlife, it's a top holiday destination for tourists. Alex dropped me at a big house in the hinterland, where my mentor and great friend Ken Ware lived with his wife Nickie.

Ken's incredible place had a state-of-the-art gym facility downstairs, better than any commercial gym I'd ever been to. I first met Ken during my mining days and he has been a pillar of guidance during my expeditions ever since. He is the founder of NeuroPhysics Therapy, which is a program designed to trigger the human system to resolve many of its issues without the use of drugs, surgery or manipulation. Ken is a former Mr Universe and current Australian powerlifting record holder who has gone on to lecture at some of the biggest non-linier science conferences in the world, where his results and findings still stun the scientific community. His programs have helped thousands of people remedy a wide variety of disorders, from easing pain and restoring movement to getting spinal patients out of wheelchairs and walking again. Out in the ocean during my row across the Atlantic, when my hands went numb from pulling on the oars, I would use NeuroPhysics Tremor Therapy to dissipate the numbness and adapt to my environment. It's truly amazing stuff.

I spent a great day on the Gold Coast catching up with Ken and getting in some training. On Day 26 I needed to get myself to Brisbane. I had a talk to give for a small book club that evening and dozens of bookshops to visit. Another friend, Phil, who owned a finance company on the coast and had been following my tour, offered me a ride. I felt almost lazy after not hitching for a few days, but I gladly accepted. Book Worms book club was my last talk of the tour.

A small crowd of book enthusiasts turned up with my books already in their hands to hear some of the stories from the horse's mouth. I had given the talk so many times by this stage that it had become second nature. Jordy, an old army buddy, turned up and sat in the crowd as well. We had served overseas together and at the end of the talk we embraced like brothers. He said to me, 'I'll be your driver while you're here, bro.'

I spent three days with Jordy bouncing around the beautiful city of Brisbane. From store to store I signed as many copies as I could and entertained the store managers in the hope of repeat business. I had a meeting with a start-up company called Before You Speak Coffee, who were looking for some exposure and thought I would be a good fit. I left the meeting with a pledge of a new sponsored kayak for an upcoming expedition and a box full of their instant coffee. I walked out of the last bookshop and my tour was officially over. It was Day 30 and I turned to Jordy and said, 'Take me to the airport brother, it's time to go home.'

◆◆◆

I sat in the departure lounge ready to fly back to Sydney. I'd travelled over 3000 kilometres around the country on the good will of the Australian public. What started as a marketing gimmick had turned into a smashing success. My book was into its second print run, I had developed a talk and delivered it a dozen times to small groups, corporate lunches and an assembly full of kids. The practice in public speaking had made me confident to pursue it as part of my career moving forward. I had listened to amazing stories from 'true blue' Aussies and learned some valuable lessons about the crafty art of hitchhiking. The top four lessons I took away from the tour were:

1. The real world is not what you see on the evening news. Ninety-nine per cent of people are honest, genuine and caring and are all just trying to get through life as best they can.

2. If you suffer from low self-esteem then hitchhiking around the country is your cure. The first time your thumb goes out and people drive by without a second glance you will feel shunned and hurt, but after a few days on the road it will cease to bother you. You will handle the rejection with ease and your esteem will be forever robust.

3. When you give something away for free it will come back to you in other ways tenfold. I gave all my talks for free and in return I was overwhelmed with offers of accommodation, food and support.

4. Remember the hitchhiking rules. Make a sign, spell the name of the town correctly, pick a spot that has a pull-over area so cars can stop safely, wear deodorant and smile when you put out your thumb.

I sat in the bustling airport reflecting on the previous month, it had been an incredible journey. The question Jillian had asked me had been rolling around in my mind for days. 'Are you searching for the thing that kills you?' I didn't have an answer for her at the time, but as I pondered it some more, I came to one. I opened my email and started writing my reply:

Jillian,

I'm not searching for death. Everything I do is about life, and getting the most out of my life. I'm searching for the experience that pushes me so close to death that I live a thousand lifetimes in a moment.

Thank you for the question,
Luke.

Chapter 12

The Murray River

His people had walked the red landscape of the Australian bush for 40,000 years. He had learned how to hunt, forage, track and survive in the tough environment from his father and grandfather. His feet were flesh against the hot earth, hardened from years of running barefoot as a child, and he was now immune to the heat and thorns. His only clothing was a kangaroo skin. His tall powerful frame was exposed to the harsh sun of the outback and his black skin glistened with sweat when he hunted. With spear in hand he was a formidable warrior and throughout the land everyone knew his name: Ngurunderi, the spirit man.

He had a camp with his two wives on the bank of the Murray River, which at the time was a small stream. One day he noticed a huge cod swimming in the shallows and he chased it in his bark canoe. As the fish tried to escape, it whipped its tail from side to side, tearing through the land, widening the river and reshaping the banks to its present size. He pursued the cod as far as Lake Alexandrina and had almost given up when he remembered his brother-in-law, Nepele, lived by the lake. He signalled him, and Nepele was able to spear the great fish.

Together the two men cut up the cod and threw the pieces into the water, creating multiple species of fish that now inhabit it, naming them as they did so. During the hunt, Ngurunderi's two wives had deserted him and he had to search for them overland. With no more use for his bark canoe, but not wanting to part with his prized possession, he noticed areas of the night sky void of stars. He lifted his canoe high over his head and placed it into the sky, forming the Milky Way. In the language of the Jaralde tribe, the word for canoe was juki, so they named the Milky Way Ngurunderi Juki.

◆◆◆

This story is one of many that are called the Dreamtime creation stories from Australia's Aboriginal people. I came across it while researching Australia's longest river for our next expedition. This simple tale gave character and heritage to a waterway I knew very little about. The Murray had not been on my radar before I asked Dad the same thought-provoking question I asked myself at the end of the Tasman row: 'If you only had five years to live, what would you do between now and then?' He answered, 'I want to go down the entire Murray River in a fishing boat.'

The river has a 2220-kilometre stretch that is navigable all year round and when Elise and I realised this, we told Dad, 'We will kayak it and you can be our support boat.' Since the Ganges paddle didn't eventuate we had both never kayaked before, and this was how the adventure was born.

I hadn't completed any big expeditions at home in the past, and I quickly realised how easy this trip was going to be to pull together. Security risks were zero, no one was going to roll up and kill us in Australia, which was a concern in other countries. Food was plentiful along the banks, every three or four days there was a country town equipped with grocery stores, banks and petrol stations. Unlike many rivers around the world, which are so polluted they can kill you or deliver a few uncomfortable days on the toilet at the least, the quality of the water in the Murray meant that if we needed to, we could drink straight from it.

We'd moved to Port Arthur in Tasmania around the same time we decided to kayak the Murray. We invited my parents to come down and live with us, and our little shack in the bush became the base of operations for the expedition. We gave ourselves three months to prepare and train for the trip, which wasn't a lot of time but as it was on home soil, logistically it was going to be a breeze. We needed two main components to get the ball rolling: a small fishing tinny for Dad and kayaks for Elise and me. Most modern-day adventures or crazy ideas begin with a search online, and this one was no different.

Dad found a boat that could be suitable on Gumtree and drove off to meet the guy. I couldn't find any suitable second-hand kayaks and settled on a new supplier north of Sydney that could ship them down to us in a week. I was fortunate at this time because a new sponsor had just come on board. Billabong Jerky had been in Australia for longer than I'd been alive. They were reshaping their marketing plan and looking for different ways to raise brand awareness. They offered to chip in with our kayaks and supply us with all the jerky we could eat for the trip. It was a perfect match. Protein was always one of the harder nutrients to guarantee on expeditions, so jerky would help fill that void nicely. I placed the order for two sea kayaks, skirts, paddles and life jackets. I received a message from Dad: 'I just bought a boat, be home soon.' The expedition was off to a flying start.

The 3.65-metre aluminium fishing boat Dad had purchased had a windshield and canopy for the rainy days we were sure to experience, and a reliable 15 horsepower Evinrude engine. He'd been a motor mechanic for 46 years, starting his apprenticeship when he was fifteen, so there weren't many things he couldn't fix. According to him, the simple outboard engine would be perfect. Dad set himself to task, stripping the boat bare and putting it back together, checking every little component and making improvements along the way.

Our kayaks arrived from Sydney and their bright yellow colour and 15-foot length were hard to miss at our local post office. A quick negotiation with the delivery truck driver and they were taken directly to our door. It was time for our maiden voyage.

Elise and I loaded up the kayaks and drove five minutes down the road to our local boat ramp. Neither of us had any experience but we'd watched a YouTube video about paddle technique the day before and felt confident. The ramp had a pontoon extending out into the water, so we carried the boats out to the end and placed them in. Elise had been a dancer in her younger years, a CrossFit athlete in her recent years, and had incredibly good balance. I played rugby, could walk uphill carrying heavy things and struggled to stand on one leg.

As we slid into our respective kayaks, it played out exactly as I thought it would. Elise looked calm and composed, while I wobbled all over the place, trying to counteract the imbalance with brute force. Once settled from the initial moment of feeling like a wombat on a tightrope, we were away. We paddled out into Long Bay and over to neighbouring Stinking Bay, named after the stench of the huge amounts of seaweed that build up on its beach. It was one of my favourite spearfishing areas. Abalone, crayfish and an abundance of fish were available to anyone willing to brave the freezing water and indifferent ocean conditions.

The backdrop of Tasmania's beautiful bush and rocky coastline was a picturesque training environment. We paddled with seals, were surrounded by birdlife and could paddle near the old convict prison inside the Port Arthur Historical Site whenever we wished. The old settlement is the final resting place of a thousand prisoners, soldiers and settlers during its life from the 1830s to 1870s. The penal colony harvested the surrounding timber and built ships for colonial expansion in Tasmania and mainland Australia.

Listed as a UNESCO World Heritage location, this is also where one of Australia's darkest days took place some 125 years after its closure as a prison. On 28 April 1996, a local outcast named Martin Bryant parked his van in the car park with dozens of tourists and families visiting for the day. He proceeded to walk into the site and gunned down everyone within range in cold blood. He killed 35 people and wounded 23 others, including women and children, before surrendering to the police the following day.

This shocking act of violence brought the nation together in agreement to ban all automatic and self-loading weapons. The government launched an immediate buy-back scheme and the population handed in thousands of guns to be destroyed. Since that terrible day we haven't had another massacre of this scale.

During our first voyage, the swell varied from flat calm to breaking waves washing over our skirts. The skirt is a thick neoprene layer that fits tight around our waists and seals over the edge of the kayak. This keeps the water out of the kayak and creates a pocket of warm air inside that would be a big benefit during the cooler winter months on the Murray. We paddled for six kilometres out and back, long enough to set my shoulders and spine on fire and give me a humble appreciation of the ocean yet again. I disembarked in the same manner as I had entered my kayak, laughing at myself and telling Elise, as I rolled across the pontoon, 'I think I'm ready.'

The following weeks were a whirlwind of preparation and training. Dad made many small repairs and alterations to his boat and we had decided on the eloquent name of *River Rat* for the vessel. Elise painted the name on the front and, if you knew my dad, it was the perfect match. Dad grew up wild and free in the outback, similar to the unique upbringing my sister and I experienced. He raced motocross, bow hunted feral pigs, was a keen fisherman and often preferred the company of the desert country over people. He worked remotely on some of Australia's biggest cattle stations and could fix anything, given the time. He cared about music, poetry and mateship but didn't put one moment of thought into clothing or his appearance. By the end of our trip he would whole-heartedly embody the river rat title.

We had four training paddles around the peninsula and I'd taken a fondness to fishing from my kayak. With a handline, some bait and putting myself over the correct rocky structures, I could have a dinner of wrasse or flathead in minutes. I appreciated the simpleness of sourcing food without an engine, fuel or cost. We could have done countless hours of training to be ready for the trip but we decided if we didn't know how to paddle by the end of 2200 kilometres there was something wrong with us. I take this approach on expeditions when death was not an immediate reality for getting it wrong.

We booked night passage on the *Spirit of Tasmania* ferry leaving from the northern town of Devonport the following week. The ferry could accommodate cars, trailers and massive trucks so it was perfect for our planned adventure. Mum was staying behind to brave the coming winter and operate our market stall on Saturdays. A short drive north from Port Arthur is the capital city of Hobart, where I operate a stall at Salamanca Markets every week. It's one of the most unique and busiest markets in Australia, and I sell my books there to avoid getting a full-time job. I love meeting people from all over the world, telling my stories and selling enough books to buy the week's groceries on my way home. Mum would take over the story telling and selling role while the three of us went off adventuring.

The day of departure arrived. We had the two kayaks mounted on the car's roof, the *River Rat* sitting on the trailer, and were loaded with all the camping gear we would need for the next six weeks. We had completed four training days with the kayaks for a grand total of 35 kilometres paddled. The average we would need to paddle once we hit the river would be close to 50 kilometres per day. We probably should have done more training, but we were fit and planning to take it slow and let the body adapt to the workload. Unlike ocean rowing, on this trip we could pull up on the bank and camp at any time during the day if we needed a rest.

After a four-hour drive to Devonport through the Tasmanian countryside, we loaded onto the ferry for a night crossing to Melbourne. It was a nine-hour voyage across the Bass Strait, and to save money we didn't book a cabin, deciding instead on a recliner lounge. This was a mistake. The lounge area was freezing and full of other travellers keen to save a few dollars and tough out a night's sleep. The recliner didn't live up to its name. After yanking on a handle it tipped backwards about two degrees and I knew there was no way I could sleep bolt upright. Elise seemed to fall asleep okay as I moved to the floor and fell asleep instantly. I was woken minutes later by a stern-looking man in a white uniform. He told me sleeping on the floor wasn't allowed and I had to return to the right-angled torture device.

I thanked him for his hospitality with a nod of my head and climbed back into the chair, resuming my original position, while he waited nearby, making sure I complied. I tried again to sleep in the recliner but a fellow traveller began having difficulties breathing and emitted banshee-like growls from her nasal cavity. This was the breaking point for me. I gathered up my blanket and pillow, vacated the freezer and wandered the empty decks until I found a restaurant devoid of patrons or staff. I built a shield out of chairs, so I couldn't be seen and made myself a bed on the floor – basically a clandestine, nautical cubbyhouse. I was asleep in minutes and enjoyed a lovely crossing.

Dad and Elise were a little worse for wear as we departed the ferry in Melbourne, but we were all excited to be on the mainland and heading to our start point. The Murray River and its adjoining rivers, the Murrumbidgee and the Darling, make up the three biggest rivers in the Murray–Darling basin. It's an enormous catchment covering one million square kilometres and drains one-seventh of Australia's landmass. The basin supplies drinking water to millions of people, allows vast agriculture and has been at the heart of Australian settlement for 190 years.

The rivers have been home to Aboriginal people for many thousands of years but the Murrumbidgee, Australia's second longest river, wasn't seen by Europeans until Charles Throsby came across it in 1821. By 1824 the explorers Hamilton Hume and William Hovell discovered the Murray River near where the town of Albury was built. Hume also discovered the Darling River, but this time in conjunction with Captain Charles Sturt, doing so in 1828 during an exploratory trip from Sydney ordered by Governor Sir Ralph Darling. Sturt returned home and detailed the role of the Darling, its bringing vast amounts of tropical rain down from Queensland in the north, and hypothesised it most likely turned south towards the sea.

On 3 November 1829, Sturt departed Sydney again, this time with convicts, soldiers, three bullock drays, a cart and saddle horses. Hume was unable to join the expedition and Sturt recruited George Macleay, son of the Colonial Secretary. The men were tasked with finding out where all the rivers flowed. They set out on a voyage of discovery beginning on the Murrumbidgee River at the town of Wagga. They built a 25-foot whaleboat and a skiff for stores, and began one of the greatest adventures of all time. Sturt wrote in his diary:

'The plains were open to the horizon. Views as boundless as the ocean. No timber but here and there a stunted gum or gloomy cypress. Neither bird nor beast inhabited these lonely regions over which the silence of the grave seemed to reign.'

We were on our own voyage of discovery as we drove four hours north-east towards Lake Hume, a man-made lake built in 1936 and named after the early explorer. The lake is located 15 kilometres east of Albury in New South Wales, and from the lake down to the sea it is supposedly navigable the entire way for the *River Rat* and our kayaks. This gave us 2220 kilometres of river to paddle until we saw the ocean.

We camped by the lake for the night and I thought about the first explorers and how they must have felt venturing into the absolute unknown. We knew we could follow the river to the ocean but to not know and keep moving forward day after day, further away from family and safety would have been an incredible experience. If I could have a taste of that pioneering adventure on this trip, I would be satisfied.

At midday on the 16th April we took our first paddle strokes away from the riverbank. The dam wall towered above us on the right and as I turned the kayak downstream the flow swept me away. I was beaming a smile and I looked at Elise who was doing the same. The adventure had begun. The river's flow was strong, and it felt great to be getting in free kilometres with little effort. While paddling in the ocean we were typically battling wind, waves and current. During my ocean row across the Atlantic, we would sometimes row non-stop for hours and stay in the same place, sometimes we would go backwards after 24 hours of work if a storm came through. Similarly, while dragging a cart across the Gobi Desert, if you stopped dragging you went nowhere, it was all up to you. This was a lovely change.

A mob of kangaroos bounded along the bank as we paddled by, and the afternoon flew past as I took in the sights, sounds and smells of the river. Dad followed behind us in the *Rat*, bottoming out once on a sandbar, hitting a submerged snag and having fun finding his river legs.

The Murray River serves as the border between New South Wales and Victoria, with each state having its own set of rules about camping. We were not allowed to camp on the NSW side as the land was all privately owned. But the Victorian side had a 60-metre section paralleling the river that was Crown land and free to use. At 4pm, after covering 28 kilometres, our longest ever paddle, we pulled up on the bank to set up camp. Elise cooked a damper – a traditional Australian bread made from flour, water and lots of butter – and I threw a line in to try to catch a fish.

According to Dad, who'd spent many years fishing country rivers, one of the best baits to use for fishing in the Murray was cheese. Matured cheese in small cubes was his suggestion and we'd brought some along for this purpose. I threw out my line and just on dark as a large group of fruit bats settled into the trees above us, I caught my first Murray cod. Not as big as the cod in the Dreamtime stories, this one was just 49 centimetres long. The size limit on cod was 55–75 centimetres, any smaller or larger and they had to be released, which I did after a trophy photo. Dad frightened off the bats by flogging the front of the *Rat* with a big stick, creating a deafening noise, and we settled down for damper, a dinner of lamb chops and our first night's sleep.

Up early at 6am, packed up and on the water by 8am, the weather was perfect with clear skies and 24 degrees Celsius. Morning routine is very similar on most expeditions, involving the process of getting out of a comfortable sleeping bag, eating breakfast, packing up and getting going. Depending on the environment, it can be very quick or take many hours. In Antarctica, it was a minimum three to four hours to get moving in the mornings due to the frigid temperatures.

We put in 30 kilometres of paddling before lunch, stopping for a hot brew and a tuna cracker on one of the many sandy beaches, then covering another 21 kilometres before setting up camp. Paddling 51 kilometres was a great day, the exact number we would need to maintain to finish the expedition in six weeks.

Captain Sturt was slowly covering kilometres along the then unknown Murrumbidgee River. With his crew of eight men in the wooden whaleboat, they navigated the fast-flowing waters with only two oars. Just as Dad was colliding with hidden snags and getting caught in trees every few hours, Sturt was having a similar experience. They sank their whaleboat on one occasion but it was recovered. Continuing on, Sturt reflected in his journal, '*A sudden wreck and defeat of the expedition appeared imminent.*'

On the morning of the fourth day, I caught a 55-centimetre Murray cod. This was legal size but with no way to refrigerate it for the day ahead I released it. Another fish plentiful in the river was the European carp. The carp was introduced to Australian rivers and had exploded in numbers thriving off the muddy banks and abundance of food. Every person we spoke to about carp hated them and considered them a rubbish fish, and it's illegal to release them once caught, they must be destroyed. I caught one and it felt like a waste to just kill it without trying it. With some butter, Elise and I cooked it up and ate it. To be honest it wasn't half bad, not the best tasting fish in the world but certainly didn't deserve its reputation. A common theme for the entire trip when we asked people about carp would go like this. 'What's carp like to eat?' 'Yuk, absolute rubbish.' 'Have you ever eaten one?' 'No way, I won't eat them.'

The river exploded with people over the Easter break, and the first few peaceful days turned into every available camping spot on the river being occupied, along with ski-boats, jet-skis and anything that floated being out on the water. I'd never seen so many people enjoying the outdoors. While it was great to see it was also frustrating, especially when multiple boats passed and threw big waves in our direction. Some camps had some of the most luxurious set-ups, containing hot showers, satellite dishes and generators. Camping no longer meant roughing it, it meant taking the whole house and all its comforts with you.

Sturt wasn't encountering fellow campers with luxurious 19th-century set-ups during his expedition, but he was encountering many Aboriginal communities living along the banks of the river. He saw tribes of varying size and disposition and in his early accounts he claimed, 'They were no real trouble.' Similar to our experience, it was frustrating with so many people around, but everyone was just enjoying a few days along the beautiful Murray before having to go back to work, and for us they were no real trouble.

I was learning a lot about how water behaved in an environment like the Murray. The river was full of snags, fallen trees and mudbanks, and it twisted back on itself over and over again. All this created back eddies, undercurrents, fast-moving sections and parts that were dead calm. I was loving it. Dad was also learning new skills as he navigated these hazards.

'How was your day?' I asked him at the end of Day Five.

'Well, I was stuck on a low reef, ran aground once and nearly went through the windscreen, motor stalled twice, I was spun 360 degrees and chucked sideways on a snag that almost sent me swimming, and a tree knocked my hat off. All in all, a great day.'

◆◆◆

Numbers are part of long-endurance expeditions as much as food and water; daily kilometres, average speeds, current flow rate, calories eaten, calories expended and the number of days until we reach the ocean. Some numbers should be avoided, such as days until completion, as that could send you mental if you focus on it too much. Along the bank of the river, however, there were numbers appearing that helped with our calculations. Since its early navigation, the river has been marked with small signs giving the distance remaining to Goolwa, the small town on the coast, and the mouth of the river. When we departed the dam, the first sign we encountered read 2220 kilometres. Every day the signs counted us down and allowed us to readily add up the daily total paddled. This was a unique feature I hadn't encountered before and made the maths easy. We could send Dad forward to a designated kilometre marker, where he could locate a camp and usually have a fire going before we arrived.

The river widened on the morning of Day Six and opened up into Lake Mulwala. On the far side of the lake was the town of Yarrawonga and its weir. This was where we needed to extract the boats and put them back in the river on the other side. The lake was big and, lucky for us, flat as we started our crossing. The calm waters were dotted with protruding branches – imagine a forest being flooded and the trees dying off to leave only their upper trunks and branches showing above the surface. This was what we were seeing, and it was eerily beautiful. The lake and the weir were built in 1939 to provide water for irrigation of the surrounding areas.

As we crossed the lake, we noticed sparrows, galahs, corellas, pelicans and black swans in abundance. The dozens of boats towing skiers dispersed them fairly rapidly, but they were beautiful when they sheltered in small bays. Elise wrote in her journal about the crossing.

> *Elise's journal:* '*A Malibu speedboat would zoom by every minute or so with one, two or three people in tow bracing for the inevitability of getting tossed from their blow-up tubes. Classic stereotypes were well and truly being met, with music from the 2000s blaring (I'm certain I heard "Barbie Girl"), the token male fist pumping and up front a few chicks sunbaking on the deck.*'

Entering the sheltered river was a relief after the chaos of the lake. As we searched for a camp I noticed a naked form on the riverbank catching the last of the day's sun. Slender legs and a white exposed backside had me double-checking to see if Elise was nearby. My eyes drifted up the lower back to the shoulders, trying to catch a glimpse of side boob, pretending not to be looking like some nosy voyeur. It was then that I noticed something out of the ordinary, a large black beard. I turned my head away and laughed to myself. The biker in the buff had fooled me. When I told Elise about the encounter later that night she gave me hell.

◆◆◆

By the end of our first week we had paddled 278 kilometres and our bodies were adapting well. My back and neck were on fire for the first part of each day, but once I warmed up all would be fine. I'd been told about the risk of shoulder and elbow tendonitis from long-distance paddling, so I was conscious of my technique and was trying to move as efficiently as my rough style would permit. The most challenging part for me physically was staying in a seated position for eight hours each day. In my normal life I didn't sit often and definitely not for long periods, so the simple act of sitting caused an annoying dull ache in my hips and legs.

We'd settled in to camp life well. We had our morning and evening routines and our system of loading and unloading the boat dialled in. Sleeping in our mountaineering tent on the ground each night was rough at first, but became a little slice of heaven after a hard day on the water.

Elise's journal: 'The nights are filled with little scratches, squawks and scurries. When I was younger these sounds used to scare me, but now I enjoy hearing nature running all around me. I'll take animal sounds over traffic or airplane noise any day. There's no quiet way to exit a tent but each morning Luke seems to think he has managed to get clothed, find his head torch and unzip, as well as re-zip, the tent without waking me. I know he thinks he's been stealthy because he then goes on to whisper, 'Good morning, mate,' to his dad, to which Clive replies in full volume voice, 'Morning, mate,' obviously aware there's no quiet way to exit a tent. They are both usually up at 5:30am. I like to stay in a bit longer. If we ever did decide to sleep in, the rooster of the bush, the kookaburra, would wake us, as it likes to have its first laugh of the day at 6am. Mornings are my favourite time out here. The river is calm and motionless, not yet having been tampered with by humans. The huge gum trees seem to peer over the banks, trying to get a glimpse of their reflection before the water begins to blur.'

So far we had seen plenty of wildlife but one animal Elise, Dad and I all wanted to see badly was a koala. I had lived in Australia my entire life and never seen one in the wild. Most people we spoke to said we had no chance of spotting them as they were too rare these days. Even my cousin Mathew's wife Megan, who was local to the area said, 'One chance in a million, I'm afraid.' I started to think the same when I considered how many people had been camping for the Easter break. The onslaught of humanity would have scared the remaining few koalas into hiding for sure.

On the morning of Day Eight, while Elise and I were discussing koalas, with me telling her, 'I don't think we will see any, there just isn't enough bushland for them,' and her replying, 'Yeah, you're right, I wish…' I cut her off mid-sentence.

'There's a koala!' I yelled.

Sitting in the fork of a big eucalyptus tree and looking straight at us was the iconic silhouette of a koala. We turned our kayaks and paddled over, our excitement building. He looked fake yet incredibly real in the same moment. He was a large male about the size of a toddler and was chewing on leaves while enjoying the morning sun. We called Dad and told him to come quick. He hit full throttle and appeared round the bend in minutes, equally excited.

We spent half an hour with our new friend before pulling ourselves away to keep moving downriver. Within ten minutes we'd spotted three more koalas; another male, a female and her joey, all close to the river. Further down from this little family were more koalas, and within the two and half hours it took us to reach the small town of Tocumwal, we had seen and spent time with 30 supposedly rare koalas. To say we were over the moon would be an understatement. I jumped on Google Maps to mark the location of the koala haven and was shocked by what I could see from above.

When I zoomed out, I noticed on one side of the river, the NSW side, that farmers had cleared the native bush right up to the water's edge, leaving barely a tree to stop erosion. On the Victorian side, where I presumed were kilometres of protected bushland, was a veneer of between 50 and 200 metres of native bush paralleling the river. This is what the koalas had left to call home. Outside of this tiny strip of vegetation the country had been cleared for hundreds of kilometres. I zoomed out even further to take in the entire state of New South Wales; from above the Murray was a green vein running through a vast agricultural land. These koalas are existing in an ever-shrinking patch of bush, and it was then I realised why we had seen so many together in one place – there was nowhere else to go.

The politics surrounding the Murray–Darling basin are hard to understand. There are many players involved, including local farmers, corporate agricultural companies, international interests and government. The Darling recently suffered huge fish kills from low water levels, supposedly due to drought conditions, mismanagement by government and over extraction of water by cotton farms. Some of these enormous enterprises syphon vast amounts of water from the river system to be stored in personal dams for later use. Trying to get a clear unbiased opinion, however, was a very hard task. Before leaving Tasmania many people, after hearing we were off to paddle the river, commented,

'I hope there is water in it.' This confused me because when we arrived at the Murray it was big, flowing and full of fish.

The media have their own agenda and often report left-leaning environmental-based stories slamming big business. I watched videos from farmers condemning the government for mismanaging the water and irrigation licences. The locals I spoke to along the banks of the river blame those up or downstream of them for either holding water back or letting too much go. One guy in New South Wales said to me, 'It's the bloody South Australians taking all the water. When you get there, tell them to send it back.' A local farmer in Victoria told me, 'The bloody New South Wales irrigators are taking all the water, that's the problem.' No one knew what was really going on.

We pulled up at a caravan park with its own private beach in Tocumwal. Dad and Mum had stayed at the camping ground on their travels in their caravan. It was five dollars each per night, which was cheap, and offered cold showers, power and fresh water for drinking. Elise and I set off into town for groceries and fuel for the boat. Tocumwal had a population of 2500 and was first settled in the 1860s. Now a popular tourist stop, it boasts a big Murray cod statue in the centre of town. In Australia we have a fondness for big things. There's a tourist trail around the country where one can view a big banana at 13 metres long, a big beer can five metres tall, big prawn, sheep, barramundi and pineapple to name only a few; all of equally outlandish proportions. In Tocumwal it was the big cod, which Elise and I happily posed with for photos.

The following day we'd covered 45 kilometres and found a camp for the night on a high bank overlooking the river. As Elise and I were discussing what type of dinner we should prepare, pasta and tuna or sausage and pasta, Dad hauled in a 56-centimetre cod. It was perfect timing, right on dinner, and before the fish realised he was now a landlubber, he was filleted and sizzling in the pan with a side of butter. Cod is by far the best fish I had ever eaten, it was melt-in-your-mouth pure deliciousness. With a belly full of freshly made damper, fish and warm tea, I slept like a baby.

VODKA & SANDSTORMS

The following morning was Anzac Day, my second during a big expedition. On 25 April 1915, Anzac units joined our Allies to try and capture the Gallipoli peninsula from the Turkish army. The ten-month campaign was an overall failure, claiming 8141 Australian lives, 2779 New Zealanders, 2700 Irish, 27,000 French and 35,000 British. A little-known fact is the opposing Turkish military lost more than all the Allies combined, with 85,000 men perishing during the costly victory. The bravery shown by all of them firmed their place in history and over a century later we stopped to remember them. Dad and I were up early on this special day, turned on the radio in the boat and stood in silence around the campfire as a bugle played the last post. We held a minute's silence and I remembered the men I had trained with and served alongside during my years in the infantry. I remembered my brothers who went on to distinguished careers, and those who died too young far from home.

Lest we forget.

By the morning of Day Twelve we started to see houseboats moored to the banks and cruising the river. A houseboat is exactly what it sounds like, a small house built on floating pontoons with an outboard engine fastened to the back. They're slow moving and a fantastic way for families to enjoy the river in comfort. They ranged from tiny caravans with the bare necessities to three-storey luxury mansions boasting a hot tub and sauna. The wind increased as we passed through an area called Picnic Point. The surrounding land was vast floodplains and where the trees had been removed it created a wind tunnel effect, which would stop us in our tracks.

Elise's journal: 'The Murray meanders its way through the earth. One bend you're facing west then the next you've done a complete 180 to the east again. The beauty of this means if you do face a headwind, it won't be long before you've changed direction and it's at your tail, nudging you along.'

We were in a routine of stopping every ten kilometres for a stretch and a snack. After one particular break, I was exiting a muddy bank when I stuffed up my manoeuvre and ended up tangled in a tree. I yanked my rudder on a branch, scratched myself in the process and tore myself free in frustration as Elise looked on laughing. As I straightened up into the current, I noticed I'd picked up a hitchhiker. A large green praying mantis was sitting on the nose of my kayak staring at me. He moved from side to side searching for a way off, but the water turned him back so he settled himself in the middle. I watched him as he watched me and in one moment it seemed as if he'd made peace with his fate, he turned around and stared ahead from his prime position. He was on the nose of the *Titanic*, off on a great adventure. We stayed together for ten kilometres until I stopped for lunch and he disembarked. He didn't even say goodbye.

During lunch Dad and I talked about the cod we were catching and wondered how big they really grew. We knew of one guy who'd caught a cod over a metre long, which was the stuff of legends. Dad also knew a keen fisherman who fished with lures from a small pedal boat. He was often out before dawn flicking baits, hunting the enormous fish from mythology. Dad had asked him once how big they grew, and he replied with a story. He'd been fishing a deep hole near a snag once and a large duck swam up to him in the water. The duck was searching for some bread, which fishermen and tourists threw to him from time to time. The fisherman turned to look at the duck just as an enormous cod came up from below and swallowed his feathered friend whole. He said the fish was a dinosaur and he'd been hunting it ever since. Dad replied, 'I've been a fisherman my whole life and never caught anything like that.'

We paddled into the towns of Echuca and Moama, where we had our first look at paddle-steamers. The *Emmy Lou*, a steamer built in the 1980s, came churning past and blasted her horn in welcome. Echuca is an Aboriginal word meaning 'meeting of the waters' and the town was the oldest inland port in Australia. It was first colonised by a convict named Henry Hopwood in 1850, who built a small punt to ferry goods and people across the river. By the 1870s Echuca was a bustling hub of trade and boasted a 400-metre timber wharf, which still stood today. The wharf would receive paddle-steamers and their goods, unload the cargo and reload it onto trains bound for Melbourne. Wool, wheat, livestock and timber were the main commodities of the time.

We received a message from Troy, aka Snappy, a friend of ours who lived in Moama. Snappy was a built guy with tattoos and a big beard. We met him in Bali while on a training holiday and he offered us a hot shower and a feed, which we gladly accepted. He was the head chef at Morrisons Winery and told us to pull up the boats at a jetty in front of their land, where he greeted us with a big smile. Thinking we would be given a cosy couch for the night we were blown away when he opened the door to our private five-bedroom home on the grounds of the winery. He then held a barbecue in our honour, invited friends and local media and we dined on some of the best food I'd eaten in a very long time. While Snappy lived up to his reputation as a top chef, I tried to eat a cob of corn that turned out to be a decoration – something called popping corn. Obviously I don't eat fine food very often. After photos and an interview for the local newspaper we shared a cold beer together and Snappy told me a story I will never forget.

He was out on the water in his tinny one day, showing his eldest daughter how to use the boat safely for her upcoming boat licence test. He lost control, fell out of the boat and wasn't wearing the kill chain at the time, which would have stopped the outboard engine. The boat powered into a turn and came straight back at him. He had two options, and only a split second to choose between them: either try and climb over the nose into the boat without falling off and getting swept into the spinning prop underneath, or push the boat away to the side and try to escape. He chose the latter, but as he pushed the boat away the spinning prop slammed into his groin. He knew instantly that he'd been hurt and swam to the bank where his daughter was waiting. He looked down and screamed at the carnage. The propeller had nicked his testicles and one ball was hanging out of the skin sack. It had also nicked his penis and opened up a deep cut. Blood was pouring out and emergency help was called immediately. He received 50 stitches to his private region, but no permanent injury and made a full recovery. Needless to say, his daughter found boat safety advice elsewhere.

We each enjoyed a warm night's sleep in a double bed, thanks to the hospitality of Snappy and his family. Not wanting to break our routine, we were back on the water early and bid them farewell. Before shoving off, I asked Snappy, 'What does the Murray River mean to you?' He said, 'The River has a way of bringing people together and connecting. It has allowed my family and me to reconnect after moving away from the city. The Murray is somewhere to sit, ponder, relax and unwind. All water masses have a way of tying places and people together, and I love the power of that.'

◆◆◆

Our goal was to hit 50-kilometre days as often as we could, but that depended on wind and river conditions. My body had adapted well to its new existence with only minor aches and pains. Every morning it would take a while for my toes and fingers to warm up. The numbness in my hands dissipated within the first few bends of the river and I would settle into a rhythm. I followed Elise's lead and began wearing thick socks for the morning paddle to fend off the coming winter temperatures. And every night before writing in my journal I would do some mobility exercises to help my body recover.

We had brought along a solid roller and a hard rubber mobility ball for this specific purpose. Utilising these, I'd roll and massage the fascia in my legs, shoulders and arms, releasing tension from the day. This was a habit I started on big climbing expeditions, and it definitely helped prevent tendonitis and injury.

At our lunchbreak Dad met a fellow kayaker and was chatting to him as we pulled up. Kent was 21 years old and was enjoying a big adventure of his own. He'd taken a year off from university and had walked to the river from Mount Kosciuszko, Australia's tallest mountain, standing 2228 metres tall. He was kayaking to Mildura, where he planned to hop on a bicycle and ride to Lake Eyre in South Australia. It was a trip of 2500 kilometres and he'd given himself six months to complete it. It was great to see a young guy out on such an incredible challenge and we shared an afternoon paddling and chatting. He was a keen outdoorsman and botanist, only paddling 20–30 kilometres per day to allow ample time to study the surrounding environment. We bade him farewell and wished him luck as we pushed on with our ambitious schedule.

For the past couple of days I'd been noticing orange flags and buoys marking submerged snags along the banks of the river. I found out these markers were for the annual ski-boat race called the Southern 80. The race attracted 900 competitors, 260 boats and tens of thousands of spectators every year. A team in the race consisted of a driver, one observer and two skiers, who would race along an 80-kilometre stretch of the river at speeds up to 200 kilometres per hour. It was NASCAR on water and on steroids. I can only imagine what navigating the narrow river around tight bends would feel like at those speeds. The event had claimed lives and its fair share of injuries over the years, and it had me contemplating humans and our desire for extreme activities. What attracted us to these sports?

Our bodies are very complex in their function but fragile in construction. We are a bag of meat and bones, and when we're thrown off cliffs wearing parachutes, hurtling down slopes on thin planks of wood, or ripping down a peaceful river on a rope at warp speeds, we're taking a big risk. Yet, when serious injuries occur we don't stop doing the activity, we just pull on a helmet, strap on a back brace and try again. I believe we have made our normal lives so comfortable and safe that we now have a desire for the unsafe and the feeling of freedom it delivers. I've spent a fair portion of my life riding the razor's edge between life and death and can understand the behaviour. When a boat comes racing passed with a skier in tow centimetres from trees and I hear people comment, 'That's crazy.' I tend to reply, 'That's living.'

◆◆◆

Twenty-six locks, weirs and barrages have been built on the Murray and we were due to hit our first lock on Day Fourteen. The locks count down from Lock Twenty-six to Lock One at the river's mouth. A river's natural rhythm is to run dry, or very low in the summer months and these constructions ensure irrigation throughout the year for surrounding farmers and towns. The locks were free to pass through at any time during daylight hours and allow the river to be entirely navigable by watercraft. A lock has a gated section in which the water can be lowered or raised to match river heights on either side. A boat is locked inside the gates, water is raised or pumped out and the craft is released again.

We were excited to see how they operated but it wasn't to be. Our first lock of the voyage, at the Torrumbarry Weir, was broken and being repaired but the lock master offered a free trailer service for the boat and kayaks. We paddled on for a few kilometres and pitched camp atop another high bank. It was five metres high and steep, on a deep bend of the river, but a previous camper had cut steps into the bank for easy access.

A storm came through overnight with high winds and torrential rain. We'd tied the kayaks to the bank, so everything was secure. Our tent was from Mountain Hardware and had survived multiple mountain expeditions and Gobi Desert sandstorms, and Dad had bought himself a small Denali mountain tent made for tough conditions. The following morning the rain had mostly cleared but we realised instantly we'd made a big rookie error. Our high bank had been turned to slush by the rain and become a slippery slope of death. I tried to recut the steps with a shovel and fill the cuttings with sticks to create some grip, but I was having a tough time.

> *Elise's journal:* 'Luke slid his way down the bank launching into my kayak and taking it with him. His fuse was lit, and it didn't take long before his shoes and socks were getting flung up the bank along with a 'useless bloody things'. I laughed (internally) when a sock got stuck halfway on the slip and slide of doom. This was the only pair of socks he'd brought with him. Packing the boat was tough but we still managed to get away by 8:30am without any rain. (Clive came to the rescue and hooked Luke's sock with his fishing rod, first go.)'

After my calm, composed loading of the boat, we shoved on and enjoyed a great day on the water, finding a camp on a sandy beach at 3pm. There would be no more high banks for us.

We passed through the country town of Swan Hill, where my grandmother had lived her entire life, where Mum was born and where I had attended some primary school once upon a time. We enjoyed a hot shower at the campground, our third for the trip, and devoured two cooked chickens from the grocery store. The price of food in these smaller rural towns was staggering. Blown away by the cost we abandoned one IGA, only to find similar prices elsewhere. The cost of basic foods was expensive, more so if we wanted to eat healthy or, dare I say it, organic.

The amount of money we were handing over for a bag of semi-healthy groceries reminded me of something Mum had recently mentioned. She travelled every twelve months to see her cardiologist after some heart issues a few years earlier, and on her latest visit the doctor told her, 'Something's going on in your home town, Mandy. I had to do one hundred back-to-back consults in a single day for heart disease there last week. I'm really worried about that town.' After our shopping trip, I realised food prices were playing a big role in the epidemic.

None of us had slept well at the caravan park that night, it was full of people and a large group of drunks were still enjoying themselves well after midnight and continued to wake me up. I always think through the consequences of my actions before confronting people and after a brief moment I decided to say something.

Elise's journal: 'Guys, it's 2am. Can you take it inside so we don't have to lie awake listening to your life story?' Luke poked his head out of the tent and put on his ultra-deep authority voice. I personally find that voice hilarious because the only time he uses it is when he's telling people off. The drunk people across from us getting told off obviously don't know that though, and he sounds like he will mess you up if you don't follow his orders. As the whispers continued Luke stayed sitting up inside the tent, waiting for them to obey. I know he's secretly thinking, 'Just go inside so I don't have to put pants on.' They went inside but I lay there awake for another few hours.

We were back on the river the next morning stocked with supplies and agreed to only camp in the bush for the remainder of the trip.

By the end of our third week on the water we had covered 852 kilometres. We were hoping to be halfway by this point but had fallen well short. The flow in the river had dropped dramatically since we entered the locked portions and had stolen ten kilometres per day off our totals. With rough estimates it was going to take us two more weeks than we'd originally planned.

My balance in my kayak was improving every day. I could launch each morning and stay completely dry most of the time. Elise and I were laughing at my balance issues when I managed to get wet and muddy after a snack break. Later while paddling I had a flashback to when I was a pretend parkour athlete trying to balance under a very different set of conditions.

Long before my life of adventure and meeting Elise, I was in the grip of drugs and living in London. One particular morning, after returning near dawn from a night spent at clubs and pubs, two friends and I ingested enough MDMA to kill a baby rhino and decided to climb onto the roof. We began leaping from roof to roof, chimney to chimney, like possessed beasts in a twisted *Mary Poppins* remake. Our parkour ambitions came to a dramatic end when my friend fell through a glass skylight and plummeted four metres into a cleaning closet. We looked down to see him lying cut and bleeding on the floor below. With much effort and noise, we managed to get him out of the skylight, stem the flow of blood and get him home, where we patched him up and called it a night. I think back on my life and shake my head at the guy I was.

◆◆◆

On Day 24 the Murray was joined by the Murrumbidgee entering from the north. The Murrumbidgee flowed down through the Australian Capital Territory and New South Wales, some 1500 kilometres, to join us on our journey to the ocean. I stopped paddling and floated through the confluence of the two great rivers and thought back to Sturt, who would have laid eyes on this exact spot for the first time 189 years earlier. His journal detailed the encounter:

'*Suddenly the Murrumbidgee took a southerly direction but in its tortuous course swept round to every point of the compass with the greatest irregularity. At 3pm Hopkinson called out that we were approaching a junction, and in less than a minute afterwards we were hurried into a broad and noble river. It was impossible for me to describe the effect of so instantaneous a change of circumstances upon us. The boats were allowed to drift along at pleasure…we continued to gaze in silent admiration on the capacious channel. We had escaped from a wreck and assured of ultimate success. We were on a high road to the south coast or to some important outlet.'*

The most enjoyable part of the day was the first hour after setting out. The water would be flat calm and reflecting the first rays of dawn as the sun poked its head above the trees. When the sun touched my skin, I felt a surge of energy and warmth that instantly boosted my morale for the day ahead; this warm surge was being enjoyed by the waterbirds as well. I had been seeing and watching pied shags every morning. They were very skittish during the day, usually disappearing below the water whenever I paddled close. But in the frigid dawn they stood on exposed logs and spread their wings to capture the warming embrace of the sun. During this open display they no longer feared me, instead we shared a moment together basking in the sun.

There were a few essentials to making life on the river more comfortable, which were also necessary to help leave a campsite as we found it. The main one was a small folding shovel for building fire pits and for taking on the daily walk into the bush to relieve ourselves. One of my biggest frustrations with campers is finding a camp full of rubbish, broken glass or old toilet paper strewn across the bushland. I have adopted a habit from my military days and applied it to camping life: 'leave no sign for the enemy.' This behaviour was born out of survival when we were being tracked by an enemy force and wanted to leave no sign in the bush for them to follow. Although the average citizen doesn't need to go to this extreme, basic habits can keep the outdoors beautiful for everyone.

I tried to never leave a single scrap of rubbish behind, not a fleck. Everything we carried or paddled into the bush had to leave with us. This included toilet paper, which I burnt or carried out. I get very upset when I find a camp with patches of toilet paper degrading on the surface of the ground. Good habits are to either bury it 15 centimetres below the surface using a small shovel, or pocket it to burn or carry out with you. When I was climbing in Antarctica and Alaska we had to carry out everything, even our faeces. This can be a measurable burden after a month on the mountain, so burying it was no problem at all.

The weather was slowly getting colder and storms more frequent. One night a storm came through while we were cosy in our sleeping bags. Then on the wind I started hearing screams, guttural growls and noises I'd never heard before. In my sleepy haze I thought Dad was trapped under a fallen tree and screaming for help, but as my mind cleared I realised it was coming from the other side of the river. Someone told me koalas made crazy grunts and noises and I assumed it must be them. The demon vocals continued throughout the night, and at dawn I crawled out of my tent to investigate. Across the river I could see a small heard of feral goats and knew they were the culprits. They were butting heads and causing havoc on the opposite bank, and a billygoat's bellows were born from the pits of hell. I cursed them for a rough night's sleep.

I've heard the saying 'there are no short cuts in life,' and that might be true. Out on the Murray, however, shortcuts were a gift and we were hunting them. We found a small waterway 50 metres long running through swampy ground. We paddled through and realised we'd cut off two kilometres of the main river by doing so. A few days later we found another shallow waterway, which shaved off four kilometres. Dad couldn't follow us in the River Rat as the water was too shallow, but the shortcuts saved us time and effort. I started using Google Maps to recce the river ahead to find any creeks we could paddle through. Purists might accuse us of cheating, but they were natural formations and our moral compass told us using them was fine. Taking the shortcuts also meant exploring areas we would otherwise have missed, like swampy sections, thick bushland and caves hidden from the main flow of the water. Gaining a few kilometres also meant a boost to morale, and an early finish to the day to go fishing.

I had been seeing carp swimming and feeding in the shallow water along muddy banks. They were huge and when they were in eating mode, they would venture into water shallow enough to expose half their bodies above the surface. This was a temptation too great for me to pass, and I began hunting them. At first I tried to corner them with my kayak and hit them with my paddle. This succeeded in getting me wet and I risked breaking my only paddle. I borrowed a wooden pole the size of a cricket stump from Dad, and this became my whacking stick. I would drift up in stealth mode to the unsuspecting carp and bring down fire and fury upon them. This too was unsuccessful. As the days went by I continued in my obsession. I contemplated using a spear, arrows, or a knife but in the end the fish gave me a clue. Whenever I cornered them, they would try to swim away at top speed, often colliding with my kayak and swimming alongside it half out of the water. This opened up their flank in very close range and allowed me an attempt at grabbing them with my bare hands. It was the closest I'd come to catching one and I wouldn't give up.

> *Elise's journal: 'Luke's carp whacking has evolved gracefully into carp grabbing. He now just tries to get as close as possible and grab the fish. I feel like I don't need to say this, but he has been unsuccessful at carp grabbing. All he really achieved was getting wetter and colder than needed.*

One of the things I was enjoying the most about the expedition was spending time with Dad. We hadn't been on an adventure together for years, not since we climbed Kilimanjaro in 2011. Most of us in our fast-paced worlds never get to spend quality time with our family, and it is so important. Every morning Dad and I would sit around the fire before dawn whispering in conversation or simply sharing silence and watching the flames. We were spending every day together, weeks on end of fishing, camping and reconnecting. Of course, our own idiosyncrasies could frustrate each other from time to time but that was all part of the journey. With the ability to communicate during more stressful times, the team grew stronger. Communication was paramount, as Elise and I had learned on the Gobi Desert expedition. We had to sit down in the sand every few weeks to air frustrations among the team or the stress could have led to destruction. We would share our grievances without personal attack, and when we finished, the weight would lift from our shoulders. This stopped small issues from becoming insurmountable problems.

I thought about team dynamics a lot while drifting along the river in the afternoons. Our earliest forms of communication were particles interacting together after the Big Bang. Single-cell organisms evolved from the cosmic chaos to eventually become Stone Age man. From grunts and growls we developed words and carved them into stone and wood. The invention of the printing press and books allowed rapid-paced sharing of ideas across the world. Next came radio, phones, computers and the internet. Instant messaging, video chat, blogs and websites allowed us to communicate like never before. Yet over the years I have seen a de-evolution of face-to-face communication skills. These skills were the essentials to harmony during big expeditions.

We resupplied in Tooleybuc and got to travel through our first lock just outside of Robinvale, on the morning of Day 27. The lock was operating, and the lock master invited us inside it with a flashing green traffic light. When we were holding onto a steel ladder, the hydraulic gates closed tight. The water was pumped out over the ensuing 20 minutes, until we were four metres lower than we were before. The gates facing downstream opened and we paddled through a squadron of pelicans sheltering nearby.

We had reached the halfway point of the journey, with roughly 1100 kilometres to go, and the scenery had changed dramatically. Elise sang power ballads at the top of her voice throughout the afternoon and the bushland gave way to red and orange cliffs, towering above us on the Victorian side. It was a welcome change. We set up camp on a pristine beach, ate damper and watched the sunset. Life couldn't have been better.

In the pre-dawn light the following morning, as I paddled away from camp, I watched a kangaroo swim across the river towards us. It left the water and stared at Dad, who was seated by the fire. They held eye contact for a good minute, two beasts from the bush showing respect, before it bounded away up the bank. The river was widening, the wildlife was plentiful and the amount of agriculture the river sustained was staggering. If the river was indeed under serious threat then the consequences of its extinction would be catastrophic.

Hundreds of thousands of people needed the water for drinking, and millions of hectares of farms relied on irrigation to grow fruit and vegetables for the cities. The dairy farmers needed it to keep producing milk in an ever-tightening market. The cotton growers and sheep farmers who'd lived on the banks for generations were bound to it by blood. The small towns, caravan parks, abattoirs, paddle-steamers, revenue from tourists, and the wildlife could all be under threat. If the droughts were getting longer and the water more vulnerable then was it time to transition to more viable industries? All I knew was that the river should be in the forefront of government policy and protected with every power we had. I was starting to realise there was too much at stake.

To break up the monotony of paddling, we stopped to check out a tourist attraction close to the bank of the river near Nangiloc. It was a rare red gum, estimated to be between 400 and 500 years old, standing 60 metres tall and almost 2.5 metres wide. Elise and I had travelled around the United States on a climbing trip and we'd visited the famous sequoia trees and Californian redwoods. We had no idea Australia had any huge trees. Standing next to the ancient tree I could feel its power and wondered about the stories it could tell. These red gum giants would have been plentiful when Sturt first passed through. Today they are so rare they have become tourist hotspots.

We'd been paddling for over a month and our bodies had adapted to the long hours of work. I wasn't in bad shape overall, though on other expeditions my body weight would be in freefall and my joints screaming out for respite. We'd found a good balance between the work we needed to do each day, the calories we could eat, and the amount of sleep needed to recover. Our daily food intake looked something like this:

3 fried eggs and oats with honey for breakfast + coffee
An apple for break one
Fruitcake for break two
Tuna and crackers for break three
Billabong jerky and trail mix for snacks while on the water
Damper at the end of the day + coffee
Tinned tuna and vegetable spaghetti for dinner (or cod and potatoes if we got lucky)
Arnott's biscuits for dessert

Sitting around a fire on a clear night and chewing on a biscuit and drinking cups of tea were some of my favourite moments. One evening just before sundown on Day 29, we were startled by an ear-splitting crack. We looked across to where the sound had originated and saw two large goats circling each other in a face-off. Like two medieval knights, they would pace away a metre or so before turning, rearing up on their hind legs and spearing into each other in a clash of heads and horns. We would see the impact before the crack reached our ears across the water. It sounded loud enough to split rock, yet they were unfazed and completed round after round of the dual. Eventually they retired to forage, and we were not sure which one had won the battle.

Dad became the storyteller around the fire each night, and he had no shortage of tales from his life growing up in the outback. He used to shoot crocodiles for a mate of his when he lived in remote regions of the Northern Territory. His friend was skilled in taxidermy and back in the eighties they were getting one dollar per inch for the crocs, which were sold to tourists. He also told us how he acquired my sister Kim's first pet budgerigar.

Living in remote areas meant being a very long way from the local pet shop. When my sister desperately wanted a pet budgie of her own, she asked Dad who, with his detailed knowledge of the Outback, located a budgie's nest high up in a tree. He kept watch over it until he saw the chicks hatch and develop to a point where they were about to fly away. He cut the tree down and it crumpled against the red earth at his feet. He located the nest among the debris, gathered up one baby bird for Kim and propped the nest up in another tree close by. The other chicks were fine, if not slightly traumatised, and flew away days later.

I'd like to say this story had a happy ending, but a week later, Kim's budgie was eaten by a python. Years later Mum had an aviary full of budgies, and all of them were devoured in a single night by a python. The snake was so fat after swallowing the birds that it couldn't escape, and was found by Mum the next morning who, in her rage, sentenced him to death. Such is life in the bush.

On Day 33 we laid eyes on the mighty Darling River, which I had read so much about. The Darling is Australia's third longest river and it winds its way 1472 kilometres from the north to join the Murray near the town of Wentworth. This was the major convergence of the two rivers and the flow picked up for a brief period before we made it to the next lock. The Darling was suffering and had received a lot of attention in the media, with the recent fish kills and dry riverbeds making primetime news. Pollution through pesticide run-off, drought and overuse of its already low water levels saw over one million fish killed in 2019. This incident, and the river's overall condition, led to an official ongoing inquiry into the management of the Murray–Darling basin.

On 23 January 1830, Sturt was close to the junction of these two rivers when their boat ground to a halt on a shallow sandbank projecting two-thirds of the way out across the river. A large number of hostile Aboriginals were crowded on the sandbank and the crew were sitting ducks to an attack. Sturt wrote, 'The men were given guns but instructed not to fire until I had discharged both my barrels.' An intervening chief from the tribe, a man of authority, swam across the stream. He persuaded the others to lower their spears and Sturt ordered a lowering of rifles. The peacemaker received a gift, guns were put away and the boat pushed off the sandbank. 'Then it was just as she floated again that our attention was withdrawn to a new and beautiful stream coming from the North.' They had reached the mouth of the Darling. Sturt records the emotion of the moment as the Aboriginals watched them: 'I directed the union jack to be hoisted and we all stood up in the boat and gave three distinct cheers.' Their mission wasn't over yet, Sturt wanted to see how far this river ran. He still didn't know if it made it to the sea.

Elise and I took our hunt for shortcuts to a new level on the morning of Day 35. I'd done a quick scan ahead using Google Maps and noticed the river completed a 180-degree turn. At one point during its turn it looped back to within 500 metres of itself. I looked at the bushland in between, then at the river's length during its turn and estimated we could cut off almost five kilometres of paddling if we completed an overland portage. I mentioned the plan to Elise, who at first was a little sceptical at my optimistic numbers. But after a few minutes of cajoling and with my 'it will be great fun' attitude, she said yes. We pulled the kayaks up onto the mudbank and laid them side by side. We put on our shoes and picking up one kayak in each hand, we started walking.

The boats were much heavier than I thought, and we needed to put them down and rest every 50 metres. We also had to navigate between trees, bush and thick grass. The sun was at its zenith and beating down on us. The humid dusty heat of the surrounding country replaced the cool water of the river. It took us 30 minutes to cross the distance between the river and luckily there was an animal trail carved into the bank, which allowed easy entry back to the water. Although sweating profusely and scratched from the scrub, it was actually fun. We slipped off our shoes, cleaned the dried blood from scratches on our legs in the water, and started paddling. We'd saved at least an hour of work and increased our daily total by five kilometres. Mission accomplished.

The river's flow was at an all-time low, and our overall speed had dropped to between four and five kilometres per hour. The extra assistance we'd received in the beginning was gone. We knew this was most likely going to happen in winter, when the environmental flow was at its lowest. Added to this were the locks holding back as much water as possible for irrigation and the result was a near stagnant body of water. This meant using our own physical abilities to make the distances each day, and

I didn't mind at all. The reward on completion would be all the sweeter.

We pulled up onto a mudbank next to the *River Rat* at the end of Day 36. The campsite wasn't ideal; there was broken glass everywhere and a nearby national parks road. Dad already had a fishing rod in the water and was in the process of reeling in a big yellow belly. It was a beautiful big fish and I said to Dad, 'One more of those and we have dinner sorted.' He told me the river was eight metres deep, perfect for fishing, and that's why he'd picked it for camp. He rebaited his line and threw it in again. Within minutes of me pulling my kayak out of the water, he had another fish lying on the mud. 'Dinner sorted,' he said to me with a big smile. After his second fish he'd run out of bait, so he gutted the two yellow bellies and used one of their livers on his hook; he wanted to keep fishing.

Elise and I climbed to the top of the bank with our tent in hand and walked over to a flat section of ground. We'd started to erect it when we heard a yell. 'Was that Dad?' I asked Elise. We heard another yell, and we walked back to the boat. As we came over the bank I saw Dad on his knees in the mud, next to him was an enormous Murray cod. I scrambled down the slope and fell to my knees beside him, instantly as excited as he was. This was a once-in-a-lifetime fish, it measured 97 centimetres and was something we'd both dreamed about. Elise doesn't fish but even she could feel the energy of the moment. People could fish their entire lives for a cod this size. Beaming like a kid at Christmas, Dad held it up for photos. The cod could have been Dad's age and belonged in the river. Dad lowered him into the water and he powered away into the deep hole from where he'd come.

We returned to our tent and as I slipped a pole into place I said to Elise, 'Imagine if he had caught one over a metre long,' I heard Dad yell again. This time I sprinted for the bank and as I came over the rise, I saw him reeling in a dinosaur. A Murray cod bigger than his last one was hooked and in the shallows. I dove into the water to help push the beast onto the bank. This cod was the ultimate prize. It measured 120 centimetres and was as thick as my waist. It had one cataract eye and scarred lips from a lifetime of battles with anglers. We were all in shock. Dad's excitement was contagious. We all took photos with the fish, which weighed at least 30 kilograms and felt powerful in my arms. He could have been 100 years old, the kind of fish in abundance under Sturt's boat in 1830 but were unique today and unobtainable for many. He was prehistoric, absolutely amazing and bestowed Dad with the title of Codfather forevermore.

I was the last to have my photo taken with him and then I bent to release him back into the river. Just as the lower lip of the giant touched the water, he whipped his tail from side to side. The power caught me off guard as the tail slapped me in the middle of my back and felt like I'd been hit in a rugby tackle. I dropped him into the shallows and he parted the water with his tail like Moses through the Red Sea. In that moment, I believed in the Dreamtime story of Ngurunderi and his giant cod. The fish disappeared below the surface, returning to the river that was his home. If there was no other reason to protect this waterway than these incredible fish, it was more than enough. They are a sacred species and I was blown away by the shared experience.

◆◆◆

During Day 38 we crossed a point in the journey where the three state borders meet and we paddled into South Australia. It was a big moment and I knew the river would soon be turning south towards the ocean. The colour of the water changed to a lighter brown because of the inflow from Lake Victoria in the north. The lake covers 12,200 hectares and is an enormous catchment feeding into the Murray. This ensures most of South Australia would receive enough water all year round. The river widened to over 100 metres and the small waterway with its muddy banks and eucalypt trees was slowly disappearing. Its new size gave it an imposing energy and it felt like I'd lost some level of control over my environment. As the river continued to grow, the wind whipped up the swell on its surface, and I knew we were at the mercy of Mother Nature.

That night our story time around the fire in South Australia focused on love letters. I told Dad how Elise and I wrote letters to each other often and hid them in places to be found later. It jogged Dad's memory about his parents, and he told us a story about how Nana Jean had written a love note for my grandfather Harry one day. She'd written the romantic gesture and hidden it in his sandwich before he went off to work. When he arrived home, Nana asked him how his day was. She was waiting for a comment about the note, yet none came. After a while she asked, 'Did you get my letter?' 'What letter?' he asked. 'The letter I wrote and put in your sandwich.' He thought for a moment, then replied in his thick English accent, 'Well, I didn't see it, so I must have eaten the bloody thing.' It was the last time she put a love letter in his food.

I really enjoyed hearing about my grandparents. They had died when I was in my teens, so I didn't have an adult relationship with them. That was also long before the current level of technology and most information about them was lost forever. Dad told me about his own grandfather as well, who was apparently a big oilman and one of the best drillers in the Middle East during the early 1900s. He had semi-retired to his small village back in England, to a terraced home where no one in the street owned cars. One day a black luxury vehicle drove into his lane and out of the car stepped a prince from one of the Arab states with a full security detail. He offered my great-grandfather his dream life – any house he wanted, cars, luxury – all he had to do was come out of retirement, move to another country and drill oil for the prince as a personal favour.

And he was apparently willing and able to do so but my great-grandmother said she wanted to stay in the village. So he never took the job. Instead they moved into a tiny unit in a high rise, he became an alcoholic and died years later telling the story about how a prince had come calling. It was a sliding doors moment that could have altered his life and the lives of the generations who followed. These moments occur in our lives at different points, and we need to be confident enough to grab them with both hands and go for the ride. It's scary when the outcome is unknown, and it could end in failure. But the flip side is a safe life, living within the comfort zone of the known. This too could end in failure, so why not take the chance.

We estimated we were two weeks from the ocean with 565 kilometres to go. The surrounding countryside was ever changing, and I noticed entire sections of the bank had been eroded away during floods. All that remained in some parts were what looked to be floating trees. The trees were held aloft metres above the ground by their own root systems. Imagine a tree had been pulled out by a giant, all the dirt was shaken loose from its roots and then stood up again. That's what we were seeing, and it was strangely beautiful. The root systems were so elaborate and robust that the trees, even though huge and weighing tonnes, were standing strong. They were holding on as long as they could before toppling into the water and creating new ecosystems for the fish and wildlife.

We entered a stage of the expedition I called 'big river suffering.' The water spanned 150 metres in places, the banks were no longer natural muddy features but flat lands lined with willow trees, and where the trees had grown thick together we couldn't access the bank. Red cliffs stretched into the distance in certain areas and at times created a wind tunnel effect that would cause havoc for us. These were the toughest conditions we'd endured throughout the paddle and with our slow physical deterioration over the last 1600 kilometres, we were showing signs of fatigue.

> *Elise's journal: 'Luke seemed to be miles ahead of me all day, I just had no oomph left in me. My wrists have been giving me grief for the past week or so and started to flare up, every stroke a sharp pain would shoot down my right thumb into my elbow. The cracks are starting to show after nearly six weeks of paddling, which was to be expected.'*

We had five more locks to navigate before the river mouth, and I started noticing strange dynamics in the water as we approached each one. For the last few hours before arriving at a lock, I would notice leaves, weeds and other debris building up on the surface. The flow would stop entirely, and I swear I could feel some back pressure that made paddling even harder. I had spoken about this with other paddlers, who agreed with what I was noticing. The lock was holding back so much water pressure that the force had to dissipate somewhere. As we paddled against the pressure into Lock Five I thought to myself, 'If a river doesn't flow, is it still classed as a river?'

On Day 41 we enjoyed the luxuries of the Riverbend Caravan Park at Renmark and decided on a sleep-in the following day. We were all fairly battered and deserved a few extra hours of rest before cracking on. I rose early as I always did and when Elise emerged from the tent something had happened to her face.

Elise's journal: 'Luke made his way out of the tent and I fell back to sleep for another two hours. When I did finally stir, something didn't feel right and as I began waking up properly, I figured out what it was. My left eye was swollen shut. Something must have bitten me in my sleep.

"*Babe, my eye won't open.*"

"*Holy shit! Hey there, Pirate Pete!*"

And so began the onslaught of pirate jokes from Luke and Clive.

"*Do you want a coffee?*"

"*Yarrrrh, me hearty!*"

Thankfully my eye sorted itself out before midday and the pirate jokes ceased – kind of.'

We found ourselves another shortcut of grand proportions midmorning on Day 42. I actually found it on Google Maps the day before and it was such a big gamble I emailed a local kayak company to ask about it. Katarapko Creek broke away from the main river and travelled 15 kilometres inland before rejoining the Murray. I wanted to make sure it was navigable the entire way before committing us to it. The company replied overnight saying it was easily navigated and one of the best paddles in the area. We locked it in and broke away from the *River Rat* just after clearing Lock Four. The creek was a picturesque copy of the upper river in its natural state. It was full of wildlife and the small amount of flow nudged us along, giving us an enjoyable break from the monotony of the big river for the afternoon. After cutting off 15 kilometres with the shortcut, we joined up with Dad as the sun was setting.

A couple of days later, during headwinds, choppy water and steady suffering, I noticed a big carp in the shallows, his back showing clear out of the water. I drifted in soundlessly and cornered him unawares. In the last second the giant fish turned and tried to get away. He collided with my kayak, swam alongside towards the back and straight into my waiting hand. I grabbed his flank, slipped my fingers underneath his gills, tightened my grip with all my strength and pulled him from the water. I'd caught a carp with my bare hands! It had only taken a month of trying. I let out a primal yell at the achievement.

> *Elise's journal:* '*I hate to admit this. I never thought it would happen. But Luke actually managed to grab a fish from the kayak with his bare hands, after weeks of trying. He was stoked with himself, as you'd imagine, and referred to the moment at least 27 more times before bed.*'

We pushed longer hours each day, trying to get as much distance in as we could. The tougher conditions slowed us down, but we wanted to keep hitting our daily targets. The trip was taking longer than we thought it would, the sameness of the big river added to the monotony and we estimated a week to go till we reached the sea.

We paddled through Lock Three on Day 44, Lock Two on Day 46, and the last of the river locks, Lock One, on Day 48. I was hoping for the flow to pick up, but it wasn't meant to be. At the end of Day 50 I added up the numbers and checked the weather. We had only 200 kilometres to go. I could almost taste the salt.

We were paddling through areas of holiday homes, all manicured to a Swiss standard and each one a carbon copy of the other. Beautiful home, boat ramp, expensive ski-boat and no one there enjoying it. I assumed many of these river homes were owned by people living and working in Melbourne. They would need to be making some serious money to afford the luxuries we saw but on the flip side they sacrificed their time to get it, leaving the boats high and dry for most of the year.

I learned more about paddling during a few days of wind and suffering than I had on the previous six weeks. How to use slipstreams as windbreaks to save energy, how to judge patterns in the swell to pick out the best route through rough water, and how to find pockets of calm where I could wait without getting pushed back by the wind. I had also learned that peeing on my toes at break times helped keep my newly developed athlete's foot under control.

We sat around the campfire that night close to a manicured estate and discussed the fundamentals of work–life balance. We all agreed that avoiding debt was the only way to be free. This was something Dad taught me at a young age. He'd never had a credit card or any debt, and Elise and I were exactly the same. Dad said his father made him, his two brothers and Nana, walk for two years when they lived in Perth while he saved enough money to buy a car for the family. I could picture my Nana pushing a trolley filled with groceries down the street all the way home with three ratbag sons in tow. Two years of walking everywhere to avoid debt and remain free. At the end of two years, Grandfather walked in with cash and bought a new car.

After our discussions solving the problems of the world, we came back to the task at hand. We estimated six days to go until we reached the sea and we still needed to cross Lake

Alexandrina before making Goolwa at the mouth. I had planned to hitchhike back to the car and trailer after we finished the paddle, but I managed to convince my cousin Matthew to drive it 800 kilometres to meet us at the end. That would save us a lot of time and hassle. Once he confirmed, we added a couple of days to our estimate and booked our ferry tickets back to Tasmania. We now had a deadline to hit.

Our final resupply was in Mannum, on Day 52. Dad managed it by himself so we could keep paddling and get the kilometres. He came up in the *River Rat* a few hours later and was laughing.

'What happened?' I asked, knowing that with my dad in a town anything was possible.

He said he was walking back from the fuel station with a jerry can full of petrol and a guy came walking towards him smoking a cigarette. The guy realised Dad was carrying fuel and started backing away, lifting his cigarette over his head clear of Dad's path. Dad saw him moving to the side and charged up, pretending to throw fuel on him. The guy freaked out, let out a yell and Dad burst out laughing. The guy eventually laughed along with him before Dad moved off chuckling at his own joke.

I laughed and shook my head as he retold the story. 'You're going to end up in jail one day with your jokes, you know,' I said.

'Yeah maybe,' he said with a grin.

The banks of the river were lined with willow trees for a few days in a row. They were thick and blocked access to the bank with abundant root systems that even a kayak couldn't get through. The willows stretched for over 40 kilometres unbroken in places and were originally introduced to fortify the levy banks and control erosion. They were brought to Australia from the northern hemisphere in the mid-1900s and had been left unchecked ever since. Reports claim 20,000 kilometres of Australia's rivers are infested with the tree. It did change the character of the river for us, from a muddy natural formation to something that felt more like an English canal. We also hadn't seen a fisherman for over a week, they didn't seem to like the willows either.

We struggled to find a gap in the trees on Day 54 and the sun was on its way down. We noticed one place where some beautiful mansions had opened up a gap and built a jetty out into the river. Next to the jetty was a patch of lush grass that looked inviting. We pulled up and Elise and I went and knocked on the doors of the two closest homes. One was vacant but the other was home to an older man named Lachy who said we were fine to camp there. He said he would tell his neighbour Linton we were staying and offered us his shower if we wanted one. I considered the state I was in and his immaculate home. I declined. Two more days without a wash wasn't going to kill me. It was a perfect camping spot for us, easy to access, soft ground for the tents and plenty of firewood.

While I was cooking up a feed, Linton arrived home and came down to say hello. He was a great guy and just as welcoming as Lachy. The land had been in his family for generations and he worked as a builder and farmer. He had emus, alpacas and kangaroos on his property, and had built eleven cabins for the tourist market. His voice softened as he told us about his blue cattle dog that was sitting at his feet.

'I had a small kangaroo joey given to me by a truck driver who hit the mum on the highway last week. I had to bottle-feed it for five days and it had become part of the family, following me around everywhere. I'd grown very attached. Yesterday I took my eyes off the little fella for five seconds, and that bastard ate it.' He pointed to the cattle dog. We were shocked, and Linton was obviously upset. I changed the subject quickly to our journey so far and our upcoming crossing of Lake Alexandrina.

Sturt had reached this same point on his expedition and had climbed a nearby knoll to view the upcoming river. Once reaching the top he recounts in his journal what he saw: 'Immediately below me was a beautiful lake which appeared to be a fitting reservoir for the noble stream which had led us to it.' He gave the lake its name after Princess Alexandrina, who would later become Queen Victoria.

We were in the water at dawn and by midmorning the river widened to the horizon and in front of us appeared an inland sea. The water spanned 64,900 hectares but with an average depth of only 2.8 metres. Its size and shallow nature made it a formidable obstacle when it was windy. I'd read one report about eleven boy scouts on a kayaking trip who were one kilometre from shore when gale-force winds hit them. The swell capsized their kayaks and the support boat, and the cold water took its toll. Four boys drowned. A terrible tragedy that highlighted the dangers of a seemingly flat and tranquil lake.

We paddled out with a northern wind at our backs and a clear weather forecast for the following 48 hours. We planned to hug the shore as much as possible, stick to channel markers and cut across sections of open water if the conditions were good. We crossed a five-kilometre stretch and a small swell began pushing us along from behind. The waves weren't breaking but I had to ride the rudder hard to keep my kayak straight. We made the shore again and pulled up for lunch. The wind dropped off and the lake became a sheet of glass. It was flat for as far as we could see, the reflection was mirror perfect and the sky turned a pinkish hue during the afternoon. Pelicans were feeding in the open water and it was an amazing feeling being out there paddling.

We made camp next to a dairy farm, collected firewood and settled into what was hopefully our last night of camping. We were 40 kilometres from the mouth and one big day from completing our journey. Overnight a swell came up and waves lapped at the shore and slapped against the boat. The noise and my active mind kept me awake for a few hours before sleep finally took me. In the morning I could hear Dad pottering about. The day was cold and rainy and the wind was blowing hard. I crawled out of my tent and made eye contact with Dad in the pre-dawn light. He said, 'Come see this, mate. We stuffed up.'

I walked over and my headlamp lit up the *River Rat*. It was full of water and sitting on the bottom. We'd grown complacent on the river and didn't put the boat in the right position to handle the waves. Tiny amounts of water had broken over the boat during the night and filled it to the top. It sank two feet and wasn't moving anywhere.

I jumped into the boat, barefoot and freezing, to fetch out the fuel jerry that was floating on the surface. I threw it to Dad and started bailing out the water like a man possessed. Once half the water was emptied the boat started to float again. I stepped out and pulled it around so the nose was pointing into the waves. I had to get by the fire to warm up, it was freezing and hypothermia was a concern. We scolded ourselves for being so stupid. After a hot breakfast I bailed out the rest of the boat until it was free of water. Dad and I drained the jerry of fuel, made sure all the fresh water was out so it wouldn't destroy the engine and refilled it. We connected the fuel, primed the engine and hoped it would start. To our great relief it spluttered to life first pull.

We sat down for another brew and discussed the conditions. It was blowing hard, whitecaps from the breaking waves covered the lake and Dad was worried about the boat's engine. If the motor died while he was out there, he would be swamped for sure. We could get swamped in the kayaks too but the waves would break over us, for Dad and the *River Rat* it was a big risk. We checked the weather, thinking we might wait a day for the conditions to improve but the next day's forecast had turned bad. The weekly forecast looked even worse. Dad said, 'I don't mind not going to the mouth, the river finished for me when we hit this huge lake.' I could understand where he was coming from, but I wanted to go all the way and put my feet on the sand and taste the salt water.

We decided to split up. Dad would take all the gear, push back into a sheltered bay where there was a small boat ramp and wait out of the wind. Elise and I would crack on and try to make it to Goolwa and ideally a hotel.

We loaded the boat and Dad shoved off, getting a battering in the process. Elise and I dressed in our waterproof gear and our rubber skirt to stop water coming in. I had mixed emotions of fear, excitement and anxiety as we shoved off into the surf. If we capsized, we were going to be in a bad position with no tent or way to warm up. I was on edge and constantly analysing the risks and how Elise was going, but I also had a huge smile on my face. I loved these moments more than anything, when success and failure was a flip of a coin and depended on our own abilities. We pushed out into open water to cross a five kilometre stretch, the whole time waiting for disaster to strike. We made it across and into a sheltered bay full of birds, where we took our first break after three hours of hard paddling.

With our waterproof clothing no match for the breaking swell, we were soaked to the bone and starting to get cold. The conditions were improving so we pushed on and aimed towards a small island about a kilometre away across open water. Ten minutes later a squall hit us with gale-force winds. We turned into the gale and battled towards the island. I was pushed backwards at times and the only saving grace was the waves were breaking from the front and not side on. After an hour of solid effort I sheltered in the thick reeds of the island, exhausted. Elise arrived shortly after, the shock showing on her face. 'What the hell was that?' she said, as she pulled up next to me. 'That's the weather that can kill you,' I replied.

Elise's journal: 'It's incredible what you can find in your reserve tank. After 55 days of paddling we angled our way through the chop, getting bucked like a raging bull by waves.'

We rested in our kayaks before pushing on again. The shore of the lake narrowed, and we entered the river with banks on either side of us. This cut the wind down and an hour later the wind direction moved to behind us and we were getting a shove along. I had phone reception during late afternoon and started to call caravan parks in Goolwa. They were all full because it was the weekend and I didn't know what we were going to do for accommodation. We were soaking wet, cold and had no tent, swags or dry clothes. I pleaded my case to a lovely lady named

Lara who owned a caravan park close to the river in an area called Hindmarsh Island. She said, 'Just come to me, leave your kayaks here and I'll drive you to a hotel in Goolwa.' It was a kind gesture and our lifeline. We were eight kilometres from her, so I hung up and we paddled on.

Just on dark we pulled our kayaks from the water and carried them 200 metres up the bank to reception at the caravan park. Lara met us at the door and made us feel at home. We couldn't thank her enough and she apologised for not having a bed for us. We put the kayaks in her shed and she drove us to a hotel in the heart of Goolwa. We checked in and I messaged Dad that we were safe. He was in his tent at a boat ramp, getting battered by the wind but he was warm. We'd made it to Goolwa after one of the most exciting days of the expedition. Elise had performed like a star, never wavering and handling everything Mother Nature threw at her. We had a hot shower, hot food and then the adrenaline dump dropped us into bed depleted.

The wind woke me during the night. It was blowing so hard I thought the roof of the hotel might come off. I thought about Dad in his tent and hoped he, and the boat, were safe and secure. In the morning I called him, and he was okay. He said it was like a cyclone during the night, but he had put the boat in a safe position. He'd also spoken to Matthew, who was picking him up in the next few hours. Before hanging up he said, 'Go and finish it off, you two.'

It was Day 56 and we had 11 kilometres to go. We carried the kayaks back to the river and just before shoving off I stopped to listen. I could hear the breaking waves of the ocean. I didn't know it at the time, but Captain Sturt had camped on this exact spot on the north side of Hindmarsh Island and slept to the sound of the pounding sea. In his journal he wrote, 'A view of boundless ocean on the morrow.'

We had a tailwind, the sun was shining and we were getting nudged along nicely. Four kilometres downstream through town, we came to the Goolwa barrage. The lock system was closed for maintenance, so we had to pull the kayaks out of the water and portage them 600 metres around. Back in the river, we had a straight shot of seven kilometres to go. I could hear the ocean to my right, on the other side of the sandbank, and scooped some water into my mouth. It tasted of salt. The river was paralleling the ocean and the mouth couldn't be far away.

Two seals swam up and played around Elise's kayak, diving under and popping up again before swimming away. The wind picked up and pushed us towards a sandbar in the distance. The land to my right opened and we beached the kayaks on the sand. We were staring at the mouth of the Murray River. I looked out at the vast ocean beyond as Sturt and the first explorers had done 189 years earlier.

Captain Charles Sturt and his team were the first Europeans to arrive at the mouth of the Murray River and had endured a true voyage of discovery. Unlike us, who were about to be collected by friends in automobiles, treated to champagne, and enjoy a hearty lunch. Sturt and his men turned their boats around and began the arduous task of rowing against the flow all the way back up the Murray, into the Murrumbidgee and to their starting point. It was a return journey of 1440 kilometres, taking over two months, which tested their resilience to the core and delivered them on the brink of starvation. They narrowly escaped catastrophe, yet Sturt went blind for six months because of the toll the river took on him. They will be forever remembered for their achievement and contribution to Australian colonisation.

I picked up Elise and hugged her. We'd completed our second big adventure together and I couldn't get the smile off my face. I had two great loves in my life, one was adventure and the other was standing beside me in the sand at the mouth of Australia's longest river.

Elise turned and caught me staring at her. Wearing a big smile she said, 'We did it, babe. We kayaked the Murray.'

What's next?

Sixteen years ago, I served as a proud soldier in the Royal Australian Infantry Corps. Eleven years ago, I was a drug addict getting hosed down by the police on the floor of a jail cell. During the ten years since that rock bottom moment, I have dedicated my life to the pursuit of adventure. I view my chosen career as an absolute privilege and even today, when someone buys my book at a speaking event, I pinch myself and reflect on how crazy life is.

The most common questions I'm asked these days are, 'What's next?' and 'Will you ever have kids?' Elise and I have talked about kids but we always seem to push it back a few more years, a few more big expeditions, and then maybe.

Whenever I soften in my convictions about my chosen life of adventure, usually after a particularly dangerous expedition, the universe sends me reminders to stay on track. The most recent ones arrived the other week, when I called my parents to see how they were going.

They'd driven 1900 kilometres through the Outback to work on a cattle station in the Northern Territory. Mum answered the phone and I could tell immediately something was wrong. Her best friend had died overnight from a blood clot at the age of 58. They'd been inseparable as kids, grown up together and were the same age. Dad took the phone from Mum when she couldn't contain her grief and he told me something else that had happened earlier that same day.

A group of guys riding motorcycles had camped near my parents overnight. They were a big group of old friends in their fifties, enjoying a road trip together. Dad had laughed and joked with them as they departed the following morning. An hour later Dad was driving along the highway and saw flashing lights up ahead. On the side of the road the bikers were gathered around one of their mates, who was lying on the ground covered in a sheet.

These two tragic events gave me clarity and reconfirmed my direction. Death can be waiting around the corner for all of us, and the reality of knowing time is precious fires a relentless enthusiasm inside me. I pulled out my list of adventure goals and as soon as I read the top three, I knew it was time. I began writing letters to the CEOs of the top 25 companies in Australia, searching for corporate partners to join me on this massive undertaking. The money I would need to fund the adventures was enormous but to these companies it would be a rounding error on their accounts.

Three weeks had passed since I mailed the letters. I opened my laptop this morning while I made my coffee and I heard the sound of emails coming in. I sat down at my desk and opened my inbox. There amongst the spam was an email with the subtitle, 'Partnership.' I read the name of the company on the email and my heart quickened. My letter had made it to the boss and I'd received a reply.

ACKNOWLEDGEMENTS

Big adventures may sometimes be executed solo, but the planning, training and logistics is a team endeavour. Taking a book from dream to reality is no exception. First and foremost, I thank my wife Elise, her unwavering support throughout countless adventures is something I am thankful for everyday. The only comment I would ever hear from Elise about my latest crazy idea would be, 'Just one adventure at a time, ok.' Thank you to my gypsy parents who still today live life on the road, you taught me country morals and values and the freedom of a simple life.

To the wordsmiths and friends who helped edit rough versions of my manuscript; Jamie Maslin, Lauren Mitchell, Zack Mellette and Eamonn Halloway. To all of my friends and extended family who I queried for details over the last 18 months, your tolerance of my pestering questions has been greatly appreciated. My editor Glenda Downing, and my designer Nada Backovic, you are both professional powerhouses and masters of your craft. Your talents and guidance were incredibly valuable and together we have produced an amazing book.

To my teammates, fellow adventurers, Sherpas and guides, you have all played an important role in my life. Sometimes we were successful and others not, but the times spent together battling against Mother Nature are now treasured memories. I look forward to the next ten years of expeditions with you.

Finally, to the readers of my books, attendees at my events and friends on social media, thank you for following along over the last decade. It has been one hell of a journey and with the help of technology we will carry on together exploring places we are yet to see and share our stories with the world. Always remember, adventure awaits and you have one life and one chance, so get out there and make the most of it.

To purchase Lukes other books
ONE LIFE ONE CHANCE and FIVE YEARS TO LIVE
visit his website www.olocadventures.com

*Stay up to date with Luke's adventures
or get in touch with him at:*

EMAIL - Luke@olocadventures.com
WEBSITE - www.olocadventures.com
INSTAGRAM - Luke_olocadventures
FACEBOOK - Luke Richmond - Adventurer

Your Certainty in Commercial Property Capital
With unrivalled market knowledge and capital partnerships from private investors to ASX-listed companies. Stamford Capital provides developers and investors with access to a broad range of financing options, and advice to ensure their transaction is successful.

Since opening our doors in 2002, Australian Sports Nutrition (ASN) has paved the way as a premium sport and health supplement supplier across Australia.

We use grass fed beef coming from the wide expanses of Australia's outback because it's perfect for making jerky. Very lean, no hormones, antibiotics or chemicals.

Highlander proudly designs and manufactures outdoor and tactical products across backpacks, clothing, sleeping bags, tents and outdoor accessories and is being sold in over 50 countries worldwide.

Stowe Australia is a leading electrical and communications installation and service contractor with a pre-eminent industry reputation for performance, quality and reliability.

beforeyouspeak

We are transforming the functional coffee space, bringing you premium instant coffee blends to help improve health, wellbeing & performance. By infusing our coffee with superfoods, you get more out of each cup!

Ken Ware NeuroPhysics Therapy is an extremely gentle, exercise-based treatment, that engages and triggers your body's natural healing processes through very light and controlled resistance training. The therapy is consistently associated with observably beneficial impacts for people with a wide variety of mild to severe conditions including disorders, injuries, diseases, and athletic performance.

Belle Property Parramatta is poised to provide property investors, building developers, and local homeowners with the very best strategic advice, alongside sophisticated real estate sales and marketing services.

www.ingramcontent.com/pod-product-compliance
Lightning Source LLC
LaVergne TN
LVHW041248080426
835510LV00009B/636